Y0-CVH-638

DISCARDED

a two-party south?

ALEXANDER HEARD

a two-party south?

CHAPEL HILL

THE UNIVERSITY OF NORTH CAROLINA PRESS

Copyright 1952
By The University of North Carolina Press

CMT

MANUFACTURED IN THE UNITED STATES OF AMERICA

For
J. K. H.

FOREWORD

IN 1946, THE BUREAU OF PUBLIC ADMINISTRATION OF THE UNIVERSITY of Alabama received a grant from the Rockefeller Foundation to study politics in the southern states. The Bureau engaged V. O. Key, Jr., to direct the research. Mr. Key, assisted by several persons, prepared the volume, *Southern Politics in State and Nation,* published in 1949 by Alfred A. Knopf, Inc.

Alexander Heard was Mr. Key's principal associate in that enterprise. In this book, Mr. Heard treats a number of topics not fully developed in the previous work. He writes chiefly about the problems and prospects of changing the South's long-standing preference for the Democratic party, whereas Mr. Key examined chiefly the nature and consequences of the one-party politics that actually prevails.

In the Foreword to *Southern Politics,* Roscoe C. Martin, who was then Director of the Bureau, set forth the conditions under which the study was initiated and conducted. In preparing this book, Mr. Heard had access to the research materials assembled for the first study. One of his important sources of information about many formal and informal aspects of southern politics has been 538 interviews conducted with politicians, public officials, and observers of politics in eleven southern states. The interviews took place between November, 1946 and February, 1948.

Mr. Heard held interviews in nine states, spending about six weeks in each state for that purpose. Donald S. Strong held the interviews in two other states. Much of the information about Republican politics and about Negro politics comes from the interviews. While no information has been published that was not obtained from at least one source agreeable to its use, almost all persons asked that they not be quoted. The sources of some of the information in the book, therefore, have not been given. The objectives and procedures of the interviews are described by Mr. Heard in *The American Political Science Review* for December, 1950. The bulk of the primary and general election returns that lie behind the statistical computations in the book appears in *Southern Primaries and Elections, 1920-1949,* a volume prepared by Mr. Heard and Mr. Strong and published by the University of Alabama Press in 1950.

The Bureau of Public Administration was pleased to facilitate the author's task during the period when he prepared a first draft of his manuscript. Subsequently he joined the faculty of the University of North Carolina where he is a Professor of Political Science. At that institution he received further aid from the Institute for Research in Social Science, in which he holds an appointment as Research Professor. While the universities have been glad to assist the author in his work, the materials and opinions presented are his, and he accepts responsibility for them.

York Willbern
Director
Bureau of Public Administration
University of Alabama

PREFACE

A NEW BREED OF ACADEMICIAN HAS COME TO THE FORE IN RECENT years. He is the broker in research, the entrepreneur who organizes men and materials to create a product somebody wants. A research entrepreneur nonpareil is Roscoe C. Martin, and I am happy to tag this book as another in a long line of works for which he deserves first credit. Mr. Martin initiated the study of southern politics mentioned in the foreword, arranged to finance it, hired the staff, and rode herd on his willing charges until all the deadlines were met. His efforts have also produced this volume.

For almost three years I worked with V. O. Key, Jr. I cannot burden Mr. Key with any responsibility for the present book, but most of what I know about its subject I learned from him, and I am sure that any insights the book contains trace their lineage to his own. He has been a tutor and friend whose generosity is beyond acknowledgment.

The book would not have been completed without the aid of the Rockefeller Foundation, the Bureau of Public Administration of the University of Alabama, and the Institute for Research in Social Science of the University of North Carolina. C. B. Robson, chairman of the Department of Political Science in the latter university, gave constant support. William K. Hubbell drew the charts and maps and Siegfried H. Ries performed the tedious task of checking the footnotes and statistics. Officials of several states supplied election returns and other information.

While I alone should be charged with what appears in the book, many others have helped, some knowingly, some perhaps without being fully aware of it. Over five hundred persons around the South have generously shared with me their thoughts and experiences in southern politics. Of this group, southerners active in Republican politics and in Negro politics have contributed most directly to the present book, for much attention is given these two phases of the region's political life.

I am particularly grateful to my friends and teachers at Columbia University, Arthur W. Macmahon and Schuyler C. Wallace, who read the manuscript and made many suggestions.

A number of other persons extended personal or official courtesies that contributed to the work. They include Harry S. Ashmore, Gordon W. Blackwell, Mary Helen Burruss, Sara H. Čadek, Hodding Carter, James W. Fesler, Frank P. Graham, Pendleton Herring, Katherine Jocher, Calvin Kytle, Robert Bolling Lambeth, Paul F. Lazarsfeld, James Mackay, Frederic Ogden, Samuel B. Olden, Jr., Leroy Percy, Joseph H. Taylor, Roger W. Shugg, George S. Steele, Donald S. Strong, Katherine Wade Thompson, Rupert B. Vance, Josephine Wilkins, York Willbern, and Edward James Woodhouse.

By grouping most of the footnotes at the back of the book I have sought to improve its readability. The general reader can safely ignore the numbered footnotes, unless for some reason he is interested in the sources of the data presented in the text, or in occasional supporting material that amplifies the text but was too cumbersome to be included in it, or in a few technical points of primary concern to social scientists. A few footnotes that will interest all readers appear in the body of the book.

Appendix I contains a statistical analysis of the Thurmond vote in the 1948 presidential campaign. The treatment is semitechnical, and since the conclusions could be summarized appropriately in the text, the detailed analysis was placed in the appendix.

PREFACE

The net result of this inquiry is a confirmation of the belief that much of the South is moving closer to competitive party politics. In addition to presenting descriptive material on several aspects of southern political life, I have tried to set forth a scheme of interpretation, a framework within which political developments in the South—a changing section of a changing nation—can be better understood. The analysis rests as much as possible on facts derived from the observation of southern political behavior. Where the facts were in doubt, I have sought to speculate in an orderly fashion with awareness of underlying assumptions. Speculations and predictions have been used as devices of analysis rather than as a way of satisfying the curiosity or of hastening the course of events. It is more important for our purposes that we be able to identify the reasons our prognoses are valid or invalid than it is that they be correct, and this can only be done by spelling out, as I have tried to do without being tedious, the system of facts and assumptions on which the expectations rest. Whatever shape the future takes, our purpose will have been served if this book makes the understanding of it easier.

Chapel Hill   ALEXANDER HEARD

CONTENTS

FOREWORD vii

PREFACE ix

the background

1. The One-Party South 3
2. The Dixiecrats: Cul-de-sac 20

southern republicans

3. Who Are They? 37
4. How Strong Are They? 54
5. Shackles on the Minority 74
6. Ballots, Second Class 83
7. Big Fish in Little Ponds 96
8. Rotten-Borough Politics 115

a gradual revolution

9. Presidential Republicans — 133
10. Materials of Revolution — 144
11. Fissures in the Democracy — 157
12. A Change in the Rules — 169

the new negro politics

13. NAACP — 181
14. Progressive Voters' Leagues — 188
15. Consolidating the Vote — 200
16. Bloc Voting — 208
17. A Lesson from History — 220
18. Southern Negroes and the Parties — 227

the future

19. The Two-Party South — 239

APPENDIX I: Sources of Dixiecratic Strength, 1948 — 251

APPENDIX II: Southern Republican Voting for President, 1916-1948 — 279

NOTES — 281

INDEX — 319

FIGURES

1. Competition for the Presidency, 1944: The Southern States Had the Strongest Preferences — 5

2. Location of Southern Republicans in the 1944 Presidential Election — 38

3. North Carolina Uplanders Opposed a Secession Convention while Slaveholders in the Lowlands Favored It — 42

4. Location of Southern Republicans in the 1904 Presidential Election — 46

5. Distribution of the "German" Population of Texas, 1890 — 51

6. Republican Percentage of the Total Presidential Vote, 1916-1948: The United States and the Southern States — 61

7. The Presidential Campaign in Texas and the Republican Vote for Governor, 1920-1948 — 136

8. Texas Dixiecrats Came from the Black Belt — 254

9. North Carolina Dixiecrats Were Strongest in Counties of Democratic Predominance with Relatively Few Negroes — 270

10. South Carolina Counties with Most Negroes Favored Truman Least — 276

TABLES

1. Supremacy of the Democratic Party in the Southern and Border States — 7
2. Decreasing Portion of the Democratic Electoral Vote Cast by the Southern States, 1876-1948 — 18
3. The Dixiecrats Form a Sector within a Section: Presidential Voting in the Southern States, 1948 — 26
4. Contrasting Political Behavior of Duplin and Sampson Counties, North Carolina: Per Cent of Vote for Republican Presidential Candidate, 1880-1948 — 49
5. Republican Percentage of the Total Vote in the Southern States, 1944 — 55
6. Southern Elections Contested by Republicans, 1920-1950, Selected Offices — 58
7. Trends in Southern Presidential Voting: Republican Percentage of Popular Vote, 1880, 1916, 1948 — 63
8. Shifts in Southern Voting for Republican Presidential Candidates, 1940-1948 — 64
9. Percentage of Total Vote for Governor Received by Republican Candidates, Southern States, 1920-1950 — 66
10. Percentage of Total Vote for United States Senator Received by Republican Candidates, Southern States, 1920-1950 — 70
11. Decline in Republican Competition for United States Representative, Southern States, 1920 and 1948 — 72

12.	Congressional Gerrymandering in Western North Carolina, 1946	78
13.	Civilian Absentee Voting in North Carolina is Most Frequent in Counties of Close Party Competition: Election of Governor, 1944	91
14.	Southern Electoral Vote and the Margin of Victory in Presidential Elections, 1880-1948	117
15.	Southern Voting for Presidential Nominees: 1940 Republican National Convention	124
16.	Southern Voting for Presidential Nominees: 1948 Republican National Convention	126
17.	Vote of Southern State Delegations on Second Ballot for Nomination of President: 1948 Republican National Convention	127
18.	Vote of Southern State Delegations on Second Ballot for Nomination of President: 1940 Republican National Convention	128
19.	Presidential Republicans, 1948, Selected Southern States	139
20.	Presidential Republicans, 1920-1948, Selected Southern States	141
21.	Decline in the Southern Negro Population, 1900-1950	150
22.	Texas Dixiecrats Were Strongest in the Black Counties, Weakest in the White Counties	256
23.	Texas Regulars Drew Votes From the Republicans in 1944	260
24.	Tennessee Dixiecrats Were Strongest Where Negroes Live	264
25.	In Virginia's Independent Cities, Anti-Byrd Democrats Tended to be Most Loyal to Truman in 1948	267
26.	Truman's Mississippi Supporters in 1948 Were Strongest in Counties of Few Negroes	275
27.	Republican Percentage of the Total Presidential Vote, 1916-1948: The United States and the Southern States	279

the background

1

THE ONE-PARTY SOUTH

UNTIL HER DEATH A SHORT WHILE AGO, AN OLD LADY GLUED ON HER postage stamps upside down. Born in the Confederacy, she did this to show her defiance of the Union whose postal service carried her mail.

Every four years, several million of this lady's fellow southerners join in electing a president of the United States. Whether Democrats or Republicans, they have marked their ballots for almost eight decades in a spirit very much like the old lady's. The Republicans, few in number, preserve their defiance toward the neighbors who voted them into a civil war. The Democrats, almost everybody else, view with impassioned distrust the party that won the war against them and set about to reconstruct their way of living. The product of this voting is the wayward child of American politics: the one-party system of the South.

The most celebrated political institution in America is its two-party system. Yet in a region of the country holding almost one-fourth of the citizens, only one political party elects its candidates to important offices and wins electoral votes in the presidential races. It has become the vogue in recent years to inveigh against this one-party politics, to charge to it all of the political defects of the region. With quickening tempo the need and prospects for a two-party system have been debated. The pundits argue under now familiar titles: "Has Truman Lost the South?", "Will the South Secede?", "The Solid South is Cracking", "The Argument for a Non-Solid South."[1] The South's politics attracts more notice than the politics of any other group of American states, and its distinguishing feature is the one-party system.

A one-party system does not mean, however, the absence of all party rivalry. At least in America, there are degrees of one-party rule, differences in the number of elections contested and in the margins of victory. We shall examine, in the chapters that follow, the extent and conditions of competitive party politics in the South, and look at the prospects for breaking down the system. There has been much hopeful hue and cry about the matter, but all the factors bearing on the development of a genuine southern party politics have not as yet been brought together for full, detailed analysis.

A number of topics of special contemporary interest will also require attention. One is the future of the States' Rights Democrats, the Dixiecrats. Another is the impact of the large number of new Negro voters. A third is the meaning for the South of proposed changes in the electoral college and in the structure of the national parties. The desertions of anti-New Deal and anti-Fair Deal Democrats to the Republican party is a fourth. Still another is the net effect of the legal handicaps and opportunities for growth that confront the Republican party in each state. Moreover, the radical differences that mark the politics of each southern state will emerge as the politics of the region are explored.

We are much preoccupied these days with systems of governance and gaze on the American political spectacle with a measure of satisfaction. Our two-party system, with all its confusions, provides governments generally capable of acting on public problems, and yet made up of persons willing to relinquish their power when directed to do so through a popular election. Over much of the world such governments do not exist. And in much of the United States people urge that improvements must be made if their government is to carry the increasing burdens heaped upon it. To understand and explain and help improve the American party system is a pressing obligation of political

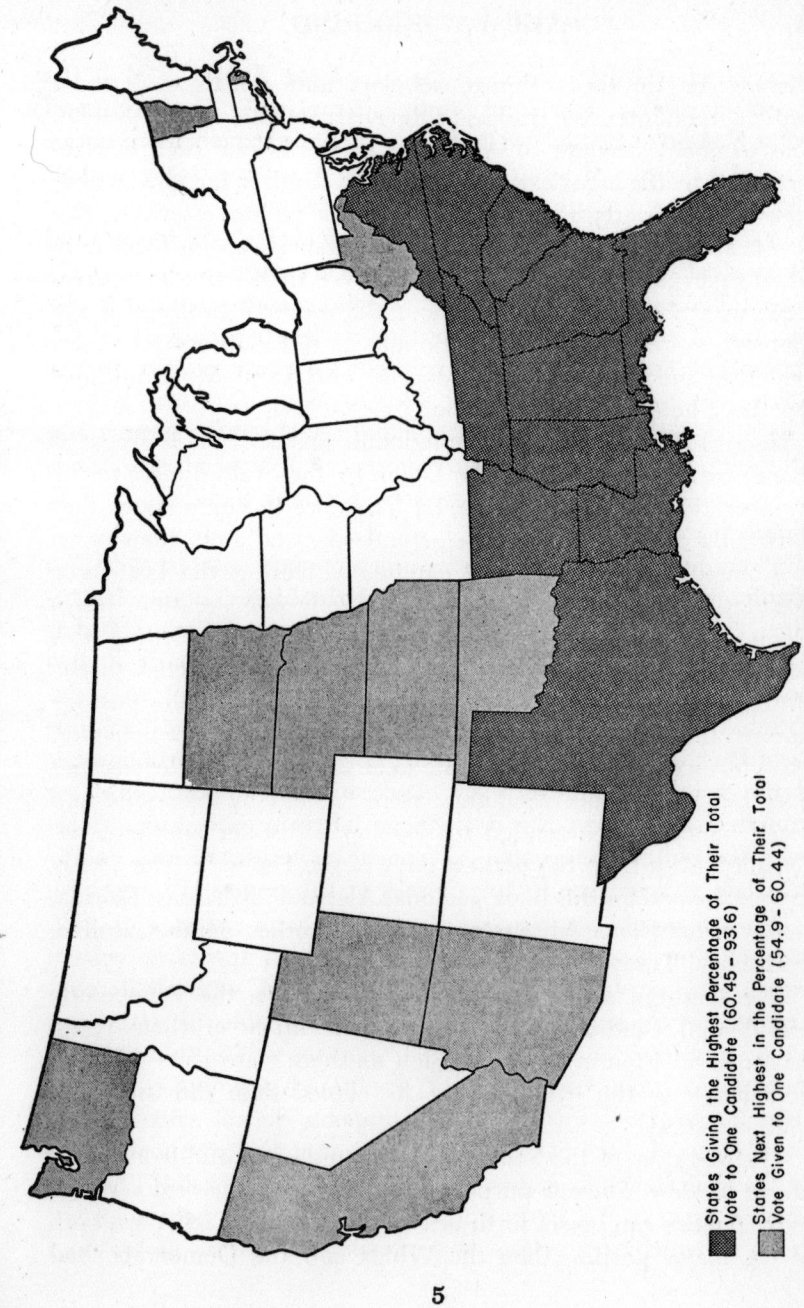

States Giving the Highest Percentage of Their Total Vote to One Candidate (60.45 - 93.6)

States Next Highest in the Percentage of Their Total Vote Given to One Candidate (54.9 - 60.44)

FIGURE 1: COMPETITION FOR THE PRESIDENCY, 1944: THE SOUTHERN STATES HAD THE STRONGEST PREFERENCES

science. To do these things, scholars and practitioners must depend upon intensive studies of the characteristics of the system. The sectional strength of American parties is one such characteristic. Sizeable areas exist, of which the South is but the largest, in which one-party rather than two-party politics prevails. The significance of these areas in the total system can be fixed only when their nature is fully understood. We shall strive to supplement what is already known about the essential outlines of the southern system, and the functioning of the majority party, by exploring the nature of the minority party and the conditions that have held it to that position.[2]

Since 1876, the eleven Confederate states have segregated themselves from the rest of the Union by their faithfulness to the Democratic party. (See Table 1.) They are the only states that during the period gave their electoral votes no more than twice to a Republican presidential candidate. During the last three decades, in only one of them, and on only one occasion, has a Democratic nominee for governor been defeated. During this period in none of them has a Republican been elected to the United States Senate. As with the little old lady of the postage stamps, the mark of the Confederacy lingers in their behavior. The eleven states share the heritage of secession and Reconstruction, but long before 1860 they were "united by economic and social bonds, which tended to develop a distinct Southern nationality, even from the earliest days of the Union."[3] The South, as thus defined for this book, includes Alabama, Arkansas, Florida, Georgia, Louisiana, Mississippi, North Carolina, South Carolina, Tennessee, Texas, and Virginia.

The southern states traditionally have given the Democratic presidential candidate a whopping percentage of their votes. As shown in Figure 1, in 1944 each southern state gave a higher percentage to the candidate of its choice than did any nonsouthern state.

The narrative of the South has been told often and from many points of view. For our purposes, the origins of the region's one-party politics can be set forth briefly. Prior to the Civil War, both of the major parties, then the Whigs and the Democrats, had

TABLE 1

Supremacy of the Democratic Party in the Southern and Border States

	Ala.	Ark.	Fla.	Ga.	La.	Miss.	N.C.	S.C.	Tenn.	Texas	Va.	Del.	Ky.	Md.	Mo.	Okla.
Number of times electoral vote cast for Republican presidential candidate, 1876-1948	0	0	2[a,b]	0	1[a]	0	1[b]	1[a]	2[b,c]	1[b]	1[b]	9	3	7	5	2[b,c,e]
Number of times Democratic nominee defeated for governor, 1919-50	0	0	0	0	0	0	0	0	1[c]	0	0	6	3	2	4	0
Number of times Democratic nominee defeated for U. S. senator, 1919-50	0	1[d]	0	0	0	0	0	0	0	0	0	6	2	3	4	3

[a] 1876.
[b] 1928.
[c] 1920.
[d] Democratic nominee defeated by another Democrat, running as an independent.
[e] Oklahoma not admitted to statehood until 1907.

roughly equal followings in the South. During the 1830's and 1840's the planters, holders of land and slaves, tended to support the Whig party while the small farmers, followers of Andrew Jackson, were found generally in the Democratic party. As the tensions over slavery, and therefore states' rights, increased, internal discord began to rack both of the major parties. The Whig party foundered, in part on sectional disagreements within it over slavery, and in the presidential election of 1856 the Republican party arose as the Democrats' principal opposition. The diverse elements of the Republican party found common cause in their opposition to slavery in the territories. In the South, conservative, slaveholding sentiment gradually shifted to the Democratic party and obtained control of it. Though the planters were in a numerical minority, and some did not agree wholeheartedly on secession, in the end most of the region went along in defense of the peculiar regional institution.

The disagreements between the northern and southern wings of the Democratic party over slavery finally split the party in 1860. Southern delegates withdrew from the national convention of that year and nominated a candidate of their own, an operation essentially like that of the Dixiecrats in 1948. The Republican party fought and won the war as the party of the Union, as the champion of the Negro. Following the war, both at home and in the Federal government, the Democratic party became the haven of the white South. Through the Democratic party in the states, southerners who had fought hardest for the Confederacy wrested local and state governments from the Republicans. The latter comprised an unhappy lot, mostly of Negroes, inadequately led; carpetbaggers, often corrupt; and many native whites who had opposed secession all along.

The position to be occupied by the newly freed Negroes in the government of the community became the emotional center of the contest. Northern Republicans advocated full Negro suffrage in part to prevent southern white votes from returning the Congress and the presidency to Democratic control. Local Democrats stood for white rule and used their party to unite whites against giving the Negro an effective political voice. Fear of the Negro as a rallying point for whites became standard equipment in combating defections from the Democratic party. Later, when the Populists threatened the hegemony of Bourbon Democrats—the whites who really ruled—their strength was undermined in several states by warnings that a split among whites would bring Negroes to power.

Though possessed of a strong following outside the region, the national Democratic party became an effective voice for the South in national politics. And the critical issue on which the voice spoke was the Negro. The Democratic party became the southern army in the field whose mission to preserve local independence in handling the Negro took precedence, so far as the South was concerned, over all other political considerations.

In all of this, the southerners most active in preserving Democratic supremacy were the whites who lived closest to the blacks. They were most sensitive to the factors of personal relationship with the former slaves. At least equally important, their economic life was inextricably entwined with that of the blacks. Each was dependent on the other. But the white man was on top, and his primacy could be assured only if he were free to run the local elections, control the local credit sources, and enforce the established etiquette of race relations.

At the origin of the southern one-party system stood the single figure of the Negro. The system was later strengthened by differences between the economic philosophies of the parties and is now shored up by inertia and its own vested rights. But the origin was the Negro, and the Negro must be supplanted by other concerns before one-party supremacy will break down.

Not a great deal is found in the books about the nature of two-party governments below the national level. It is impossible without intensive, special inquiries to compare in detail the results of one-party politics in the South with the results of two-party politics in other states. There is a rainbow of varieties among the one-party governments of the South, and the chances favor an equally assorted set of political arrangements in two-party states. It is quite clear, nevertheless, that the South receives from its one-party politics government distinguished by several features not usually associated with organized party politics. In a defensive mood, southerners are wont to claim that the contests between individuals in their Democratic primaries are equivalent to the contests between parties in the general elections elsewhere in the country. The competitive vigor of some southern primaries is surely not surpassed. It is a misconception, however, to hold that elected officials who bob in and out of office on their own buoyancy will provide the same kind of government as do officials who have behind them a powerful political party with a broad, continuing program and members in all branches of the government to help carry it out.

The way the South governs itself has become almost as vexing a problem to modern America as the Irish question was to Victorian England. It is always coming up but it never gets settled. To emphasize the importance of the prevailing political system, and consequently the importance of any changes in it that might be made, here, paraphrased in raw outline, are what seemed to V. O. Key to be the chief effects *on the South* of its one-party rule:

Localism is accentuated in the election of officials. In a two-party state the geographical distribution of party strength is usually well stabilized. The sectional pulling power of a candidate presumably represents attachments of his party to sectional interests. In the primary in a one-party state, a candidate relies heavily on personal appeals, not the least of which is to his "friends and neighbors." He enjoys local popularity that may at times reflect a sectional interest, but generally has no relation to significant issues, class divisions, or to the qualities of the candidate.

The voters have trouble knowing what the candidates stand for. In a primary, the group of politicians and supporters backing a candidate is called a faction. The factions are usually transitory groupings that do not appear year after year, have no continuity in name, in leadership, or in voter-following. The voters have greater difficulty learning what the primary candidates represent by way of program and ability than they do in a two-party state where the record of a party and its stable set of adherents identify the party's general orientation and policies.

"Party responsibility" is absent. In party politics, the parties as well as the candidates go before the voters. When a party's slate, standing on the party's platform, is elected, the party has some ability and definite responsibility to carry out its program. In the South's primaries, almost always the chief executive, the other elective administrative officers, and the legislators are elected independently of each other. They may stand for any number of different things and there exists no party mechanism to bring them into line behind an integrated program.

Campaign appeals tend to be based on personalities rather than issues. There is much shifting from one political alliance to another. Factions form and dissolve and re-form in seemingly meaningless patterns. Politicians who are against each other one year may be with each other the next. It is therefore difficult to apply the principle of "throwing the rascals out" in punishment for the policies they have followed, for the line between the "ins" and the "outs" is not always clear. As a result, campaigns usually revolve more around personalities than programs and issues.

The quality of leadership that rises to the top in a competitive party system may be quite different from the kind that succeeds in a one-party, primary system. Long established party traditions, a career party hierarchy, and the need of the party to look to the future, bring to the front candidates who are likely to be "reasonable" and conformist in character. Such representatives of the party have a responsibility to the party that put them in power. They are influenced in their actions by the admonitions of party leaders. Political leaders in the one-party melee find a premium on stunts that attract attention. The demagogue is encouraged, and once in office he is unrestrained by any responsibility to the party machinery. The free-wheeling individuality of some southern governors would not be tolerated by the party leadership in other states.

The lack of need to think of the future on the part of those in office may encourage a carefree attitude in the distribution of government perquisites. No party's reputation is at stake if favoritism is employed in the award of contracts; get while the getting is good may be the attitude.

In the absence of the organized political force that parties represent, freer play is given to pressures on government officials. Legislators, for instance, when subject to rigorous party discipline, are less susceptible to the inducements of lobbyists than if every legislator is out for himself. When a party becomes subservient to special interests, it has the power to serve those interests more successfully, perhaps, than they can be served in the one-party anarchy. Individual pressures are likely to be more effective, however, on both legislative and administrative officials in a one-party state.

Government administration tends to become highly unstable in a one-party system. Successive unconnected "administrations" often accompanied by changes in personnel and policies on many fronts make it extremely difficult to undertake long-range programs. The movement grows up to isolate particular activities from "politics," with the result that state government becomes disintegrated and incapable of putting into effect a united program.

In net effect, the South's politics appears to operate to the disadvantage of those who "have not," or who "have less," in the society.

The grand contest in state government is pretty much one of public expenditures and tax sources. The interests of lower income groups are served by public programs in their behalf which must be financed ultimately by those who are better off. The problem of the "haves," therefore, is chiefly one of keeping government activities down. The process of obstruction is facilitated by the undisciplined nature of one-party politics.

The obverse of this condition is lack of power for carrying out a sustained program on behalf of the "have nots." Political parties provide a means for organizing and overcoming opposition. Such organization is particularly necessary in representing the interests of those lacking economic power.

In disorganized politics, voters are buffeted from pillar to post by the transitory appeals of candidates. The underprivileged have no guideposts, that is, party labels, by which to know their true friends. Irrelevant appeals flourish, and those whose interests require positive governmental action suffer.

The lack of party responsibility among legislators and administrators operates to the advantage of the "haves," for they have the means with which to seek special influence.

An integral feature of southern politics is its low voting participation. This condition results at least in part from the absence of party competition. The absence from the electorate of large numbers of poor whites, plus the absence of huge numbers of Negroes, weights the electorate in favor of the "haves." Politicians would feel more need to cultivate lower income groups if more of them voted.

One-party politics encourages the dormancy of issues and contributes to an issueless politics. A submissive politics pleases the holders of power under the status quo. Were they challenged more strongly and more frequently to justify the exercise of their power they would presumably wield it more responsibly.[4]

Needless to say, the features of one-party government that are described here do not obtain in all of the states to the same extent. Moreover, the characteristics that are imputed to two-party governments are not found nicely displayed in all such states all the time. We may find that some of the imagined advantages of organized parties in state politics are cancelled because national issues often determine the lines of rivalry between the parties, and divisions among voters on national issues may not coincide with meaningful divisions on state issues. The evaluation of one- and two-party politics can be extended when additional comparative studies are made that take into account the varieties of American two-party politics as well as those of the one-party South.

The relationship between the party system and the administrative efficiency of government is, for one example, a phase of the problem we know little about. Is government in one-party states necessarily less efficient than government in other states? We have some impressions, but impressions are often misleading. Consider county government. After a trek through half-a-dozen sun-baked, tobacco-stained courthouses in the rural South, the casual visitor might conclude that indeed this was it: the rock bottom in shoddy government. But Paul Wager, who has studied county government across the whole nation, has observed that "All in all, county government in the South has perhaps made more progress and is more receptive to new ideas than in any other part of the country."[5] If this is true, does the nature of the politics play a part in it?

The sociologists talk about the "power structure" of a community, the real but informal hierarchy of economically, socially, and politically influential people who "run" the community. Analyses of the functioning of the power structure under varying conditions of party government would further expose—better than any other inquiry—the real meaning of the one-party system. There are some who argue that political parties are superficial ornaments to the basic way a society is organized. Election victories and defeats are froth compared to the real struggles for power and the world's goods. It matters not whether the South has one or a dozen parties so long as in net effect the political system remains favorable to the existing power structure. So long as conservative southerners, the argument runs, can maintain the status quo in important social and economic arrangements they don't give a nip what party tags the successful candidates wear.

In answer, it can be said that in a democracy the only power many plain people have lies in their votes, and they can make their votes best felt through a strong party system. That is the essence of Mr. Key's conclusions. Operating under democratic procedures through well organized parties they can even revolutionize their society, as our friends in Britain have shown. Whether for better or for worse is not the point. The point is that the nature of the party system is of crucial importance to the most fundamental issues of a democratic society. Exploration of the precise connection between social structure and power structure on the one hand and the way politics is organized and fought out on the other would illuminate further the consequences for the South of its present political system.[6]

Let us look at the varieties of southern one-party systems. There are wide divergencies in the types of factionalism that prevail inside the Democratic party. At one extreme stand Virginia and Tennessee. In both a relatively formal, dual factionalism has existed. The Byrd organization in Virginia possesses continuity and cohesion very much akin to that of a party. Aligned against it, the opposition faction holds a core of leadership and a body of doctrine that asserts itself campaign after campaign. The intra-Democratic contests of Tennessee have also usually been two-sided. Mr. Crump's organization is of an entirely different character from that of Senator Byrd, but it too has held together campaign after campaign, introducing at least some aspects of responsible government. In both states during the last generation, only two major candidates have usually offered for the Democratic nomination in the important state-wide races: the machine candidate and the opposition candidate.

In sharp contrast, at the other end of the factional spectrum stands Florida where in recent years as many as eleven and fourteen candidates have run in the same race for the gubernatorial nomination. In such a state each race begins afresh. The confusion of alliances, the oddness of the bedfellows, becomes hilarious. The other states range between the two extremes of Virginia and Florida. In some, like Alabama, sectional alignments have at times given the primaries a degree of rationality based on economic interest. In some, powerful personalities, like Eugene Talmadge, by their magnetism and skill build followings that for a while approach the nature of a party. These diversities set each state off from the other. Running through them all, nevertheless, in varying degrees and combinations, are the features of one-party politics that we have listed.

A stronger second party in the South need not result in defeat of the Democrats to yield significant results. A healthy minority party, though seldom winning an election, produces within the majority party greater cohesiveness, a greater tendency toward the corporate spirit that characterizes the internal operations of the major parties in two-party areas. North Carolina, Virginia, and Tennessee are the southern states in which Democrats meet with the most significant Republican opposition. The Democratic party in those three states possesses an orderly and rather clearly defined factionalism. Unquestionably other factors influence this condition, but the presence of a common enemy seems to drive the Democrats together, creating a sense of "party" unknown in most of the South. As the sense of party increases, consciousness of party responsibility and capacity for concerted action across the whole governmental front also increase. As the party comes to have meaning in the competitive sense, those who man its machinery and conduct its external relations gain significance that they lack in states where the Democratic party is just one big tent within which all the politics is played. A struggle within the party develops for control of the party machinery, the committee memberships, chairmanships, and campaign posts. Democrats in areas where they face opposition for local offices cling for succor to the Democratic state administration, laying the basis for factional unity among the "ins." The basis is laid for rational, factional rivalry between those who control the government and the party organization and those who would like to do so. Within the majority party these factions take on some order and continuity and even look a little like sub-parties. As such, they bring to the politics some of the advantages of organized parties.

Modifications in the one-party system would affect national politics—Congressional and presidential—as well as state affairs. Many southern Congressmen secure renomination without making even a primary race. No organized opposition regularly challenges their right to office by raising contemporary issues. They lean for support more on personal popularity and a personal organization than do candidates who run as the chosen representatives of their party. William G. Carleton has pointed out that shifts from Right to Left and from Left to Right take place within the southern Democratic party in reflection of trends that elsewhere in the country are read in the rise of one party and the decline of the other.[7] Nevertheless, the insulation of southern Congressmen from party politics results in the return to Washington of numerous legislators who are only mildly compelled to heed contemporary drifts in the attitudes of their constituents.

The low levels of voting that accompany southern one-party politics produce constituencies weighted in favor of the more substantial citizens of the community. Generally, voting participation rises with economic and social status. A small electorate, as a result, generally contains higher proportions of the upper and middle economic brackets than of the lower ones. In only a few spots around the region have the effects of this tendency been successfully counteracted by the political activities of labor unions. The absence of parties that normally conduct sustained campaigns for votes among the lesser groups further increases the political importance of conservative voters.

Moreover, it seems probable that the southern Congressman is less subject to the pressures of party discipline applied by national party leaders. The bossless character of most southern politics deprives the national leadership of a channel, the state party boss, for holding the party member in line. Furthermore, feelings of cohesiveness are less intense than they would be if the member were forced regularly to fight shoulder to shoulder with his running mates for party victory. Changes in these conditions might improve the representative character of the Congress as well as its ability to enact the program of the majority party.

Complaints against the South's one-party politics have come from various sources. Those on the Left have pointed to the disadvantages suffered by Negroes and nonvoting whites because of the low participation in elections. Business-minded citizens have noted that competition is always healthy, and have urged that both government administration and government policy would be improved by the growth of a strong second party. The most important condemnation of the existing system in recent times has come, ironically, from those who have in all probability benefited greatest from it. These cries from the Right have not arisen from dissatisfaction with the governments of the states, but rather from a sense of frustration in presidential politics.

The dependence of the Democratic party on the South in presidential politics has been diminishing. Under Franklin Roosevelt the party became, in fact, statistically independent of the South. Its success in garnering electoral votes for F.D.R. outside of the region would have given him victory each time even if the electoral votes of all the former Confederate states had been transferred to the Republican candidate. By contrast, in previous times of defeat the solid votes of the South comprised a large percentage of those won by Democratic candidates, and in the elections of Cleveland, and in Wilson's 1916 race, the South never contributed less than 40 per cent of the Democratic total. As may be seen in Table 2, from 1932 to 1948 the percentage never exceeded thirty.

The triumph of Truman in 1948 suggests that a fundamental shift in the balance of political power may have taken place.

The country no longer is "normally Republican." The accessions of Democratic strength outside the South that this condition indicates have led to the greatest stresses within the party since Reconstruction.

TABLE 2

THE DECREASING PORTION OF THE DEMOCRATIC ELECTORAL VOTE CAST BY THE SOUTHERN STATES, 1876-1948

Year	Total Democratic electoral vote	Southern Democratic electoral vote	Percentage southern
1876	184	76	41.3
1880	155	95	61.2
1884	219	107	48.9
1888	168	107	63.6
1892	277	112	40.4
1896	176	112	63.6
1900	155	112	72.3
1904	140	120	85.7
1908	162	120	74.0
1912	435	126	29.0
1916	277	126	45.5
1920	127	114	89.8
1924	136	126	92.6
1928	87	64	73.6
1932	472	124	26.3
1936	523	124	23.7
1940	449	124	27.6
1944	432	127	29.4
1948	303	88	29.0

The historic role of the Democratic party is liberal. Each of the four Democratic presidents since the Civil War has been, in his time, a liberal. Under Roosevelt and Truman the party's role —shifting from agrarian liberalism to industrial liberalism—has led to policies objectionable in conservative southern circles. Southerners have complained that on racial matters in particular they no longer have a controlling voice in national councils. They sense that nonsouthern party chiefs think only of the margin of victory in doubtful states. As a remedy, these southerners prescribe making the South doubtful too. If the Democratic party were forced to bid for southern votes, and if the Republican party had the opportunity to bid for southern votes, they assert, the South would gain more sympathetic recognition of its peculiar problem. Also, they say, Democrats would be forced to give a more conservative cast to their policies in general if they hoped to keep their hold on the South.

An uncertain southern outcome would inevitably make presidents and presidential candidates more solicitious of the region, as few would deny. It is doubtful, however, that alterations in national party policies can be achieved so long as the demands of dissatisfied southerners regarding the Negro run counter to the settled views of the rest of the country. Under these circumstances, competition for the southern presidential vote would probably produce more significant effects on the internal politics of the southern states—by stimulating party rivalry for state offices—than on the platforms of the presidential candidates.

It is significant that those who have hamstrung the Democratic party most severely in the South have so far avoided going over to the Republicans. The Dixiecrats in 1948 tried to preserve the party status quo in state politics. At the same time, they tried to improve their bargaining position in national politics by threatening the status quo. Their actions resulted in a crisis of southern politics. The crisis may not be as grave as some who had a hand in bringing it about would have us think, yet it signifies certain ferments and poses a challenge to the traditional form of one-party rule.

2

THE DIXIECRATS: CUL-DE-SAC

THERE HAVE BEEN VARIOUS PROPOSALS FOR REFORMING SOUTHERN politics. The obstacles to Republican growth are so great that many opponents of the Democrats turn elsewhere seeking a way to crack the one-party mold. When the Dixiecrats' Strom Thurmond ran for president in 1948, there was much talk about the rise of a new party, a party dedicated in the regional interest to the hobbling of Democrats.

The vision looked beyond a revised Democratic party in which the South gained a position of increased influence. It looked to the creation of an entirely new political organization that would bring to the South at least some of the advantages of vigorous party competition. In any analysis of the prospects for developing a second party in the region, account must first be taken of the Dixiecrats. What, precisely, are they, and what is their future?

Theirs has been, without question, the most vociferous minority political movement in the South since the Populists were dragged from the scene in the politically grim nineties. In 1948, they garnered the electoral votes of four of the eleven southern states, and won more than a fifth of the region's popular votes.

Despite this showing, few people seem agreed on exactly what the Dixiecrats are. Sometimes they have acted like a separate political party, sometimes like an organized faction operating across state lines within the Democratic party. Sometimes they have looked like a new and higher order of pressure group. The truth is, they have been different things at different times in different places.

Their big meeting in Birmingham on July 17, 1948, was called a "conference." There they adopted a "declaration of principles" and "recommended" Governor J. Strom Thurmond of South Carolina for president and Governor Fielding Wright of Mississippi for vice president, neither of whom had been nominated by any other group. As a result of the recommendation, electors pledged to Thurmond and Wright were placed on the ballot in a number of states and the Dixiecrats put up a vigorous campaign in their behalf. All this looked very much like the doings of a political party, yet Dixiecratic leaders wavered throughout in accepting the status of party. In the middle of the campaign, in which their target was the Democratic nominee, the press reported that "States Rights leaders, including Governor J. Strom Thurmond, of South Carolina, the party's presidential nominee, decided . . . to keep alive their political group beyond the November election, but to 'work within the framework of the national Democratic party.'" These leaders talked about the future of their "party,"[1] yet elsewhere in the South States' Righters proclaimed they were not a "party" but rather a "revolt" within the Democratic party.[2]

In the spring following the election approximately five hundred Dixiecrats of Alabama and nearby states met in Dothan at an "appreciation dinner" honoring members of Congress who had opposed civil rights legislation sponsored by the Democratic president and endorsed in the Democratic platform. A principal speaker was the most prominent Dixiecratic spokesman among journalists, John Temple Graves. Mr. Graves invited his gathering to think kindly of the Republicans. Perhaps with them, he intimated, lies the future of the States' Rights Democrats. "Gentlemen, let us not wince any more when we hear the word Republican." The nucleus of a new party already exists, he continued, in the teaming of southern Democrats and Republican conservatives against President Truman's civil rights and labor proposals. The meeting absorbed this sentiment and resolved: "We declare that we will join hands with any national group or party, who sincerely embraces states' rights and constitutional government. We declare that principle is above any party. We invite all Americans to work with us."[3] When the press interpreted the proceedings as a gesture by the Dixiecrats toward the GOP, growls of protest brought a disclaimer from the chairman of the dinner committee. The Dixiecratic appeal, he pointed out, was to all Americans, not just Republicans, and those whom the dinner had honored were all Democrats.[4]

The Dixiecrats off and on announced plans to set up an office in Washington from which they would campaign to spread the "principles of constitutional government" and gain membership in every state in the Union. To be called the States' Rights Institute, or perhaps Bureau, it was "also expected to serve as a lobbying headquarters from which to fight President Truman's 'civil rights' legislation."[5]

The strategy of the movement was to capture the name and machinery of the Democratic party in each southern state. It was mainly the partial success of these efforts that confuses the clear definition of the Dixiecrats. Had Thurmond and Wright everywhere run on their own ticket, their status as representatives of a new political party would have been unquestioned. In Alabama, Louisiana, Mississippi, and South Carolina, however, the Dixiecrats succeeded in having the electors named by the regular Democratic machinery instructed for Thurmond and Wright. Persons in those states who marked the conventional Democratic ticket thus did not vote for the nominees of the Democratic National Convention. In justification, the Dixiecrats argued that the Democratic party is confederate in character; the state organizations have the right to secede; they can support whomever they want for president. Their success in putting this doctrine into effect in four states made the movement a revolt within the party as well as a bolt from the party.

Thurmond mustered a plurality only in those four states. The southern voters' allegiance to party label is fierce, recurring examples of which we shall see as we go along.[6] The real presidential fight in the South, therefore, took place at the point of deciding what electors were to go under what party label. The significant competition engendered by the Dixiecrats thus occurred *within* the Democratic party rather than *with* it. Partisans of the national leadership were slow on the draw, and skillful procedural maneuver played a decisive part in the outcome in Alabama and apparently in Louisiana, though in the latter state some seemingly significant in-fighting never made its way into print. Any attempt to repeat the strategy would undoubtedly find the supporters of the national party more alert in protecting their right to the party name.

These actions of bolt and revolt led to speculation over the disciplinary measures Democratic leaders would take toward nominal Democrats who had supported Thurmond. Senator McGrath, as chairman of the Democratic National Committee, early announced that there would be few whom he would bar from positions of leadership in the party organization. The most active leaders, such as Governor Thurmond, yes; but the "great bulk" of those who had supported the States' Rights ticket had "understandable reasons" that would not prevent their return to the party.[7] In August, 1949 the national committee expunged the names of six southern members for failure to support the nominees of the national convention: the four members from Mississippi and South Carolina and the committeemen from Louisiana and Alabama, the latter having resigned sometime before.[8] At the same time, there was talk of purging the "rebel" leaders in the state organizations in order to get a "loyal, functioning, pro-Truman party organization in every Southern State."[9] Pro-Truman Democrats were encouraged informally in their efforts to recapture the party machinery in the states where it had been lost, though a spokesman for the national committee announced that the committee "does not intervene in the activities of state Democratic committees."[10] Especially in Mississippi, a hot fight raged over party posts and perquisites.* In reality, the issue at

* In that state, pro-Truman replacements in certain party posts later embarrassed their sponsor by laying themselves open to charges of selling Federal appointments.

the state level would be settled as a factional fight in the future primaries and conventions at which party officers, delegates, and electors were chosen.

In Congress, the practices of the major parties toward wayward members have shown little consistency throughout our history. A desire to punish the unfaithful conflicts with the necessities of parliamentary management. Bolters have not always been punished. When they have been chastened by deprivation of committee assignments, loss of seniority, or exclusion from the caucus, they have often been restored to grace after only a short period.[11] Most southern members of Congress kept their skirts clear in 1948 either by abstaining from the presidential campaign or by supporting Truman. Senator Eastland of Mississippi was reportedly the only senator who took the stump for Thurmond, though a number of members of the lower house were prominent in his behalf.[12] Despite early intimations to the contrary, the Dixiecrats were given regular committee assignments as Democrats, including chairmanships, and any other sanctions imposed were considerably short of a purge. The press reported, for instance, that Speaker Rayburn had rejected the request of Representative Colmer of Mississippi for a place on the Rules Committee with the statement: "As a Dixiecrat you don't have much claim for consideration."[13] Nevertheless, Mr. Colmer received the Rules Committee assignment.

In the matter of patronage, the attitude of the Administration was more severe. After the new Congress had been in session four months, the *New York Times* summarized the situation by saying that members who had openly opposed Truman would get no jobs, those who had supported him would get some rewards, and those who had neither opposed nor favored him would receive consideration. In accord with this policy the Democratic National Committee had failed to act on repeated requests of Senator Eastland for patronage,[14] and some members of the Mississippi and South Carolina delegations in the House had been relieved of the privilege, or burden, of making appointments. The question of patronage early became tied up with the efforts to put the President's program through the 81st Congress. Democrats who opposed his program, Mr. Truman said, wouldn't have much say about handing out jobs.[15] That, of course, was at the heart of the whole matter of disciplining the Dixiecrats. The Administration needed votes, then and for the future, and could ill afford to antagonize any that might not otherwise be lost to it. Therein lies the classic compulsion for the preservation of the two-party alignment in Congress.

Whether the 1948 Dixiecrats consider themselves a new party or merely an autonomous faction inside the old party, and whatever the attitude of the regular Democrats toward them, it is clear that any potentialities they have in southern politics are limited to the Deep South. Dixiecratic leaders have insisted from the beginning that theirs is a national movement,[16] but in fact it is exclusively sectional. The 1948 election results show that. Thurmond and Wright received 1,169,312 votes, 2.4 per cent of all cast. Of their total vote, 98.8 per cent came from the eleven southern states. They received one or more votes in only nine states outside of the South, and their greatest success in those nine was found in the border state of Kentucky, where their percentage was 1.3 per cent of the total. In the main, the candidates confined their campaign appearances to the southern states. Some gestures to the outside were made, but hardly on a serious scale. Former Governor Sam Jones of Louisiana made a sortie into North Dakota,[17] but won only 374 votes for Thurmond.

The Dixiecrats were not only confined to the South, but largely to a sector within that region. As Table 3 shows, they were concentrated in the band of states across the Deep South. Thurmond carried Alabama, Louisiana, Mississippi, and South Carolina (and received their 38 electoral votes plus one from a recalcitrant Tennessee elector). The four states held 55.3 per cent of all voters for Thurmond. In each of them he ran under the regular Democratic label. In six of the seven states where he appeared on a separate ticket, his vote trailed the Republicans as well as the Democrats. That the Dixiecrats were successful in capturing the party label in some states and not in others in itself constitutes a rough indication of differences among the states. But had Thurmond appeared everywhere on the same type of ticket the disparities would not have been so wide.

TABLE 3

THE DIXIECRATS FORM A SECTOR WITHIN A SECTION: PRESIDENTIAL VOTING IN THE SOUTHERN STATES, 1948 [18]

State	Percentage of popular votes for:			
	Thurmond	Truman	Dewey	Wallace
Mississippi	87.2	10.1	2.6	0.1
Alabama	79.8	——	19.0	0.7
South Carolina	72.0	24.1	3.8	0.1
Louisiana	49.1	32.7	17.5	0.7
Georgia	20.3	60.8	18.3	0.4
Arkansas	16.5	61.7	21.0	0.3
Florida	15.6	48.8	33.6	2.0
Tennessee	13.4	49.2	36.9	0.3
Virginia	10.3	47.9	41.0	0.8
Texas	9.3	65.4	24.6	0.3
North Carolina	8.8	58.0	32.7	0.5
SOUTH	22.6	50.0	26.6	0.6
UNITED STATES	2.4	49.5	45.1	2.37
Percentage of candidate's total vote cast in South	98.8	10.6	6.2	2.6

The returns of the 1948 election reveal another cardinal fact about the Dixiecrats: Despite much oratory to the contrary, their basic appeal lay in fears of the Negro. Former Governor Frank Dixon of Alabama, a chief of the movement (some Alabamians called his followers "Dixoncrats"), laid the cards squarely on the table when he declared that the States' Rights candidates had and needed no platform other than opposition to the President's civil rights program, "the most vital single issue facing the country at this time." [19] Generally, however, the Dixiecrats accompanied their fight against Federal civil rights action with a crusade for the principle of states' rights. They were fighting for individual liberty, local self-government, domestic tranquility, human decency, and constitutional processes, all threatened in one way or another by the President's proposals. The motives of some were doubtless ulterior, but Governor Thurmond reflected the attitude of many of his supporters when he said during the campaign:

... we consider so-called civil rights legislation *and many other like questions* to be reserved to the States by the Constitution. Anyone who insinuates that there is any other intention in the States' Rights movement than that of *protecting and preserving this constitutional guarantee* must undoubtedly be attempting to smear our movement....[20]

Nevertheless, when the votes were in, they showed that appeals to race consciousness had reaped their reward. In state after state the Dixiecrats won their greatest support among the whites who live closest to large numbers of Negroes. Later on, in Chapter 11, we shall look more closely at the nature of Dixiecratic motivation and leadership. And in Appendix I may be found a statistical analysis of Dixiecratic strength. For the moment, we need only to remember what that analysis shows: that among the voters, at the grass roots, as is the fashion to say, the Dixiecrats had one principal, effective appeal, the appeal to fear and dislike of people of different color. Southern concern over the Negro is the most deeply rooted source of political contention in American history. In some degree, we pray increasingly small, the concern will persist indefinitely.[21] A movement appealing to those worried about the Negro will be assured of an audience and of at least a measure of support for a long time to come.

What the Dixiecrats accomplished in 1948 is debatable. They did not succeed in their announced aim to throw the presidential election into the House of Representatives. Nor did they embarrass President Truman by a humiliating defeat. The electoral votes captured by Thurmond gave new warning of the sensitivity of certain elements in the South to the race issue skillfully played upon, just as the southern votes for Senator Russell in the Democratic national convention had done. A foundation for possible future action was laid, but the relative failure of the movement to attract votes damaged its prestige and revealed the narrow limits of its appeal. National Democratic leaders were alerted to the possible loss of southern electoral votes in the future, but the terms in which the Dixiecrats framed their demands in 1948 would give the national leaders little opportunity to make peace. Under these circumstances it looked to many southerners as though the only effect the movement could have on a presidential race would be the election of a Republican president, either in the electoral college or in the House of Representatives.

It is doubtful that the furor kicked up by the Dixiecrats greatly affected the Congress except to increase friction between the President and a few southern members. The forensics no doubt shackled any tendencies toward adventuresomeness that some southern liberals may have had, but the pattern of southern Congressional action on civil rights legislation had been set for two generations. On social legislation, periodic coalitions between some southern Democrats and some Republicans had long since become familiar. The Dixiecrats perhaps provided a screen behind which special interests worked, but special interests had long been working through sympathetic legislators. The purpose proclaimed by one spokesman, that of educating "the people of this nation on the perilous departure from constitutional government advocated by the three nominees of the Philadelphia conventions," [22] seemed a rightful one for a political movement but not one whose fulfillment could be discerned from the election results.

The sharpening of factional lines within the Democratic party may ultimately prove in several of the states to be the most significant result of the whole fracas. The fight over loyalty to the President split the party wide open in several states and gave form to liberal and conservative factional divisions. From the beginning, some observers saw the movement aimed at the defeat in 1950 of southern liberals, like Senators Hill and Pepper, by forcing them to the unpopular side of the race question.[23]

The fuss may have served a function neither the Dixiecrats nor their opponents fully acknowledged. Many of the persons prominent in the movement had long nursed grievances against the Roosevelt and Truman administrations. They were resentful on many scores, of which Federal interest in racial matters was only one. They had been frothing at tax, labor, and economic policies long before a Federal civil rights program was offered. Many were sure in their hearts that Federal intervention was being proposed in matters that should be left to state action. Many of them would have been Republicans had they not lived in a region where the one-party system limited their opportunities to strike back. Some of these people found in the States' Rights movement an outlet for pent-up emotion. They found in the waving of Confederate flags and the playing of Dixie an emotional catharsis whose principal effect may have been to prepare them better to accept inevitable disappointment. Honorable defeat after a great battle can be more easily withstood than abject submission.[24] The Dixiecratic movement gave these people a channel of protest within the confines of the one-party system. To that extent, the movement interrupted a migration to the Republican party of persons who, after four elections, had determined against further succor to a Democratic president. At the same time, the movement offered a stepping-stone away from the national Democracy for other souls, also unhappy, but not yet ready to take the chilling plunge of voting Republican.

Granting these things, do the Dixiecrats have a future as a southern third party?

Writing in 1925, Professor Arthur N. Holcombe of Harvard University described a number of obstacles to the multiplication of parties in American national politics.

In the first place, ... the constitutional basis of national politics is such as to exclude from the jurisdiction of the federal government many of the issues which engage the attention of national party leaders in other countries. Problems of religion and race, which have led to the formation of more than one political party abroad ... do not furnish issues with which a party in power can readily deal by means of the legal authority at its disposal. Such issues must be fought out, if at all, in the field of state and local politics.[25]

Since this statement was written, Federal regulation and legislation has extended to many fields theretofore believed reserved for state action. The Constitution has been interpreted to admit national responsibility for an increasingly wide range of matters. Federal action taken in the past to protect the Negro has generally been circumvented in the South, but more recent proposals have been drawn with an eye to their enforcement. Although the constitutionality of some parts of President Truman's civil rights program is the subject of hot debate, his insistence, and the insistence of the Democratic National Convention, on bringing the welfare of Negroes as a group into the arena of active Federal politics has altered the scene viewed by Professor Holcombe in the 1920's.

He was no doubt thinking of minor parties abroad formed around racial minorities, rather than formed in opposition to government action favorable to minorities. Nevertheless, the deep feelings aroused by racial identities give durability to the minor party sentiment in both cases. As long as Federal civil rights legislation is a subject of debate there will remain in the areas of the South containing the greatest proportions of Negroes a political resentment capable of some kind of organized expression. We have noted that the States' Righters of 1948 found their strength in this sentiment.

Historically, minor parties have arisen in the United States when the major parties have failed to represent adequately the views of a determined group of citizens. Most frequently they have arisen in protest against economic and social conditions that have borne with special heaviness on certain segments of the population.[26] These protests have generally come from groups on the Left, especially since the Civil War. There has been a strong sectional flavor to American politics throughout all our history, and to our minor parties as well. Many have reared up to champion a sectional viewpoint.[27] Time and again, however, in the history of minor parties and protest groups generally, the goals they fought for have been absorbed by the major parties and they themselves have passed away.[28]

The States' Rights Democrats differ from the usual American minor party in several ways. Only in part a separate party, their formal objectives have so far been limited to presidential politics. They have tried to go in at the top to capture a going party organization rather than to build up a corps of voters from the bottom. Their protest is from the Right and grows from a unique sectional appeal of such a nature that neither major party can concede to it without seriously endangering its popularity outside the South.

The Dixiecrats can keep alive indefinitely at least some elements of revolt within the Democratic party, but in doing so they will not contribute to the development of an organized party system in the South. Third parties in America are doomed so long as our present constitutional arrangements are maintained.[29] The only new parties in our history that have survived filled a vacuum left by the disintegration of one of the older major parties. And the South has been less sympathetic to maverick movements than any other section of the country. Even the Populists—whose program arose from the needs of oppressed and poverty-stricken farmers, plentiful in the South—fared less well in that section than in the West.[30]

If the Dixiecrats indefinitely continue their semi-separate, anomalous political maneuvers, they will formalize dissension within the Democratic party and seal it off in a cul-de-sac where its opportunities for effective protest are extremely problematical. Many persons of substance who by all rights should take the lead in revitalizing the Republican party in the South will be neutralized.

In a very restricted area, perhaps confined to the state of Mississippi, they might for a considerable period control the selection of Democratic electors and use their votes in the electoral college to seek concessions from the major parties.[31] In possession of the Democratic machinery in one or more states, the Dixiecrats might even form something of a sectional confederation of state Democratic parties to work within or outside the national party.*

Such a course would in a few southern states give greater form and continuity to factions within the Democratic party and lead to better organized intraparty politics. But the use of the race issue by the Dixiecrats—and it would be inevitable, despite the injection of other issues—would demoralize the politics and minimize attention to other issues. As a channel to *competitive party politics*, the States' Righters, as an organized movement or as a separate party, have little to offer.†

For those with the courage to face it, the hope of the South for real party politics rests in the Republican party. Some of the courageous envision the shift toward the GOP as a painfully

* Charles Wallace Collins, a member of the Alabama bar resident in Maryland, has written the most elaborate statement of the viewpoint held by many Dixiecrats. *Whither Solid South?* (New Orleans: Pelican Publishing Company, 1947), chap. 17, proposes two possible courses for the South: creation of a regional party by taking over the machinery of the Democratic party in the southern states and (1) throwing the election of president and vice president into Congress whenever possible by putting up its own candidates and voting for them in the electoral college, and (2) eliminating the presidential campaign from the South by having electors instructed by the state legislatures, special electoral commissions, or a regional convention, perhaps at the time of the "northern election" but possibly between it and the meeting of the electoral college. Despite Mr. Collins's suggestion of a forty-ninth state in Africa to handle the Negroes, his book is seriously written and should be consulted by any who seek to understand the thinking behind the whole Dixiecratic phenomenon.

† The province of Quebec is in certain respects similar to the South in the united political front it presents to the rest of the country. Dominion legislators elected from Quebec have usually been overwhelmingly of the same party and their support has been necessary for a parliamentary majority. The province has shifted its political preference wholesale from one party to the other in the past, and respectful consideration is given by the national parties to the factors of national origin and religion that set off the province. A Dixiecratic sector party in the South would not, however, occupy a comparable position. The singleness of program of the Dixiecrats, their numerical weakness, and the differences between the American and Canadian party systems would render a permanent Dixiecratic group less effective. See Robert MacGregor Dawson, *The Government of Canada* (Toronto: The University of Toronto Press, 1948), chap. 21.

gradual one; others speak of a great, sudden revolt inside the Democratic party against the northern city bosses and labor leaders. Whatever the speed, such a shift is usually conceived as part of a radical change in the composition of American political parties: a realignment more along lines of economic class interests, after the manner of the British, breaking down the traditional sectional orientations. Before looking closely into these matters, however, we must examine the chief character in the drama: the Republican party.

southern republicans

3

WHO ARE THEY?

To many citizens of the South, a Republican is a curiosity. They may have heard about the Negro undertaker who goes to Republican conventions, or the eccentric railroad official who came from Ohio; but a genuine, breathing Republican is a rarity in most of the counties of the region. In the elections after 1936 some rich folks surprisingly let out that they voted for Willkie or Dewey, and there was a lot of talk against Roosevelt and Truman, but most people who took the trouble to notice figured it didn't amount to much. There weren't really many complainers, and the Democrats always win anyway. Even the Republicans up in the hills have been looked upon as curiosities, rather than as political opponents, by the Democrats in the lowlands. In many localities it is easy to answer the question: Who are the Republicans?; because there aren't any.

We shall have no trouble in the next chapter putting our finger on the Republican concentrations, and measuring their strength. The origins of southern Republicans claim our attention now. These nonconformists are of several types: mountaineers, residents of the South's highland areas; Negroes, loyal to the party of the Emancipator; migrants from outside, who have resisted the incentives to merge with their new neighbors; descendants of the Populist uprising who could not stomach a return to the

■ 50 per cent or more of total vote Republican

▨ 35 - 49.9 per cent of total vote Republican

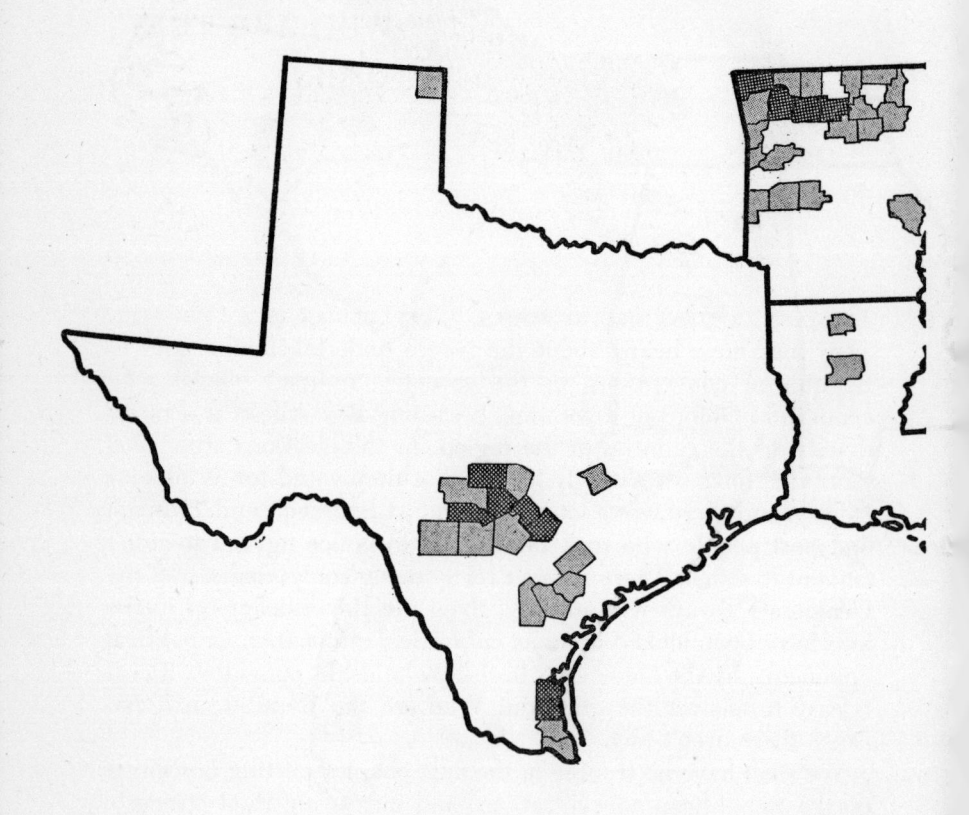

FIGURE 2: THE LOCATION OF SOUTHERN

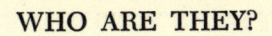

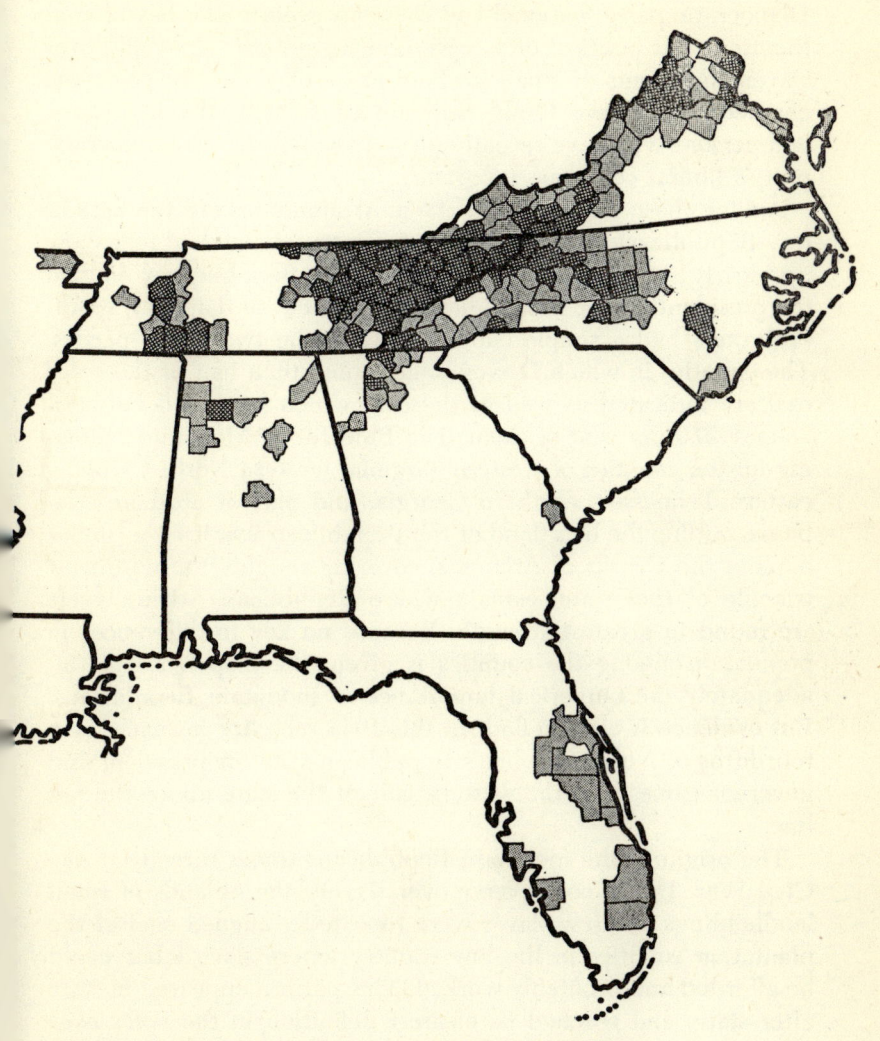

REPUBLICANS IN THE 1944 PRESIDENTIAL ELECTION

Democratic party; national and religious groups who have found themselves at political odds with their neighbors, especially over slavery; residents of small lowland areas of a deviate economic character who have found common cause with the highlands; and persons who have recently turned away from the Democratic party's liberal economic programs.

Among these groups by far the most numerous are the hereditary Republicans of the highlands.* These independent folk show up clearly in the map in Figure 2 where Republican voting in the presidential race of 1944 has been plotted. In that year, southern voters had a simple choice between the two major parties. The counties in which Dewey polled more than half of the votes cast are indicated as well as those in which he polled between 35 and 49.9 per cent of them. The Blue Ridge Mountains, plowing up the counties of western Virginia, western North Carolina, eastern Tennessee, northern Georgia, and part of northern Alabama, outline the heartland of the Republican South. In a similar manner the Ozarks of Arkansas, covering roughly the northwest triangle of that state, explain where Republican Arkansawyers are found in greatest strength. Because no key to differences in population among the counties is given, the map bespeaks inadequately the numerical importance of mountain Republicans. But evidence is easy to find. In this 1944 race, for instance, over four-fifths of North Carolina's Republican vote for president and governor came from the western half of the state above the fall line.

The origin of the mountain Republicans traces directly to the Civil War. In the controversy over slavery the uplands of small landholdings and few slaves were repeatedly aligned against the plantation counties in the low country where slave labor could be afforded and profitably worked. This pattern appeared in state after state, and reached its clearest definition in the votes over secession. Meanwhile, the Republican party grew from its birth in 1854 to the party of victory in 1860. It was a party of varied

* Two important types of Republicans, Negro Republicans and "presidential Republicans," are not treated in this chapter. See chapters 17 and 9 respectively.

adherents, ranging from small-farmer radicals through old-line conservative Whigs to eastern industrialists. Common opposition to the extension of slavery in the territories bound these elements together. In 1856 the party platform came out stoutly against slavery and polygamy—"the twin relics of barbarism"—but could find agreement on no other vital problem.[1] On the sole issue of the Negro (excusing the men of many wives) the Republican party was founded and it achieved success in 1860 against an opposition deeply divided by the same issue. When the slavery issue evolved to the question of secession, the stoutest opposition in the South came from the hill folk who had least to lose from a national policy adverse to slavery. They wanted to mind their own business and stay in the Union.

The relationship between slaveholding and secession is illustrated by the pair of North Carolina maps in Figure 3. One map shows the counties with more than 40 per cent of their population composed of slaves in 1860. The other map shows the counties that voted in February, 1861 against calling a state convention to consider the secession question. The bulk of the votes against a convention that might lead to secession came from above the fall line, from the piedmont plateau and the highlands. The bulk of the votes for the convention came from the counties of many slaves.

During the war and its aftermath, the Republican party became the champion of the Unionists. When secession became a fact, some southerners who opposed it nevertheless joined the Confederacy and fought the good fight. Others went off to join the Union armies or remained at home and resisted Confederate conscription. There was much bitterness. Counties tried to secede from states, and within counties there was civil conflict,[2] tiny in its proportions but more keenly felt and longer remembered because it was intimate. When the states tried to enforce conscription, resentment and reprisals on both sides set trains of emotion burning, and some of them still burn. The literature of the Confederacy abounds with stories that explain the emotional origins of southern Democratic loyalties. It is well to remember that they are paralleled by indelible resentments *against* the

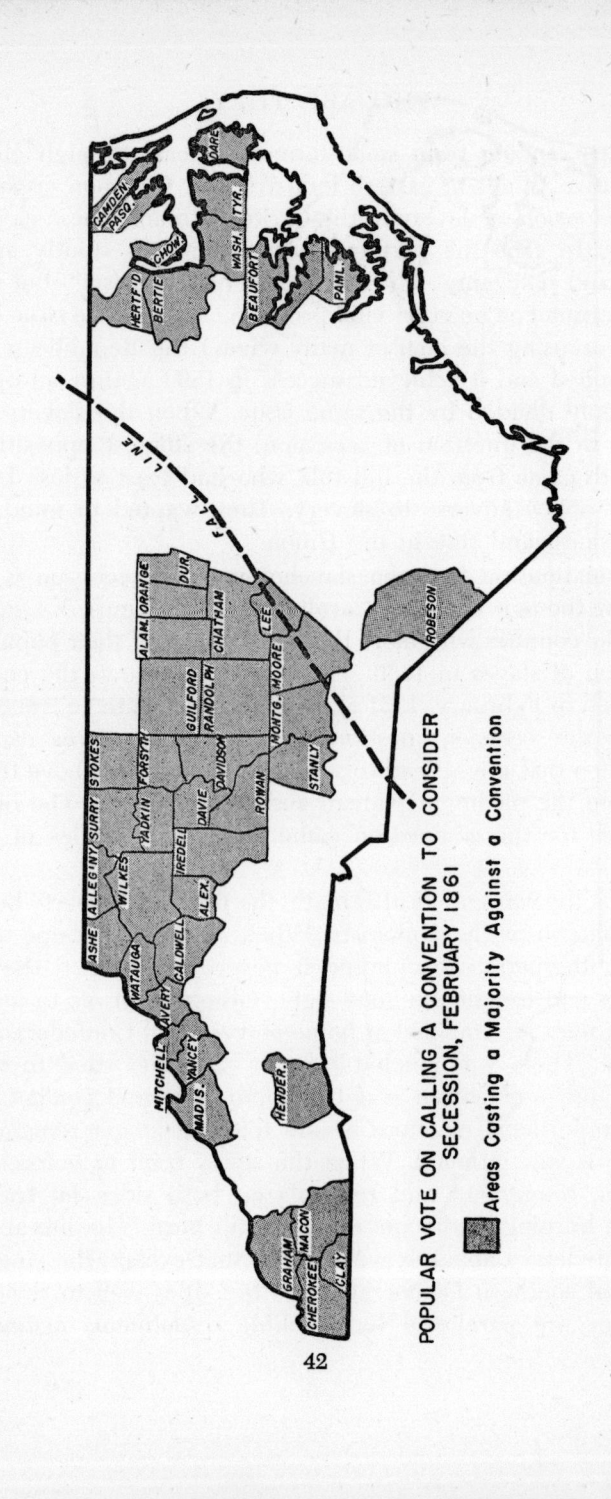

POPULAR VOTE ON CALLING A CONVENTION TO CONSIDER SECESSION, FEBRUARY 1861

Areas Casting a Majority Against a Convention

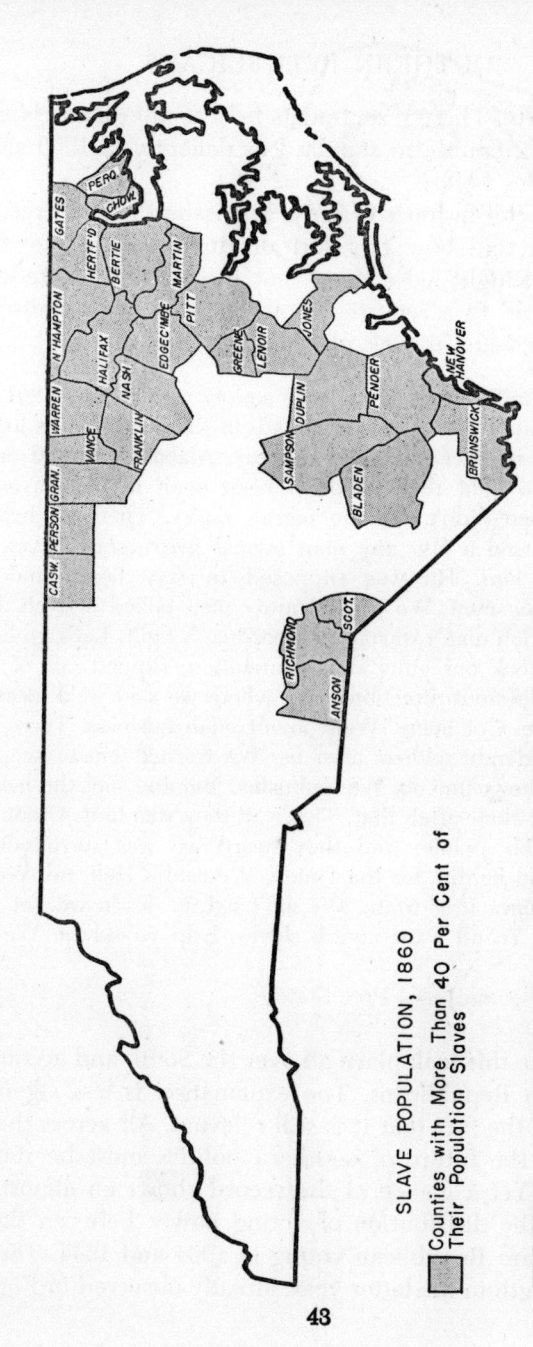

SLAVE POPULATION, 1860
Counties with More Than 40 Per Cent of
Their Population Slaves

FIGURE 3: NORTH CAROLINA UPLANDERS OPPOSED A SECESSION CONVENTION WHILE SLAVEHOLDERS IN THE LOWLANDS FAVORED IT

Democratic party. These resentments held families and clans and counties to the Republican standard as defiantly in 1950 as they did nine decades before.

A local character in Jones County, Mississippi ("The Free State of Jones") has told how this sort of Republican came about. "Cap'n" Newt Knight led a band that resisted the Confederacy. His story, as told to a reporter about 1920, is more amusing in retrospect than when it took place.

Confederacy drafted a lot of us Jones county men back in 1861. Sent around a sergeant with a couple of squads of riflemen; told us to come along. Marched us over near Montgomery, Alabama. Found out we was supposed to fight the Nawth to keep ouah nigrah slaves. We Jones county men didn't own no nigrah slaves. Then we hear the Confederacy passed a law any man owned five nigrah slaves, they wouldn't draft him. He was supposed to stay home and raise vittles for fighting men. We Jones county men talked it oveh. I told 'em: "This is a rich man's war and a poor man's fight. Let's go home." One night we took our guns and ammynition, slipped out of camp one at a time, different directions, met where we said we'd meet, and we started home. Got home. Went about ouah business. Three times they sent Confederate soldiers after us. We warned 'em to keep outa Jones county. They came on. We ambushed 'em and shot the hell outa 'em. They let us alone afteh that. That's all they was to it. Union army came along afteh awhile; said they heard we was surrounded by Johnny Rebs and fightin' for the Union. We said: "Hell, no. We ain't Union. We're Jones Free State. We ain't fightin' less'n we got a real reason to fight. Yo'-all want nigrah slaves, help yo'-selves. We don't own none."

So that's how-come Jones Free State.[3]

Incidents like this took place all over the South and account for many southern Republicans. The explanation is less significant, however, than the fact that it is still relevant. All across the land men say that the future of southern politics must be different from its past. Yet a glance at the record shows an almost drab continuity in the distribution of voting power between the two parties. Compare Republican voting in 1904 and 1944. The high points of strength in the latter year, already observed in Figure 2, correspond remarkably to the counties casting a majority for the party's presidential candidate in the earlier year as shown in Figure 4.[4] The election of 1904 was chosen for comparison because it was the first national election after the subsidence of the Populists (although some Populist votes were cast, and as a consequence Republicans had a plurality in a few counties not shown on the map) and the first in which the bulk of the disfranchising measures—effective mostly on Negroes, most of them Republicans—were in effect. All over the world hereditary influences affect party affiliation, but the intensity of hereditary Democratic and Republican strength in the South should sober those tempted to believe party realignments can occur overnight. Only the deepest upheavals jar voters loose from their habitual moorings.

The two maps we have been looking at show other pockets of Republicanism scattered around the South. These little enclaves are intriguing. The dark-shaded area appearing in eastern North Carolina on both maps is Sampson County. The ghosts of the Populists still walk in Sampson. In a normally Democratic section, it stands out like a sore thumb. Its deviate political behavior especially deserves notice because of its large number of Negroes (34.6 per cent in 1940) living in a predominantly rural county (92.5 per cent rural in 1940). The rural black belts of the South are the seats of Democratic supremacy. Yet, election after election, Sampson departs from its neighbors to give the Republican candidates a thumping vote.

The explanation lies in a decision of the county's most prominent citizen at the turn of the present century. So runs the local story. Marion Butler was elected a United States senator in 1894 by the Fusion forces, a combination of Republicans and Populists. Earlier a Democrat, he had been captured by the Populist vision. The six years before the end of the century saw as bitter politics as any state has witnessed,[5] and Butler suffered such personal and political abuse at the hands of his Democratic opponents that when Populism collapsed he led his following into the Republican party. That the phenomenon was not purely personal is suggested by several other counties in the South where Populism

46   SOUTHERN REPUBLICANS

■ Counties Casting a Majority for
The Republican Presidential Candidate

Note:
County lines are those of 1935; adjustments not made for changes since 1904

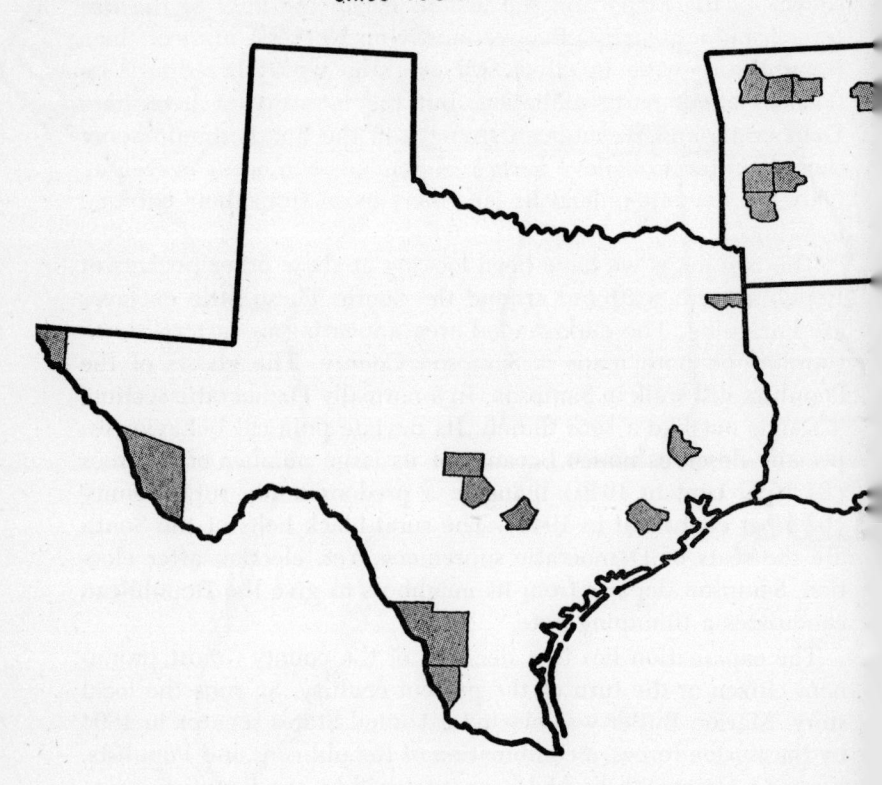

FIGURE 4: THE LOCATION OF SOUTHERN

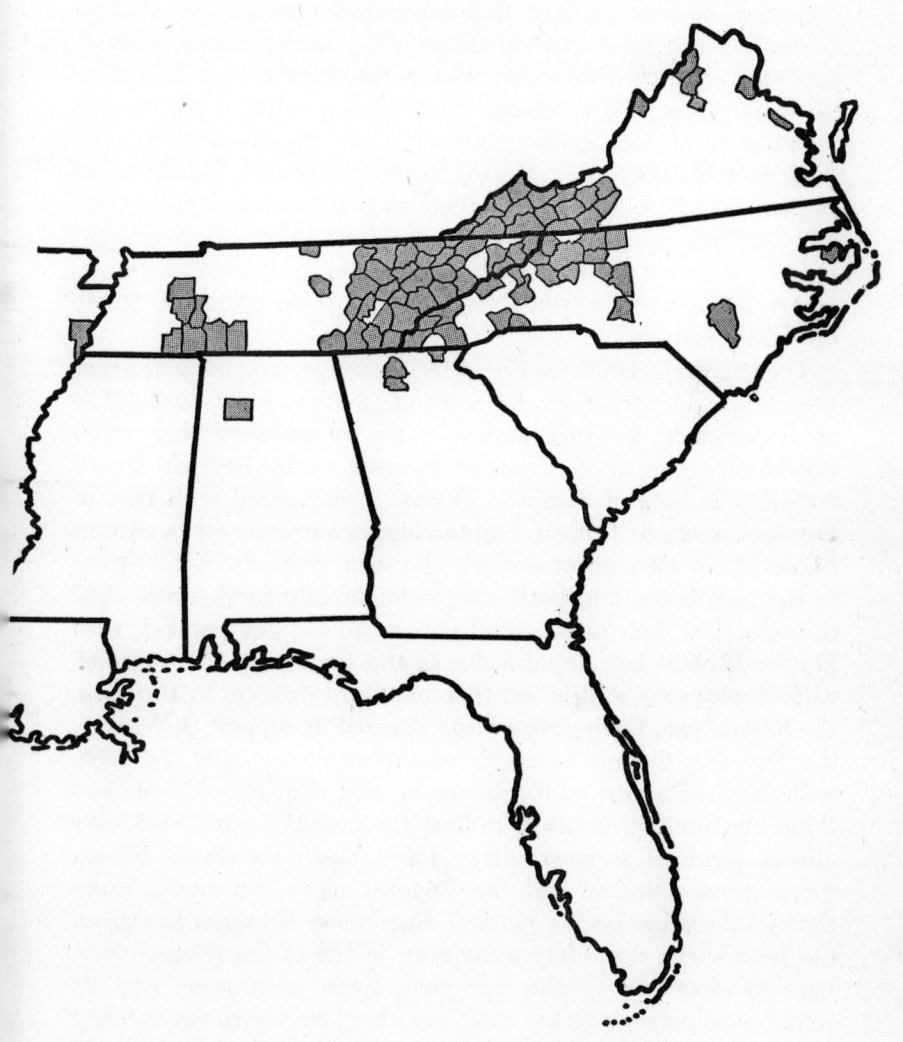

REPUBLICANS IN THE 1904 PRESIDENTIAL ELECTION

flourished and which show Republican tendencies today. Chilton County in central Alabama, along with others further north in that state, harbored Populists who turned Republican. The more southern of the two Louisiana parishes appearing in Figure 2 is Winn, seat of Louisiana Populism [6] and, not incidentally, the birthplace of Huey Long. During the Fusion period, Populists and Republicans had more to join them in politics than merely common opposition to the Democrats. Habitual Republicans scratching out a living on the southern hillsides had good reason to embrace Populist doctrines, which were designed to aid small, oppressed farmers.

The persistence of these Republican enclaves dramatizes further the seemingly perpetual character of political habits once they are established. Political action in the proportions of a social revolution seems to be necessary to upset established patterns of voting. The vote of Sampson County is compared with that of Duplin County in Table 4. Duplin adjoins Sampson on its eastern border. They have approximately the same proportion of Negroes in the population and both are predominantly rural. From 1880 through 1896 their presidential voting ran roughly parallel, with Duplin slightly less Republican. In the three-way race of 1892, each county gave a little less than one-third its votes to Harrison, the Republican. Each gave a large share of its support to Weaver, the Populist, though Sampson was more enthusiastic. In 1896, with the field narrowed to two again, and with Republicans and Populists fused in North Carolina, the counties gave McKinley almost identical support. After 1896, North Carolina's Fusion forces were defeated and the Populist party destroyed. From then on there has been a marked divergence. Sampson has given the Republican candidate a majority in ten of the thirteen subsequent elections. Duplin has gone Republican once, and its Republican percentage has run from about twenty to about thirty points behind that of Sampson in every election. In a rational politics, presumably the counties would behave more or less alike, and for several elections they did. But politics is not always rational, and the notions fixed on the county by an honored and powerful citizen still prevailed half a century later. There is some-

WHO ARE THEY?

TABLE 4

CONTRASTING POLITICAL BEHAVIOR OF DUPLIN AND SAMPSON COUNTIES, NORTH CAROLINA: PER CENT OF VOTE FOR REPUBLICAN PRESIDENTIAL CANDIDATE, 1880-1948 [7]

Year	Sampson	Duplin
1880	43.4	37.9
1884	38.4	34.5
1888	40.2	33.9
1892	29.9[a]	30.1[b]
1896	68.7	67.7
1900	61.4	36.5
1904	62.2	37.0
1908	64.9	44.8
1912	67.3[c]	38.5[d]
1916	66.6	45.6
1920	70.4	44.2
1924	60.8	34.2
1928	70.9	52.4
1932	45.1	19.9
1936	45.5	20.9
1940	53.1	18.9
1944	59.0	20.8
1948	46.8	14.2
Per cent Negro, 1940	34.6	35.6
Per cent rural, 1940	92.5	100.0

[a] Populist candidate received 39.0 per cent.
[b] Populist candidate received 25.6 per cent.
[c] 2.2 per cent of this for Taft, remainder for Roosevelt.
[d] 1.6 per cent of this for Taft, remainder for Roosevelt.

thing ironical, yet instructive, about the descendants of radical Populists who vote for Dewey and Bricker in preference to Roosevelt and Truman.

There are Republican high points in the South that are explained neither by topography nor by Populist ancestry.* Among

* Two low points have explanations, too. Polk County, Tennessee, and Wise County, Virginia, surrounded by Republican strongholds, stand out on

these are the "German" counties of south central Texas. But their Republican origins emphasize further the tenacity of political habits once fixed. The section of Texas most heavily Republican was settled by large numbers of Germans during the Republic and early days of statehood. They were for the most part political liberals in the spirit of 1848. They disapproved of slaveholding, and, as the controversy leading to the Civil War developed, became Unionists. During the war they suffered brutalities at the hands of the Confederates similar to those experienced by the mountaineers. For the most part previously Democratic, many of them turned to the Republican party and large numbers have remained Republicans since.[8] They have exhibited other common political preferences from time to time, like their strong vote for prohibition repeal in 1935 and a leaning toward conservative candidates like O'Daniel and Jester in Texas' Democratic primaries.* Their vote used to account in part for the election of Texas' long-time Republican member of Congress, Representative Wurzbach.

The exact location of the Germans of today is hard to place. Migrations, in and out, as well as cultural diffusion serve to wear down the effects of the original settlements. The best approximation of their presence is offered by the census of 1890, when the statistics of national origin showed them in the counties marked in Figure 5.[9] (They no longer show up in the census, of course, as immigrants and descendants of immigrants.) Compare these counties with those shown by Figure 2 as having strong Republican leanings in 1944.†

---

the map in Figure 2 as giving 35 per cent or less of their votes to the GOP. In 1944 both counties were dominated by a Democratic machine, each the most notorious in its state. Buncombe County in western North Carolina, shown with a Democratic majority, contains the city of Asheville.

* Seventeen German counties (those on the map in Figure 5, excluding Bexar and Travis) were ranked by their vote in several elections. The percentage of the median county in the group, compared with the state percentage, in three races follows: for prohibition repeal, 1935, German county, 83.0, state, 54.2; for O'Daniel for Senate, 1942, German county, 64.3, state, 51.0; for Jester for governor, 1946, German county, 75.8, state, 66.3.

† It should be borne in mind that there have been particularly large popu-

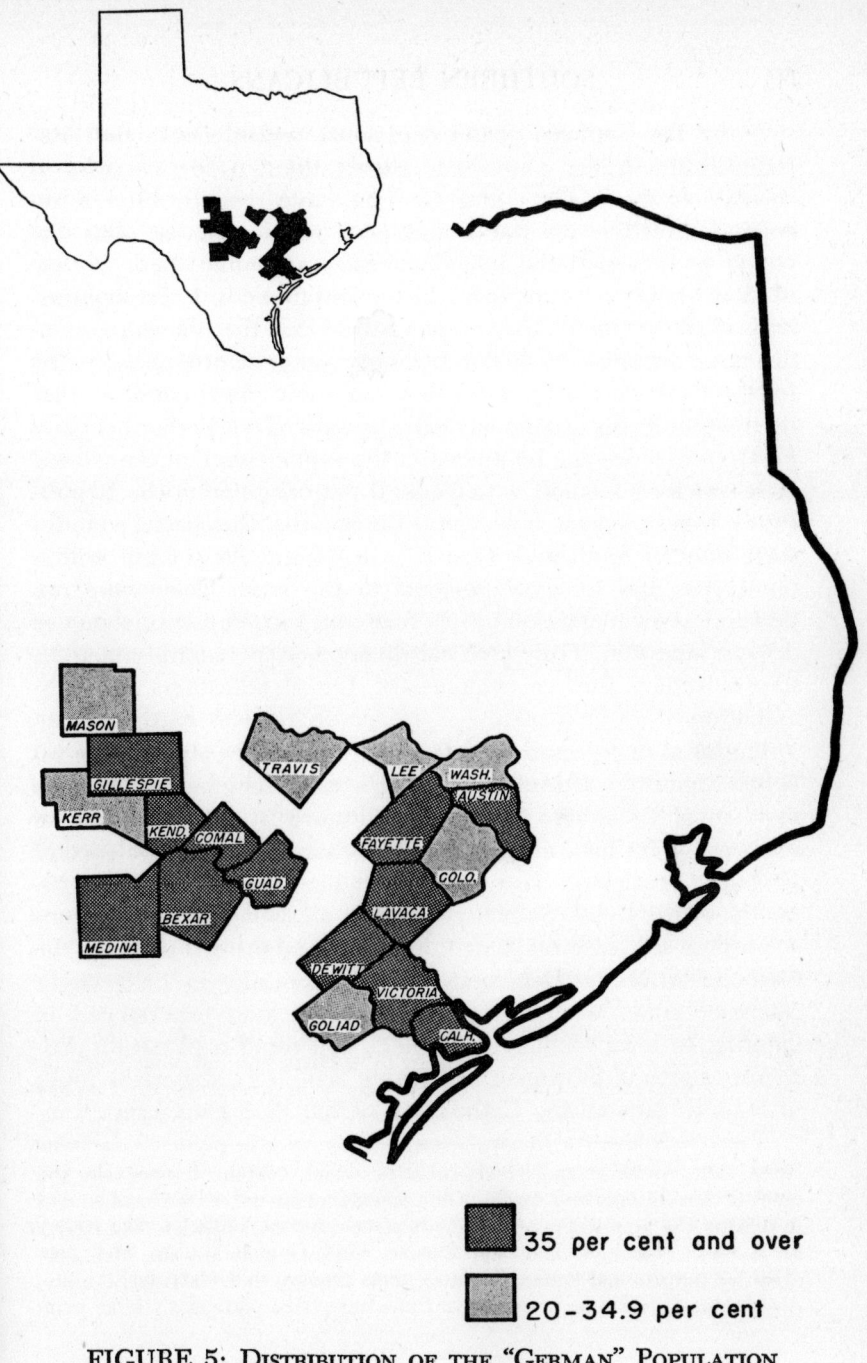

FIGURE 5: DISTRIBUTION OF THE "GERMAN" POPULATION OF TEXAS, 1890

Along the southern coasts occasional tendencies toward Republicanism do not conform to expectations. A few counties in coastal North Carolina and Georgia have demonstrated a recurring affection for the Republican party at odds with the voting behavior of the inland counties adjoining them. A few of them show up on the maps in Figures 2 and 4. Local explanations vary. In North Carolina one is told that the tidewater counties were occupied by Federal troops who generated a sympathy for the GOP that lasted after they had gone. Be it admitted that occupation forces usually have an opposite effect. Perhaps slightly greater credence can be placed in the suggestion that the coastal area was long favored with Federal patronage from the Republicans. More relevant, however, is the fact that the coastal counties were ones of few slaves (see Figure 3) and do not fall within the cotton and tobacco crescents to the west. They were not dependent on plantation agriculture and turned a cool shoulder toward secession. Their political divergence, perceptible in 1861, lingers today, further evidence of the steadfastness of party affiliation.

The local interpretation of Georgia's coastal Republicanism involves inherited attitudes again, this time religious. A lifetime resident of Effingham County (see Figure 2) could suggest no explanation for his county's behavior other than the prevalence of Lutheran sentiment. The county had been settled in the eighteenth century by Salzburgers and a strong religious consciousness still endures. Our informant thought a dislike for the Catholicism of the Democratic party, especially in 1928, might influence some voters. A state politician long experienced in catering to local feelings gave much the same explanation. Lutherans north of Savannah and strong Scotch Presbyterians south of it both resented the Catholicism of the 1928 Democratic can-

---

lation shifts in Bexar and Travis counties, which contain, respectively, the cities of San Antonio and Austin. The percentages from the 1890 census used in making the map in Figure 5 include some other nationalities. The figures for Bexar, Calhoun, Goliad, and Victoria counties include some Mexicans; those for Fayette and Lavaca counties, some Czechs; that for Travis County, some Swedes.

didate. Voters in these counties, however, have more than a transient affinity for the Republican party. Intensive local inquiry might turn up economic and social factors not otherwise perceptible. The high proportion of Negroes in some of the counties gives them special interest to the analyst. The significant fact remains, nevertheless, that here are fixed allegiances, and, as research into political behavior has increasingly demonstrated, the allegiances do not necessarily originate in so-called "rational" political incentives.

It would be most unnatural if southern politics were not affected by population shifts. Of course it is. All of Florida except the northern strip bordering Alabama and Georgia has been opened and settled since the Civil War. The state contains more than twice as many citizens born outside its borders (48.1 per cent in 1940) as any other southern state. Though the largest numbers have come from nearby states, many of the migrants have come from Republican areas of the East and Middle West, and many of those have brought their politics with them. The patches of Florida Republican strength on the map in Figure 2 represent, in the main, a different type of Republican voter than we have been discussing. The lesser importance in Florida of fixed political traditions and a more diverse, dynamic economic life have made it easier for outsiders to hold on to their politics than in most of the South.

Republican immigrants are not confined to Florida. They are important in the fruit and vegetable country of Texas' lower Rio Grande Valley. Hints toward Republican sympathies in southwest Louisiana are explained locally by the numbers of outsiders who were attracted to the state several decades ago by its timber resources. Similarly, the upswing in the Republican vote in certain south Mississippi counties in 1928 was explained by the activities of persons attracted from the North by the lumber industry. In the broad sweep of southern politics, however, relatively few Republican votes come from immigrants.

So much for the origins of southern Republicans. And now—how strong are they?

4

HOW STRONG ARE THEY?

TO SPEAK OF "THE" REPUBLICAN PARTY IN THE SOUTH IS LIKE SPEAKing of "the" American novel. There is more than one, and no one is exactly like the others. There is a type, perhaps, but within it individualities cut so deeply as to render the type almost meaningless.

Ancestral origins account for some of the differences in Republicanism from state to state. The principal differences, however, spring from the wide variations in the party's strength. The number of Republican voters varies from state to state in the South just as it varies from section to section in the nation. In a few states, they are numerous enough to make the thought of winning an election somewhat more real than a fairy tale. In others, they number so few that the party is little more than a fiction. The possibilities of strengthening the party vary correspondingly from state to state.

This chapter is concerned mostly with election returns. We shall learn from them the levels of Republican activity in each southern state and shall also look for hints of a sustained rise or fall in party strength in each of the states.

The first of these matters can be disposed of relatively quickly. Table 5 shows the Republican share of the vote for president in 1944, along with that for governor in the same year (or in the closest year in which a governor was elected). The table does not employ the results of 1948 because in some states the Dixiecratic vote may have disturbed the normal distribution of strength between the major parties. In Table 5, the states of the region

TABLE 5

REPUBLICAN PERCENTAGE OF THE TOTAL VOTE IN THE SOUTHERN STATES, 1944

State	For president	For governor[a]
Tennessee	39.2	36.0
Virginia	37.4	31.0 (1945)
North Carolina	33.3	30.4
Arkansas	29.8	14.0
Florida	29.7	21.1
Texas	16.8[b]	9.1
Louisiana	19.4	No candidate
Alabama	18.2	11.3 (1946)
Georgia	17.2	[c] (1946)
Mississippi	6.4[d]	No candidate (1943)
South Carolina	4.5	No candidate (1946)

[a] 1944, unless otherwise specified.

[b] Does not include vote for Texas Regulars, an anti-New Deal uninstructed slate, that polled 11.8 per cent of the votes. See pp. 159, 258-61, below.

[c] Democratic candidate received over 99 per cent of the votes.

[d] Includes vote for both regular Republican (2.08 per cent) and Independent Republican (4.36 per cent) slates.

fall into three groups. In what we shall call the Upper South—Tennessee, Virginia, and North Carolina—the Republican party polled more than 30 per cent of the total vote for both president and governor. In three other states, Arkansas, Florida, and Texas, the party was somewhat weaker, though almost 30 per cent of the voters opposed the Democratic presidential nominee, and in each case the Republican nominee for governor drew more than a token vote. In the third group, the party was weakest of all. These states, the Deep South—Louisiana, Alabama, Georgia,

Mississippi, and South Carolina—all gave less than 20 per cent of their votes to the Republican presidential aspirant and none save Alabama had a meaningful Republican candidate for governor. Over all the South, the turnout of voters in general elections falls where competition between the parties is lopsided. This means that Republican voters in the Upper South not only contribute a larger proportion of those who vote, but that those who vote constitute a larger proportion of the potential electorate.

It takes no sage to see that party politics differ in South Carolina where Governor Dewey received 4 per cent of the votes from that in Tennessee where he attracted 39 per cent of them. These differences among the states are continuing ones, remaining about the same election after election. See, for illustration, the graphs in Figure 6 on page 61. Casual observers frequently gloss over the differences, but we would do well to keep them constantly in mind. They mean that any shifts in the political balance in the South will almost certainly take place piecemeal. They suggest also that forces conducive to two-party politics in one state may be ineffectual in another.

The turnout of voters in the presidential and gubernatorial races does not reflect completely the varieties of Republicanism among the states. The phenomenon of "presidential Republicans," revealed in the disparity between the vote for president and governor, is taken up at some length in chapter 9. There are also variations resulting from the way the Republican voters are distributed in a state. Thus, Florida, 29.7 per cent Republican in 1944, had no counties in which Dewey received a majority and only 12 (out of 67) in which he received over 35 per cent of the votes. In contrast, Arkansas, with virtually an identical Republican percentage in the state as a whole, held four counties with over 50 per cent for Dewey and 18 more (out of 75) that gave him between 35 and 49.9 per cent. Manifestly, the Republicans in Florida are more evenly dispersed than those in Arkansas.

Concentrations of Republican strength are significant in so far as they give the party a foothold in local government. A substantial geographical base conduces to party virility. To Republican politicos in such areas, politics is not whimsey, but a way

HOW STRONG ARE THEY?

of gaining and losing office. A handful of counties regularly giving a majority to the Republican presidential nominee, sending Republicans to the legislature, perhaps even to Congress, and capturing local government patronage provides a party nucleus in touch with political realities. In states without Republican officeholders the party tends to become a sort of social club operating without reference to the electorate.

Tennessee, Virginia, and North Carolina possess the largest areas of heavy Republican concentration. Data are not available on the extent of Republican control of county and municipal governments, but the number of Republican state legislators holding office in 1950 offers an index of Republican local supremacy. Of 132 Tennessee legislators, 23 were Republican; of 170 North Carolina legislators, 15 were Republican; of 140 in Virginia, 9 were Republican. The legislatures of Arkansas, Georgia, and Alabama had one Republican each, and those of Florida, Louisiana, Mississippi, South Carolina, and Texas had none at all.[1]

Republican parties around the South are further differentiated by the extent to which they contest elections. Even in the deepest southern states, if they possess the will, Republicans can put up candidates for major offices and with moderate efforts generate a respectable degree of support for them. Table 6 presents a tabulation of the elections for United States representative, United States senator, and governor in each southern state from 1920 through 1950. It shows the number of contests for each office and the percentage of the contests in which a Republican nominee received 5 per cent or more of the votes.

The states of the Upper South, by this measure too, have the most virile Republicanism. North Carolina Republicans had a candidate for governor and one for senator every year throughout the period. In roughly seven-eighths of the Congressional district contests they had a candidate who polled 5 per cent or more of the votes. Tennessee and Virginia followed closely behind North Carolina, and at the other end of the scale the Deep South states of Louisiana, Georgia, Mississippi, and South Carolina witnessed almost no Republican candidacies.

These disparities further stress the fact that building a second party does not present identical problems in all the states. In those accustomed to a fight over state or Congressional offices, no matter how perfunctory, there develops a set of voters and cam-

TABLE 6
SOUTHERN ELECTIONS CONTESTED BY REPUBLICANS, 1920-1950, SELECTED OFFICES

State	The number of elections held and the percentage of them in which a Republican candidate received 5 per cent or more of the votes, for:					
	U.S. representative		U.S. senator		Governor	
North Carolina	175	86.3	13	100.0	8	100.0
Tennessee	155	60.6	13	92.3	16	93.8[a]
Virginia	150	61.3	13	69.2	8	100.0
Florida	79	51.9	13	69.2	8	87.5
Texas	319	40.4	11	72.7	16	81.3
Arkansas	112	31.3	12	58.3	16	87.5
Alabama	150	34.7	14	64.3	8	87.5
Louisiana	128	4.7	12	16.7	8	0.0
Georgia	160[b]	6.3	13	15.4	15	0.0
Mississippi	118	4.2	11	9.1	8[c]	0.0
South Carolina	102	5.9	12	0.0	10	0.0

[a] In 1950 there was no Republican nominee, but a candidate on the "Good Government Ticket" polled 21.9 per cent of the votes.
[b] 1922-50.
[c] 1919-47.

paign workers habituated to Republican politics. They offer a framework in which the mechanics of party politics can be developed. Given a going organization, the number of voters may be expanded by hard work and shrewd politicking. Where no sizeable going organization exists, the problem of building the party lies not only in a shortage of voters, but also in the difficulty of developing machinery, skill, leadership, financial resources, and all the other sinews of political warfare.

A search for trends in Republican voting during the three decades after 1920 will improve our perspective on the relative vigor of Republicanism over the South. In some states Republican percentages are so tiny that trends mean little. And always there is the danger that chance variations will mislead. But while a search in the elections figures for hints of things to come may not give assured predictions, it will deepen our understanding of the Republican position. Has all the late hullabaloo about the Democratic party actually strengthened the Republicans? Democratic solidarity may be wearing away by attrition. On the other hand, by the process of stimulus-and-response, Republican challenges may be met as firmly as they are offered, and the net effect of growing Republican sentiment may be an invigorated Democratic party rather than a run of Republican victories.

Two approaches must be taken. Voting in presidential elections is one index; voting in state and Congressional elections is another. Republican voting for president from 1916 through 1948 in each of our eleven states has been plotted on three graphs in Figure 6.* They trace the rise and fall in the percentage of the popular vote cast for the Republican candidate at each election. The top graph shows the states where the party is strongest; the lower graph, those where it is weakest; the middle graph, the others. On each of the graphs there appears a line for the Republican percentage in the nation as a whole.

The graphs reveal several things about southern Republicanism. The party's strength in the region fluctuates with the party's strength in the nation. At every election between 1916 and 1932 the curve of each state turned up or down with the national curve. Subsequently, during the era of overwhelming Democratic dominance, the state and national fluctuations from election to election narrowed, and in some states the party gained or lost strength contrary to the trend in the nation. Thus, in Texas, Arkansas, Georgia, and Louisiana, the party drew a slightly larger percentage of the votes at the 1936 polling than it had in

* The data from which the graphs were made are contained in Appendix II.

1932, in contrast to the nation-wide fall. Contrary also to the national trend, the North Carolina Republican percentage declined between 1936 and 1940, as did that of Texas between 1940 and 1944. The 1948 election brought increases in Georgia, Alabama, Texas, Florida, and Virginia against a slight decline in the nation and despite the candidacy of the Dixiecrat.

Regardless of the aberrations, clearly the factors that determine the party's appeal in the rest of the United States also operate in the South. This is true although in many southern states there is little solicitation of votes except that overflowing from other regions through the press, radio, television and movies. This fact is most important where the Republicans have a sufficient foothold to make occasional victory possible. In the Upper South, aggressive leadership might turn a national trend into victory at home. Presidential politics in the South, despite its lopsidedness, is not as isolated from the national scene as is sometimes assumed.

The graphs also demonstrate, however, that influences affect Republican voting in individual southern states and throughout the region that do not affect the national appeal of the party in the same way. Such a conclusion emerges from comparing changes in the national Republican percentage between presidential elections—the amount the Republican percentage rose or fell—with corresponding changes in the individual states. On many occasions Republican strength in a state veered more sharply than in the nation.* The small Republican vote in some states gives the comparisons limited meaning. A small body of voters may at times fluctuate in size more sharply than a larger

---

* For example, between 1936 and 1940 the Republican presidential vote rose 8.2 per cent in the nation and fell 2.3 per cent in Georgia. Thus Georgia's fluctuation varied from that of the country by 10.5 per cent. Except for shifts involving 1928, this was the greatest divergence during the period. The maximum divergences from the national trend in the other years were: between 1916-20, 9.3 per cent (Louisiana); 1920-24, 5.1 per cent (South Carolina); 1932-36, 8.6 per cent (Arkansas); 1940-44, 7.6 per cent (Arkansas); 1944-48, 8.6 per cent (Texas).

FIGURE 6: REPUBLICAN PERCENTAGE OF TOTAL PRESIDENTIAL VOTE, 1916-1948: U. S. AND SOUTHERN STATES⟶

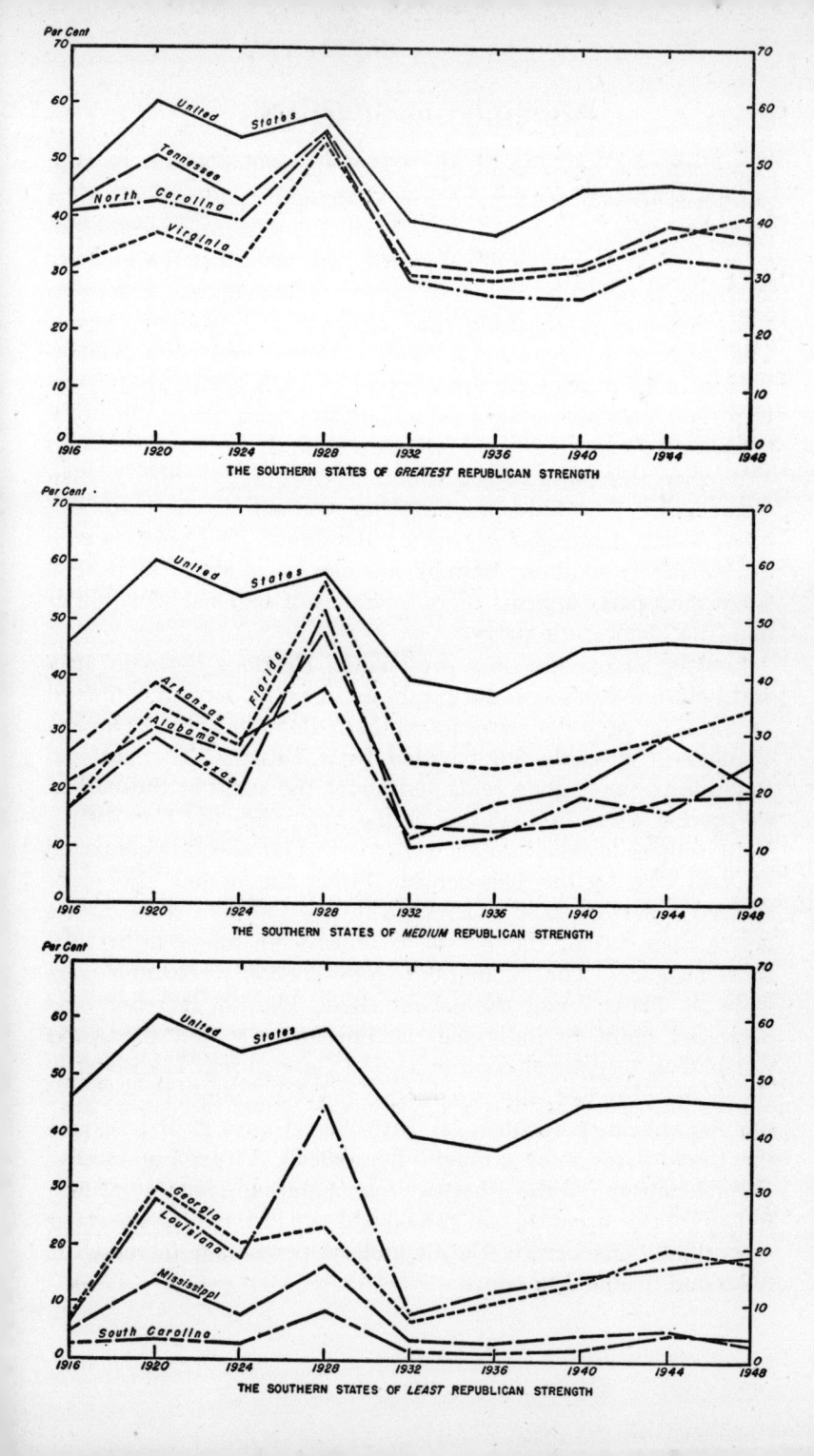

THE SOUTHERN STATES OF *GREATEST* REPUBLICAN STRENGTH

THE SOUTHERN STATES OF *MEDIUM* REPUBLICAN STRENGTH

THE SOUTHERN STATES OF *LEAST* REPUBLICAN STRENGTH

group. On the other hand, the handicaps under which the Republicans operate in such states as Mississippi and South Carolina make an increase of even a handful of Republicans something of a feat. In any event, political realists will note that the low Republican percentage in some places would permit enormous gains without approaching the national, or a winning, figure. The greatest divergencies between national and state fluctuations of course involved the election of 1928. Southern Republican percentages, almost unanimously, rose more abruptly between 1924 and 1928, and fell more abruptly between 1928 and 1932, than did those of the country.[2] Governor Smith's Roman Catholicism, East Side provincialism, and attitude toward prohibition had a peculiar impact on the South. The point is well to remember: southern Republicans can be mightily reinforced when their party appears more solicitous of regional sensibilities than the Democratic party.

Looking across the nine presidential elections between 1916 and 1948, one can see in the graphs no sustained tendency toward an increase, or a decrease, in southern Republicanism. The net changes in strength can be read from Table 7. The national Republican percentage remained about the same at the end of the period (45.1 in 1948) as at the beginning (46.1 in 1916). Both of these terminal points were marked by a closely contested election won by the Democrats. During the period, the party showed a net decrease in strength in five southern states and a net increase in six, though the changes were minor in at least three instances. The fluctuations from election to election were wide, as Table 7 and the graphs show. The net increases and decreases point to individual circumstances within the states rather than to general conditions. (In Georgia and Louisiana, it should be observed, the Progressive ticket substantially reduced the Republican percentage in 1916. See Appendix II.) Among the three states most strongly Republican, Virginia gained in Republicanism and the other two lost; among the four states next in Republican strength, two gained and two lost; among the states most solidly Democratic, the Republican percentage increased in three and declined in one.

TABLE 7

Trends in Southern Presidential Voting:
Republican Percentage of Popular Vote, 1880, 1916, 1948

State	1880 [3]	1916	Elections between 1916-1948 Highest Republican percentage received	Elections between 1916-1948 Lowest Republican percentage received	1948
Virginia	39.5	32.1	53.9	29.4	41.0
Tennessee	44.5	42.8	55.3	30.8	36.9
North Carolina	48.0	41.7	54.9	26.0	32.7
Florida	45.8	18.1	56.8	23.9	33.6
Texas	23.9	17.4	52.0	11.4	24.6
Arkansas	40.0	28.0	38.6	12.5	21.0
Alabama	37.0	21.9	48.5	12.8	19.0
Georgia	34.3	7.1	44.0	7.1	18.3
Louisiana	37.1	7.0	30.5	7.0	17.5
South Carolina	34.0	2.4	8.5	1.4	3.8
Mississippi	29.9	4.9	17.3	2.6	2.6
UNITED STATES	48.3	46.1	60.3	36.5	45.1

As a matter of record, the percentage of the popular vote received by the Republican presidential candidate in 1880 is included in Table 7. Except in Virginia and Texas, the decline since this election, the first after Reconstruction, has been general. The party had a respectable following in every state in 1880. It was weakest, however, and its decline has been sharpest, in the Deep South. The disfranchisement of Negroes hurt the party in all states, but perhaps most in certain of the areas where they were most numerous. The Republican rise in Texas has been influenced by the settlement since 1880 of the western half of the state and by the development of its great concentration of wealth—factors not prevalent in the rest of the South, with the partial exception of Florida.

More important than trends over the whole period are the

tendencies revealed by the 1944 and 1948 elections. Since 1940, the resentment that has developed in some southern circles against the New and Fair Deals seems to have expressed itself partly in a mild increase in southern Republican sentiment, an increase

TABLE 8

SHIFTS IN SOUTHERN VOTING FOR REPUBLICAN PRESIDENTIAL CANDIDATES, 1940-1948

State	Increase (+) and decline (−) in percentage of total vote received compared with previous election 1944	1948	Net change between 1940 and 1948
Virginia	+ 5.9	+ 3.6	+ 9.5
Tennessee	+ 6.9	− 2.3	+ 4.6
North Carolina	+ 7.3	− 0.6	+ 6.7
Florida	+ 3.7	+ 3.9	+ 7.6
Texas	− 2.2	+ 7.8	+ 5.6
Arkansas	+ 8.8	− 8.8	0.0
Alabama	+ 3.8	+ 0.8	+ 4.6
Georgia	+ 2.3	+ 1.1	+ 3.4
Louisiana	+ 5.3	− 1.9	+ 3.4
South Carolina	+ 2.6	− 0.7	+ 1.9
Mississippi	+ 2.2	− 3.8	− 1.6
UNITED STATES	+ 1.2	− 0.8	+ 0.4

as compared to the Republican vote in the nation. Table 8 presents the change in the percentage of the total vote received by the Republican presidential candidate in the United States and in each of the southern states between the elections of 1940 and 1944, between those of 1944 and 1948, and the net change between 1940 and 1948.

In every state of the South save one the Republicans gained a larger percentage of the total vote between 1940 and 1944 than they did in the country as a whole. The election in Texas, the exception, was affected by a slate of electors known as the Texas Regulars. The slate had one objective, to obstruct the candidacy of Franklin Roosevelt, and the county election returns indicate that Republicans as well as unhappy Democrats were attracted to it. Thus, Washington County, where the Texas Regulars were strongest, cast 52.2 per cent of its votes in 1944 for the Regulars and 13.3 per cent for the Republicans. Its Republican percentage in 1940 was 56.3 and in 1948 was 50.9. The returns of the four counties next highest in Texas Regular strength (Austin, Midland, Colorado, Matagorda) conform generally to the same pattern. (See Appendix I, pp. 260-61.)

In 1948 the Republican percentage in the country slipped by 0.8 from the 1944 level. In the South, a continuation of the 1944 upward trend may have been interrupted by the Dixiecratic candidate. Thurmond appealed to dissatisfied Democrats, the natural recruits of the Republicans. Though he drew his greatest strength from the areas traditionally least Republican, perhaps his candidacy affected Republican fortunes.

The Dixiecrats ran strongest in Mississippi, South Carolina, and Louisiana (and of course Alabama, where no Truman electors appeared on the ballot).* The Mississippi Republican percentage, pitiful as it already was, went down sharply. The South Carolina percentage declined about the same as the nation's and the Louisiana percentage fell somewhat more. The Dixiecrats ran weakest in North Carolina, Texas, and Virginia; the Republican percentage declined less in North Carolina than in the nation and in the other two states the Republicans showed an increase. Among the remaining five states, Alabama, Florida, and Georgia showed a strengthening, and Tennessee and Arkansas showed a marked weakening of the GOP.

Although the table shows that between 1940 and 1948 Republican voting strengthened notably in parts of the South, the bare figures *prove* nothing, and those tempted to read a serious

* See Table 3, p. 26, for the Dixiecratic percentage of the total vote in each state.

TABLE

Percentage of Total Vote for Candidates, Southern

State	1920	1922	1924	1926	1928	1930	1932	1934
Virginia[c]	31.3		25.9		37.0		24.3	
Tennessee	54.9	42.1	42.8	35.2	38.9	35.6	30.5	[d]
North Carolina	42.8		38.7		44.4		29.9	
Florida	19.9[f]		17.2		39.0		32.1	
Texas	18.7	18.0	41.1	11.9	17.0	19.8	37.4	3.1
Arkansas	24.4	21.9	20.0	23.5	22.7	18.5	8.9	9.4
Alabama		21.3		18.6		[j]		12.7

[a] During this period there was no Republican candidate in Georgia. There was none in Mississippi except in 1947, when the "Independent Republican" received 2.5 per cent of the votes. There was none in South Carolina except in 1938 when one received 0.6 per cent of the votes. In Louisiana, Republican candidates have run in the following years, and received these percentages of the vote: 1920, 2.4; 1924, 2.1; 1928, 3.9; 1940, 0.6.

[b] Of the elections in which there was a Republican candidate.

[c] Virginia elects its governor quadrenially in the year following the presidential election.

portent into them should remember that 1928 was followed by 1932.

A major presidential candidate automatically attracts a quota of votes, regardless of the vigor of his local campaign managers. A party's efforts to capture state offices constitutes a truer test of party virility. Scrutiny of the returns of southern gubernatorial elections will further illuminate differences in the Republicans from state to state and will permit a second search for signs of Republican growth.

Again the states fall into three groups. Republican candidates for governor in Virginia, Tennessee, and North Carolina have consistently drawn higher proportions of the vote than in other states. (See Table 9.) On the average, in the thirty years after

9

GOVERNOR RECEIVED BY REPUBLICAN
STATES, 1920-1950[a]

1936	1938	1940	1942	1944	1946	1948	1950	Average[b]
	15.8		17.7		31.0		27.4	26.3
18.9	28.3	27.9	29.8	36.0	31.9	33.1	[e]	34.7
33.3		24.3		30.4		26.4		33.5
19.1	[g]			21.1		16.6		23.6
7.0	2.3	5.5	3.2	9.1	8.8	14.7	10.1	14.2
14.6	4.8[h]	10.9	[i]	14.0	15.9	10.8	15.9	15.7
	12.4		10.5		11.3		8.9	13.7

[d] The unsuccessful candidate for the Democratic nomination ran in the general election, receiving 38.2 per cent of the votes.

[e] No Republican nominee, but a candidate on the "Good Government Ticket" polled 21.9 per cent of the votes.

[f] Includes "Republican" and "Republican, White."

[g] Candidate withdrew.

[h] An Independent received 8.5 per cent.

[i] No Republican candidate.

[j] A Hoovercrat, barred from the Democratic primaries, ran as an independent and received 38.2 per cent of the votes.

1920 they polled about a fourth of the votes in Virginia and about a third of the votes in the other two states. Republican candidates in Florida, Texas, Arkansas, and Alabama fall into a second group, averaging in the same period between one-seventh and less than one-fourth of the votes. In Louisiana, Georgia, Mississippi, and South Carolina, Republican candidates either did not appear on the ballot or attracted minuscule support. Ability and willingness to contest for the state's highest office during thirty years reflects not only the character of the party's leadership in a state but also something of the problem of building it into a serious political movement. The details of the gubernatorial voting buttress the obvious conclusion that competitive politics can be developed most readily in the border states. To all intents and purposes there is no Republican party in states that fail to put up candidates for the governorship.*

During the years 1920-50, the proportion of the votes cast for Republican candidates for governor declined in most of the states. The period begins in the pinnacle era of Republicanism in the nation and ends with the Democrats still in power after five successful presidential campaigns. The potency of Republican gubernatorial candidates followed roughly the potency of the party's presidential candidates: greatest during the twenties, least during the thirties. This pattern prevailed most neatly in Virginia, Tennessee, and Texas,† and in all three cases the Republican percentage was lower at the end of the period than at the beginning.

In some ways, North Carolina party politics possesses greater vigor than found elsewhere in the region. Yet the Republican bid for the governorship has gradually declined since 1920. The percentage of the popular votes received has fluctuated regularly up and down, but the persistent trend has been downward. Florida, Alabama, and Arkansas enthusiasm for Republican candidates pursued a more uneven pattern. In all three cases, how-

* The time of holding gubernatorial elections may affect the Republican turnout. The presence of a concurrent presidential campaign might be expected to bring out a larger Republican vote for governor than appears in off years. In such a case, Republicans in states like North Carolina and Florida, that elect governors every four years along with presidential electors, would make a better showing than Republicans in a state like Alabama where the governor is elected in the even year between presidential elections. The tenuous nature of the notion is shown by the Tennessee returns in Table 9. The Republican percentage for governor does not bob up neatly in presidential years and down in other years in that state. In Texas, however, a regular fluctuation seems to be the case. Probably the more genuine the bid for state office, the less dependent on the national campaign is the interest shown in the local race.

† With regard to Texas, the 1924 and 1932 contests require special mention. In both years Democrats, dissatisfied with the Democratic nominee, "Ma" Ferguson, openly bolted the ticket to support the Republican candidate. In each instance the fight became one between two factions of the Democratic party as well as between the Democratic and Republican nominees.

HOW STRONG ARE THEY?

ever, the vote for governor declined during the thirties from earlier highs and did not revive in the forties. These figures reveal plainly that the Republicans have not gained in state politics from the dissensions within the Democratic party.

To complete the record, Table 10 presents the percentage of the total vote that southern Republican candidates for the United States Senate received between 1920 and 1950. The general pattern conforms to that of the vote for governor. Comparisons are most meaningful in the years the Republicans had candidates running for both offices. For most of the period, the vote for the two offices in North Carolina and Tennessee followed each other closely. The Republican senatorial vote in Virginia ran behind the party's gubernatorial vote. The character of the Virginia senators no doubt explains the situation in that state. Glass, in office virtually all of the period, possessed an unassailable personal following founded on a long career and enormous prestige. Byrd, in office much of the period, had the backing of America's most tightly disciplined state machine. Both senators were conservatively inclined. In many elections they were more effective proponents of Republicanism than any candidates that party might have put forward.

In Alabama, senatorial voting ran about the same as gubernatorial voting in the same year. The situation was similar in Texas on several occasions, with notable exceptions in 1924 and 1948. In the former year many Democrats bolted the ticket to vote against "Ma" Ferguson for governor, a special case involving a split in the Democratic ranks. In the latter year, many Democrats voted for the Republican senatorial candidate in protest over the narrow margin by which the Democrat had won his party's nomination. The unsuccessful candidate for the Democratic nomination charged fraud and announced his support of the Republican in the general election. In Florida and Arkansas, the Republican percentages of the vote for the two offices often diverged, though cast in the same year. It should be remembered, with respect to both Table 9 and Table 10, that the averages shown ignore the years in which no candidate ran, thus limiting their usefulness for comparative purposes.

TABLE

PERCENTAGE OF TOTAL VOTE FOR UNITED
CANDIDATES, SOUTHERN

State	1920	1922[b]	1924	1926	1928	1930	1932	1934
Virginia	8.7[d]	26.9	24.2		[e]	[e]	26.7[f]	20.9
Tennessee		32.0	42.6		40.7	27.1[h]		35.8[i]
North Carolina	42.5		38.4	39.5		39.4	31.4[j]	
Florida	26.0	11.7		12.8	31.5		[e]	[e]
Texas		33.1	14.6		18.6	12.7		2.8
Arkansas	34.1		26.5	15.2		[e]	10.3	
Alabama	33.1[p]		20.5	19.1		[e]	13.8	

[a] During this period, there were no Republican candidates in Louisiana except in a special election in 1948 when one received 25.0 per cent of the votes; and in the regular election of 1950, when one received 12.3 per cent of the votes. There was none in Mississippi except in 1922, when the Republican attracted 5.4 per cent of the votes. The only candidates in Georgia ran in 1920 and 1932, polling 5.1 and 7.2 per cent of the votes in the respective years. Republican candidates received votes in South Carolina in the following years, in the percentages indicated: 1932, 1.9; 1936, 0.6; 1938, 1.1; 1944, 3.2; 1948, 3.6. Independent candidates not noted for any states.

[b] This year only, percentage of major party vote.

[c] Of the special and regular elections in which there was a Republican candidate.

[d] A special election.

[e] No Republican candidate.

[f] This was a special election held in 1933.

[g] A special election also held this year, Republican receiving 29.1 per cent of the votes.

Tables similar to those above could be presented for the Congressional district races. They would show little in addition to what is revealed by the gubernatorial and senatorial figures. Only in East Tennessee's first and second Congressional districts do southern Republicans regularly win House seats. Suffice it to examine the 1920 and 1948 voting summarized in Table 11.

10
STATES SENATOR RECEIVED BY REPUBLICAN
STATES, 1920-1950ᵃ

1936	1938	1940	1942	1944	1946	1948	1950	Averageᶜ
4.7		e	6.5		30.5ᵍ	32.0		*21.0*
19.4	26.2ᵈ	29.2	21.5		26.2	33.9		*32.7*
29.2	36.2		34.1	29.7		28.8	31.3ᵏ	*34.2*
19.1ᵐ	17.6	e		28.7	21.3		21.2	*21.1*
7.1		5.7	4.4ⁿ		11.5	32.9		*13.0*
15.9ᵒ	10.4		e	14.9		e	e	*18.2*
12.8	13.6ⁱ		e	16.9	q	16.0	e	*19.5*

ʰ A special election also held this year, Republican receiving 25.6 per cent of the votes.

ⁱ A special election also held this year, no Republican running.

ʲ A special election held concurrently between same candidates, Republican again receiving 31.4 per cent of the votes.

ᵏ A special election also held this year, Republican receiving 32.6 per cent of the votes.

ᵐ A special election; a second special election also held this year, no Republican running.

ⁿ A special election was held in 1941, Republican receiving an infinitesimal vote.

ᵒ A special election was held in 1937, no Republican running.

ᵖ A special election also held this year, Republican receiving 29.5 per cent of the votes.

ᵠ A special election held this year, no Republican running.

Again the states group themselves as before, with the Upper South states heading the list and the Deep South bringing up the rear. Though 1920 was a year of Republican resurgence, and 1948 a year of defeat, the difference in the Republican competition for seats in the House between the two years cannot be ignored. Although 1948 was the year when Democrats and Republicans alike expected the GOP to recover control of Federal patronage, in every state except North Carolina a smaller share

TABLE 11

DECLINE IN REPUBLICAN COMPETITION FOR UNITED STATES REPRESENTATIVE, SOUTHERN STATES, 1920 AND 1948[a]

State	1920 No. of districts in state	1920 No. of districts with candidates	1920 Average per cent vote received[b]	1948 No. of districts in state	1948 No. of districts with candidates	1948 Average per cent vote received[b]
Virginia	10	10	30.4	9	7	34.4
Tennessee	10	10	47.1	10	7	40.2
North Carolina	10	10	38.6	12	12	25.5
Florida	4	4	15.7	6	4	22.6
Texas	18	12	21.3	21	9	10.9
Arkansas	7	7	32.6	7	3	19.1
Alabama	10	7	30.9	9	4	14.3

[a] Louisiana had no Republican candidates in 1920, and one in 1948 who polled 33.4 per cent of the votes. Mississippi had four in 1920, averaging 5.1 per cent of the votes, and one in 1948, polling 1.6 per cent. South Carolina had two in 1920, averaging 7.8 per cent, six in 1948, averaging 4.6 per cent. Georgia returns for 1920 are not available. In 1922, two Republicans offered, averaging 5.9 per cent; in 1948, none.

[b] The average of the Republican percentage of the total vote only for the districts in which a Republican candidate offered.

of the state's Congressional seats was bid for by Republicans than in 1920. In the states other than Virginia and Florida, the average Republican vote in the districts with contests also fell. The rise in the average percentage in Virginia parallels the general strengthening of the Republican position in that state. The rise in Florida accords with the tendency of the presidential vote in that state.

The review, in this chapter, of southern voting in general elections has revealed several characteristics of the Republican party in the South. First, there are fairly consistent variations in the party's virility from state to state. Moreover, in presidential elections the party in the South shows fluctuations in common with the party in the nation as a whole, as well as aberrations from the national pattern. In some states, the Republican presidential percentage declined and in others it increased between 1916 and 1948, but most interesting, and perhaps most significant, was a tendency toward an increase between 1940 and 1948 as compared with the party throughout the nation. In other races—elections of governor, United States senator, and United States representative—the Republicans generally showed less, and declining, vigor. Part of the explanation for these things could be found in the conditions under which the Republicans worked.

5

SHACKLES ON THE MINORITY

The statistics of Republican voting hint only tentatively at changes in the political balance of the South. The prospect that Democratic dominance will decline must rest, rather, on a developing clash of interests so closely touching the hearts of men, or their pocketbooks, that ultimately political habits will be changed.

Habits become prejudices, however, or the other way around, and a dominant group, like the Democratic party, encourages community attitudes and formulates public policies designed to perpetuate the established way. To picture the present Democratic party as a "dominant group" in most southern states would be mildly ludicrous, since almost everybody is a Democrat and there is no one left to be dominated. But looking across seventy-five years, Democrats have had to gain and retain their position in as hotly fought a politics as the country records. The victory dearly won is not lightly lost, and the party has dug in at every juncture to protect its superiority.

Southern Republicans operate under election laws enacted and administered by governments that are, for all intents and purposes, unanimously Democratic. They are the objects of a bias that only recently has ceased to view their party as the agent of an occupying power. And they meet the resistances encountered by any challenge to the status quo. Political repression, economic coercion, and social ostracism are familiar to minority parties everywhere. They exist in the South, too, and southern Republican leaders point to these shackles to justify the apathy that pervades their efforts to build a strong party. In periodic fits of frustration they cry out against the social and legal handicaps under which they labor. And rightly, too.

Consider the secretary of the Democratic state committee in one state. He said, quite simply, that he would like to vote Republican. Most Americans who think and live and act as he does are Republicans. The Democratic party has become, according to him, the party of Negroes, labor, and all the people who can't or won't make a living. They're not his kind. But if he voted Republican once, he says, and even if the Republicans won in that election, he might as well "turn in his papers" and abandon any ambition for a successful law practice. Not all Democrats are as forthright, but in the ninth decade after Appomattox the predicament was repeated thousands of times in every southern state.

An ancient prejudice against Republicans endures in the present as a community convention, one of the folkways. The convention is fortified by the calculated maneuvers of southerners who see a political, economic, or social advantage in the status quo, who see a means to gain against competitors who have trespassed on the code. And so, when a small-town Georgia Ford dealer has the temerity to favor a Republican presidential candidate, he loses "17 trade-in customers" to the Chevrolet dealer across the square. A retail merchant attributes a drop of one-third in his trade to the fact that he bolted the Democratic ticket. A Yankee emigrant raised hay successfully in the Alabama black belt until he disclosed that he always voted the Republican ticket. An "informal boycott" went into effect and after that he had trouble selling his crop. A Texan of substance fairly hated F.D.R. He expressed good will toward the Republican party but protested, "If you join, you lose your influence."

The tenacity of political bias is a wonder to behold, but southern Democrats have not relied on it alone. They have passed laws that put their opponents at a paralyzing disadvantage. Numerous legal stitches that hold both Republicans and Democrats in their places will appear as our story goes forward. The sanctions against party disloyalty, for example, will be noted in chapter 9, where presidential Republicans are examined. Legal definitions of "political party" sometimes force Republicans to finance their own primaries while the state pays for those of the larger party, a burden on state leaders discussed in chapter 7. And always there are the suffrage requirements as they affect both whites and Negroes.

In the rest of this chapter and the one that follows, other legal handicaps that shackle the minority will be examined in some detail. The use of the powers of government for party advantage is as old as party government itself, but seldom in a modern democracy have they been used more deliberately to repress opposition than in the South since the Civil War. Of course, a pitcher with a thirty-run lead in the first inning can go easy on the one-armed batter, and Democrats are playfully generous with the Republicans on occasion. Wherever the threat is genuine, however, the attitude stiffens. Some of the existing arrangements that seem to lack significance because of the puny Republican threat serve to remind us of olden battles, first against scalawags and carpetbaggers and later against Populists and Fusionists.

The gerrymander is an ancient if not honorable political weapon. It is the process by which a party's votes are so divided and consolidated in drawing election district lines that the party fails to elect as large a share of officials as its strength would seem to justify. The concentration of Republicans in eastern Tennessee, western Virginia, and western North Carolina might be expected to guarantee their party a measure of success in local and district politics. In fact, the Republicans do control numerous mountain counties. But in district politics—the election of U. S. representatives, state legislators, prosecuting attorneys, and the like—they usually find they have been outmaneuvered.

North Carolina's famed "bacon strip" Congressional districts offer a lesson in political tactics as well as the most dramatic example of southern gerrymandering. Republicans flourish in the counties along the Blue Ridge, running from southwest to northeast. A set of districts roughly paralleling each other has been drawn running at right angles to the mountains, that is, from northwest to southeast. A county or two of strong Republican leanings in the top of the district is thus joined with enough counties of Democratic predominance in the lower part of the district to insure a Democratic majority. The districts are generally one county wide and extend upwards of a hundred miles in length.

The effectiveness of the system was demonstrated in the 1946 Congressional elections. Most of the state's Republicans cluster in the eighth, ninth, tenth, eleventh, and twelfth districts. Despite the fact that Republican candidates polled 43.4 per cent of the 282,435 votes cast in those districts, only Democrats won. How this result was achieved is illustrated by Table 12 which displays the vote in the eighth and tenth districts. The party majority in each county is shown. In the tenth district the large Democratic vote of Mecklenburg County, which contains the city of Charlotte, was required to overcome the net Republican majority in the rest of the district. In the years of presidential elections the Democratic vote increases much more than does the Republican vote, especially in Mecklenburg, and the results are not so close. In the fantastic eighth district (whose odd shape is barely outdone by Governor Gerry's salamander pictured in Webster's dictionary), the votes of four Republican counties in the upper end of the district are outweighed by a host of Democratic majorities that run 165 miles to the south and east.

The most jolting instance of gerrymandering among less important districts occurs in North Carolina's seventeenth judicial district. This Republican district is split into two noncontiguous parts, a western wing made up of Mitchell and Avery counties and an eastern wing made up of Wilkes, Yadkin, and Davie. The Republicans claim that the county formerly connecting the two wings, Watauga, was dropped in 1931 because the Republican solicitor of the district brought bills of indictment against the Democratic election officials in that county. The legislature hastily removed the county from his jurisdiction and placed it in the

TABLE 12
Congressional Gerrymandering in Western North Carolina, 1946

County	Republican majorities	Democratic majorities
8th District		
Wilkes	3011	
Yadkin	1494	
Davie	484	
Davidson	227	
Montgomery		618
Union		1432
Anson		1619
Richmond		1926
Moore		1158
Lee		1236
Hoke		775
Scotland		1067
DISTRICT		4615
Total Votes Cast: 55,225		
10th District		
Mitchell	1041	
Avery	1563	
Burke		1221
Catawba		531
Lincoln		721
Mecklenburg		3649
DISTRICT		3518
Total Votes Cast: 45,710		

safe sixteenth district where the solicitor was a Democrat. The Republicans charge that in 1935 Alexander County was similarly transferred from the seventeenth to the safe fifteenth district to avoid indictments brought by the same Republican solicitor.[1]

In drawing and revising district lines, Democratic politicians must consider the strategy of intraparty politics as well as their relationship to the Republicans. Candidates who have worked hard to develop a following in their district, one that wins in the primaries, resist efforts to dismember their district, whatever the motive. They may defer to party welfare, however, if the danger is sufficiently clear.

Congressional redistricting becomes necessary when a state loses or gains in its representation following the decennial census. On those occasions the Democrats have the chance to make prudent adjustments. In 1928, Republicans were elected to the national House of Representatives from the second, seventh, and ninth Virginia districts. In 1930 the Republican from the second district was re-elected. In the apportionment following the 1930 census Virginia lost one representative and the state was not redistricted by the time of the 1932 election. In that year nine members of Congress were elected at large, thereby, incidentally, insuring a solid Democratic delegation. When the new apportionment was finally made it did not alter the second district, which contains the city of Norfolk, but it redistributed the counties of western Virginia to make less likely the future election of Republicans from that section. Traditionally, the strongest Republican area is the "Fighting Ninth" district. In 1928, Wythe County gave Hoover a larger majority than any other county or independent city in the district. The new apportionment severed Wythe and attached it to the more dependably Democratic fifth district. The seventh district emerged in 1934 completely transformed. It had given Hoover a majority of 234, or 50.4 per cent of the votes. Had it been constituted then as it was later, he would have lost by 720 votes and received 49.1 per cent of the total.

Further opportunity for prejudicial practices, closely related to the gerrymander, arises in the apportionment of seats in the state legislatures. One hears mutterings in Tennessee, for instance, that inequality exists in the allotment of legislative seats between the Republican and Democratic sections of that state. Detailed studies would undoubtedly turn up numerous examples of inequitable apportionment, some of which might have a partisan slant. It is not to be expected, however, that Republicans should have a share of legislative seats corresponding to their proportion of the state's voters. Under a perfect apportionment they might have no seats at all if the Republican voters were spread evenly in Democratic strongholds. The geographical concentrations of Republicans in the three Upper South states, however, suggest that a fair apportionment would give them a share of seats at least approaching their relative strength in the state. A rough notion of the actual situation can be obtained by comparing the percentage of legislators who are Republicans in each house of the Virginia, Tennessee, and North Carolina legislatures with the proportion of the state vote given the Republican candidate for governor who ran at the same time. Here are the data for two years:

State	Percentage of state vote given Republican candidate for governor		Legislatures elected at same time as governor: percentage of membership Republican			
			Lower house		Upper house	
	1944	1948	1944	1948	1944	1948
Tennessee	36.0	33.1	24.2	19.2	15.2	12.1
North Carolina	30.4	26.4	11.7	9.2	6.0	4.0
Virginia[a]	31.0	27.4	6.0	7.0	8.3	5.0

[a] Virginia races held in 1945 and 1949.

The inference is strong, though not conclusive, that a less partial drawing of district lines would increase Republican representation in the upper houses in Tennessee and North Carolina, bringing it closer to the level in the lower house. A mathematically exact apportionment would probably, especially in Virginia, increase the number of Republicans in both houses. The importance of legislative apportionment, of course, extends far beyond its effects on the minority party. Underrepresentation of urban areas and overrepresentation of black belts are two characteristics of southern legislatures whose importance can hardly be exaggerated.[2]

On gerrymander and apportionment matters, nevertheless, Tennessee's Republicans get a comparatively fair break. They are better represented in the legislature than their fellows in other southern states. They rule virtually without challenge in the first and second Congressional districts. Of course they have preeminence in too many counties to be split up easily, but perhaps a contributing explanation lies in the much noted modus vivendi that Tennessee's Republican and Democratic politicians are reported to have worked out for purposes of mutual protection.* In North Carolina and Virginia, the Democratic party has taken its corporate responsibilities more seriously. Especially in North Carolina are Democrats wont to look upon Republicans as a dire threat who deserve not an inch lest they aspire to take a yard.

A political party cannot sustain itself unless it can support its politicians. It must do so in lean years as well as fat if it would attract men of ambition and ability. American parties have been able to survive long periods of political drought by holding on to geographical areas in which they predominate all or most of the time. The Democratic party, no matter how badly defeated in a national election, has always retained a sizeable corps of trained personnel in the South. Upstate New York and downstate Illinois assure the Republicans a base of operations when Democrats control those states. If the Republicans in the Appalachian sections of the Upper South could reap the full benefits of their local superiority, the chances of developing a virile party would be enhanced. That alone would not suffice, as Tennessee may testify, but the possession of district and legislative jobs now denied to Republicans in Virginia and North Carolina by discriminatory devices would give the party additional stamina, prestige, and hope, perhaps enough to make it a genuine opposition party.

There is no reason to think a wave of good fellowship will sweep out of the lowlands, righting ancient wrongs and promising for the future to do nothing that isn't cricket. On the contrary,

---

* See below, pp. 107-9.

Democrats will continue to enforce their present advantages wherever they can. One of their most telling weapons is the control they enjoy in state legislatures over the local legislation of Republican members. In this way they threaten the little influence the Republican member thinks he has. They have even been known to hint at redrawing existing districts to further handicap their opponents. The air of hopelessness in which the Republicans work was reflected by a news story in 1951. The Republican delegation to the North Carolina General Assembly introduced legislation to reshape the Congressional districts. The news story announcing the bill began: "The General Assembly had a new contender yesterday for the title of bill least likely to succeed."[3]

6
BALLOTS, SECOND CLASS

IN A DEMOCRATIC SOCIETY, THE REDRESS OF SUCH GRIEVANCES AS WE have been discussing ultimately depends on the integrity and sense of justice of the citizens. The means of recourse is the ballot box. But what if it, too, be corrupted? In many sections of the South, Republicans claim that Democratic control of voting procedures has turned Republicans into second-class voters casting second-class ballots.

Ben W. Hooper, Republican Governor of Tennessee from 1911 to 1915, wrote in 1946:

> The Tennessee electorate is in imminent danger of being choked and strangled by the reeking filth and muck of fraudulent elections. And close on the heels of fraud will always follow the force necessary to secure submission to the fraud.
> The Republican party of the state has been reduced to a condition of harmless impotency, and the Democratic party no longer functions from bottom to top but from top to bottom.
> A system of government that begins with the destruction of the minority party always ends up with the destruction of the majority party as well. Wherever this process takes place, the factual results are the same. Genuine popular government is dead....
> The low political estate to which Tennesseans have descended derives from the inherent weakness of the election laws and their unconscionably undemocratic administration.[1]

Corruption is probably no greater in Tennessee than the investigations of the Governor's neighbor, Senator Kefauver, disclosed it to be in some other parts of the United States in 1950 and 1951. And it should be noted that Tennessee legislatures, spurred by such charges as these, have modified some of the election laws. But if Governor Hooper's findings in 1946 were even partly representative of southern politics generally, only truly heroic Republicans would not resign themselves to the role of a permanent, hopeless minority.

Probably Democrats enjoy their greatest advantage in control over election officials. A high Republican in Arkansas tells a story that illustrates the possibilities of such control. A group of north Arkansas lawyers came to Republican state authorities to ask their help in running a candidate for circuit judge. Under Arkansas law then applying, the State Board of Elections, composed of seven ex officio state officials—hence always Democrats—appointed three county commissioners of elections. The law required that one of the commissioners come from the minority party. In close counties, the board customarily appointed as the Republican commissioner not a party member recommended by the county Republican committee, but a "Republican" favorably known to local Democrats. The north Arkansas lawyers felt the Republican members in some of the counties of the circuit would have to be changed if their candidate were to have a chance. Republican officials went before the State Board of Elections to make the request. They were incredulous at being told "right out in open meeting" that no changes could be made without first consulting the Democratic candidates in each of the counties affected.

Top Republicans asserted that the future of their party required a revision of the election laws. They did not complain so much that in counties with Republican majorities Democrats were assured a two to one majority among the election commissioners. They would settle for just one Republican, if he were a real one. In 1948 they sponsored successfully an initiated act that revised both Arkansas' state and county election boards. The new act reconstituted the state board to consist of the governor, attorney general, secretary of state, Democratic state chairman and Republican state chairman, and the county boards to consist of the county chairman of each of the two parties and a third member appointed by the state board.[2]

State control of elections has much to commend it from the standpoint of effective administration. Only in a remote sense, however, did concern for administrative efficiency prompt southern states to vest in state authority the appointive power over local election supervisors. Precisely for purposes of partisan advantage, like those served in Arkansas, were the arrangements made.[3] In six more southern states, control over local election officials runs back to state authorities. The low estate of Republicanism in Louisiana, Mississippi, and South Carolina renders the subject of only latent interest in those states.[4] Yet Democrats in the saddle show no quarter. The state chairman of the South Carolina Republican party could cry in 1944 "that despite repeated requests to all governors of South Carolina since 1930, not one single Republican has been appointed as a member of the minority party to be a member in any county of the federal election board, nor have any Republicans been named as judges or clerks at the polling precincts."[5]

North Carolina, Tennessee, and Virginia also lack local autonomy in the selection of election officials.[6] In these states, as in Arkansas, politicians place a premium on control over the balloting. The county boards name the judges and clerks who hold the election, i.e., who interpret the voters' lists, count the ballots, and tally the totals. North Carolina's governor appoints a bipartisan state board of elections. The state board appoints a county board of two Democrats and one Republican in each county, including the western counties where races are hot, and where the Republicans often win. The appointees come from a list of three nominees submitted by each county party committee. The Tennessee General Assembly elects a state board of supervisors of elections composed of one member from each of the two major parties, and a third member. The Assembly is Democratic, so the third member is Democratic. Each of the three members designates a person in each county to serve on a county board. The form in

Virginia varies but the meaning remains the same. County and city electoral boards are designated by the circuit and corporation courts. Of the three members on each board, two must be of the party whose candidate won the most recent gubernatorial election. The judges who make the appointments are elected by the legislature. Since Virginia's governors and legislatures are invariably Democratic, Democrats in doubtful counties can generally depend on sympathetic election officials. In the remaining southern states—Alabama, Florida, Georgia, and Texas—elections are under the supervision of local officers, some ex officio and some appointed by other local authority.

The selection of officials to handle the registration of voters is closely akin to the selection of election officials, but with less partisan significance. In all the southern states save South Carolina and Alabama, they are chosen locally, though in Tennessee, Virginia, and North Carolina the county electoral boards named by state authorities choose them. The governor of South Carolina appoints county registration boards in his state, subject to senatorial approval, and in Alabama the governor joins with the state auditor and commissioner of agriculture in naming the three registrars for each county.[7] Only spasmodically have Republicans alleged that fraud is practiced against them in registration procedures. Charges have occasionally arisen in Florida and North Carolina around the registering of Negroes who also were, or might have been, Republicans. In the latter state, the Republican state executive committee has charged that the Democratic registrars unfairly facilitate the registration of Democrats, especially when a new county enrollment has been called for.[8] In 1946 Alabama adopted a measure, known as the "Boswell Amendment," to give local boards of registrars enough discretion in determining the qualifications of voters to keep down the number of Negro voters. Republicans, along with labor unions and other minority groups, expressed fears that some of them as well as some of the Negroes might be disfranchised. The amendment was later declared unconstitutional. Arkansas and Texas have depended on poll tax lists rather than registration lists for identifying voters at the polls. Charges are seldom encountered, however, that the poll tax is administered in a manner discriminatory against Republicans. Some leaders feel that the tax, as a suffrage limitation and as a tool of organization politics, nevertheless contributes to the difficulties of building their party.

A description of the requirements of law is not sufficient to explain the operation of election machinery. The latitude inherent in the decentralized character of elections administration insures variety in the application of the law. Wide differences in electoral customs develop from county to county. All over the South, politicians testify that some counties are long habituated to fraud in elections, that others, adjacent to them, have an equally long history of rectitude. An explanation of how this comes about might add up to an impressive disquisition on the power of personality in a community. That it comes about should give caution to any generalizations about the conduct of elections.

Opportunity for fraud does not mean that fraud occurs. And then there is more than one type of fraud. To stuff the ballot boxes may be possible, when one has charge of them, but many will hesitate before running the risk of detection. An official can keep the polling place open a little after closing, however, and accommodate a handful of late voters without creating much of a stir. He can give friendly help in the voting booth. He might even slip a digit in recording the tallies. The range of opportunity for partisan advantage in control of electoral machinery is as wide as a man's conscience and as narrow as his opponent's alertness and opportunity to check him. A book could be filled with charges of fraud in general elections that would emphasize the significance of control over the election machinery.

The more heated the competition, the more significant the control. The extent to which fraud exists in the general elections is therefore most important in the three states of the Upper South. Anyone who reads the daily papers knows of the high incidence of gunplay in the politics of east Tennessee.* Less dramatic

---

* McMinn County and Polk County have been scenes of the most sanguinary recent outbursts. In the former county, GI's, armed and shooting, ousted the local Cantrell machine when the machine's election officers decided to count the ballots in private. The fantastic story is told by Theodore

evidence of fraud, however, has led Republican leaders like former Governor Hooper to ascribe the failure of their party in state politics to the election system. Perhaps more would do so but for the "understandings" between the two parties in the section. Governor Hooper listed "a few" of the election law violations that he says were committed, "some of them repeatedly," in Cocke County, Tennessee, between 1940 and 1945. Allowing that some of the fraud occurred in the primaries, excerpts from the Governor's list make his concern for his party's welfare seem reasonable:

Purposely delaying notices of appointment to election officers; failing to get election supplies and ballots to precincts; sending an insufficient number of ballots to a precinct; failing to bring in and canvass returns from certain precincts; a candidate holding his own election in his own home with members of his household as election officers; refusing to permit election officers to be legally sworn by an authorized officer; appointment of election officers notorious as election law violators; illegally marking hundreds of ballots; election holders refusing to certify the ballots they marked; forging a county court record to obtain poll tax exemptions; padding election scrolls with hundreds of forged names and thus changing the result of several elections, particularly a local option election; stuffing ballot boxes with illegal ballots; removing legally cast ballots from a ballot box; casting a large number of fraudulent absentee ballots, many of them in the names of men in the armed forces of our country; voting in both the Republican and Democratic primaries on the same day; voting in more than one precinct in the same election; the voting of hundreds of Republicans in Democratic primaries ... [9]

H. White, "The Battle of Athens, Tennessee," *Harper's Magazine*, 194 (Jan., 1947), 54-61. Subsequently, T. Burkett Ivins, an associate of Cantrell, shot the nephew of a political enemy. Ivins claimed self-defense, but he never got to trial. He stepped on the starter of his automobile one day and set off a fatal explosion. Investigators concluded the explosion had no political implications. Ivins, said the Etowah police chief, "was in office a long time and made a lot of enemies. He had killed seven or eight men, most of them as sheriff."—*Arkansas Gazette* (Little Rock), October 4, 1947. In Polk County, home of the notorious Biggs machine, the National Guard was called out to restore order after the August, 1948 elections which saw three election-day killings.

The remedy for all of this, Mr. Hooper says, is "agitation, education, and organization.... It should be remembered that practically every fraud that is committed in our elections is a violation of some law, and we still have courts and juries." [10] Some of his fellow Republicans, however, question the efficacy of an appeal to courts and juries that are manned by Democrats or by others in cahoots with the Democrats. But few deny that a greater part in the conduct of elections would improve their party's chances of winning.

Wholesale charges of fraud are not as widespread in North Carolina and Virginia as in Tennessee. In fact, North Carolina has evinced through its State Board of Elections greater determination to maintain clean elections than any other state in the South. The hue and cry in that state has revolved almost exclusively around absentee voting.* Similarly, in Virginia the most frequent charges concern the casting of "mail ballots," as they are called in that commonwealth. The procedures for absentee voting are more susceptible to manipulation than any others in the conduct of elections. The designation of local election officials by Democrats thus assumes special importance in those two states.

The North Carolina election board took cognizance of this feature in its recommendations to the governor and General Assembly in 1947, 1949, and 1951. In 1939 the board had proposed abolition of civilian absentee voting in the primaries and the legislature had abolished it. In 1947 the board began recommending that civilian absentee voting be eliminated from the general elections as well. It had concluded, reluctantly, that since 1939 absentee ballot scandals had been "frequent enough to cause serious damage to the election machinery, and to all of those persons responsible for elections in the state."

The civilian absentee ballot is the single cause of most election troubles. . . .

The greatest evil of the civilian absentee ballot lies in the ever

* Though not entirely. In Madison County in 1950 Republicans charged fraud in the election of sheriff and state representative, and took a somewhat dim view of the way the State Board of Elections handled the protests.—*News and Observer* (Raleigh), November 29, 1950.

present temptation which it presents, and in the all pervading suspicion which it breeds.

Our election machinery is party machinery. On every election board or body the majority party has majority representation and has control. The minority party has minority representation and sometimes a loud voice of protest. The election officials are chosen from partisan party workers and chosen by party leaders. The election officials are interested in politics.

Otherwise they would not have been chosen. Otherwise, probably, they would not have accepted the onerous and inadequately remunerative election jobs. . . . But the origin of election officials makes for quick tempers and volatile suspicions.[11]

Republican legislators concurred with the board's recommendations, in fact included as part of their announced program "Absolute repeal of the absentee ballot law." [12] Democrats, in private conversation and publicly, conceded that things sometimes got pretty raw out in the west, and something, but not too much, ought to be done about it. The Raleigh *News and Observer,* however, yielding to none in its Democracy, argued that the law "should be made crook proof or be repealed. The time has come when the Democratic party must clean house in a few counties which are disgraced by dishonest practices in connection with the absentee ballot." [13]

That something was up in the closely contested counties no one denied. In 1951 the State Board of Elections noted that "in a number of close counties in the last general election as many as 20 per cent of the total votes were cast by absentee ballots." [14] In the 1944 gubernatorial race (for which year the data are available) 25 of the state's 100 counties cast a higher number of absentee votes (civilian and military) than the plurality of the winning candidate in the county. In the same election there were 18 counties in which 5 per cent or more of the votes were cast by civilian absentee ballot. (See Table 13.) Clay County hit an amazing percentage, 17.4, while Swain's was 11.9. In all of these 18 counties serious bipartisan contests took place: the Republican candidate received at least 35 per cent of the votes and the Democrat received at least 40 per cent of them. In contrast, there were 21 counties in which less than 1 per cent of the votes were cast by absent civilians. In 20 of those the leading candidate in the county received more than 75 per cent of the votes. In the other, the winner polled 59.2 per cent. With the outcome assured in local races, both parties had less incentive to get out the vote, absentee or otherwise. And it was natural that alert electioneering by both sides in the close counties would increase the number of absentee voters. What seemed to support the election board's contention that things were amiss was that not all close counties had high absentee totals. There were 13 counties, in addition to the 18 mentioned above, in which Republicans cast at least 35 per cent and Democrats at least 40 per cent of the total votes. In all 13 the civilian absentee ballots fell below 5 per cent, in eight instances below 3 per cent, and in one instance below 1 per cent of those cast.

TABLE 13

CIVILIAN ABSENTEE VOTING IN NORTH CAROLINA IS MOST FREQUENT IN COUNTIES OF CLOSE PARTY COMPETITION: ELECTION OF GOVERNOR, 1944

Percentage of total vote cast by civilian absentee ballot	Number of counties giving a specified percentage of their vote to the Republican candidate			
	0-34.9	35-59.9	60-74.9	75-100
5.0 and over		18		
3.0-4.9	5	5		
1.0-2.9	39	7	4	1
Under 1.0	19	1		1

Statistics on absentee voting in Virginia are not available. Virginia Republicans, however, are convinced they wind up with the fewest mail ballots. Democrats agree, though usually in private. The GOP sponsored legislation in 1948 to abolish absentee voting altogether. It charged that modifications made in 1946 had proved unworkable and the only solution was to repeal the law.

"Earle Lutz, GOP State executive director, said the absent voting setup is so open to fraud that the good name of the State is at stake." [15] A Democratic counterattack took the form of a bill sponsored by state Senator M. M. Long. His proposal would have removed some of the safeguards, such as an affidavit or two, erected around the ballot by the 1946 General Assembly. It was reported that officials had found the law cumbersome to administer and wished greater freedom in handling the ballots. Senator Long's sponsorship was considered understandable. He came from Wise County in southwestern Virginia, the most notorious county in the state for election shenanigans. The Republican state committee had just lodged charges with the State Board of Elections against "widespread violations of election laws in Wise County" in the previous general election. Included was the assertion "that specified persons carried absent voters ballots to the homes of persons who had not applied for them and illegally solicited these persons to vote; ... the GOP committee had information that 682 mail ballots were obtained from the Wise electoral board but only 578 were used." [16] The *Richmond Times-Dispatch* observed that 2,300 absent ballots were cast in one Wise County election as compared with 50 in Richmond, whose population was four times as great.[17] It may be said in summary that the surest sign of the importance of absentee voting has been the reluctance of Democratic legislatures in both Virginia and North Carolina to abolish the privilege or to safeguard it more securely.

In the previous chapter, we contended that southern Republicans on occasion have been subject to reprisals for their political views. If this be true, we must note the extent of nonsecret voting in southern general elections. Most of the democratic world, and most of the Democratic South, has come to accept the secret ballot as essential to the democratic process. That a man should be free to vote as he pleases, and that his ballot shall be counted as cast, are axioms now seldom disputed in the United States.

The form of the ballot is not the only consideration. The use of voting booths, orderliness at the polls, and the attitude of election officials in preserving secrecy affect the ability of a voter to mark his ballot with confidence that his choice will remain unknown. Where inadequate laws regulate the ballot, election officials naturally enjoy the widest opportunity to maintain or violate ballot secrecy. In such areas the privilege of appointing the election officials can be of considerable partisan importance.

Voters in nine of the eleven southern states could in 1950 cast a ballot with the assurance that no one would peek into the box later and find out who voted it. That is to say, the ballot had no distinguishing marks or numbers that could be checked against the voter's name to find out how he voted.[18] In South Carolina until 1950, each party provided its own ballots. A voter went to the polls and selected the ballot of the party he wished to vote for, thereby proclaiming his intentions to the onlookers.[19] South Carolina is a Deep South state where feelings against Republicans are strong. The absence of a secret ballot perhaps accounted in part for the infinitesimal Republican vote in the state. The vote may not increase greatly with secret balloting, but Republican leaders have felt that a secret ballot is essential to make conversions. They felt it so strongly in 1944 that the state chairman, acting for the party, offered to pay the cost of providing the whole state with conventional single ballots listing the candidates of all parties.[20] The Democrats, in control of the state government, did not take him up. The Democratic state convention of 1948, nevertheless, resolved in favor of extending the Australian ballot, long used in the primaries, to the general election,[21] and in 1950 the legislature did so.

Arkansas, a state with a number of bipartisan counties, long used an extraordinary ballot form, abandoned after 1948. The official ballot had a duplicate, replete with carbon paper. The carbon copy was signed by the voter. To make things certain, it also carried a number that was noted by the voter's name on the register of voters. The duplicates were preserved in separate containers, to be opened, it was provided, in case of contest.[22]

Those who favor nonsecret ballots insist that fraud can be prevented only if it is possible in investigations after the election to link up the ballots with the persons who cast them. Texas law until 1949 required the election judge to write on each ballot the number opposite the voter's name on the voter's list.[23] In protesting a proposed change in 1947, the chairman of the state Democratic executive committee stated: "The so-called secret ballot bill insures secrecy of the ballot which is, of course, to be desired. But in insuring secrecy of the ballot it works a much greater evil in that it destroys present means of detecting fraud in elections. The mischief the bill would work outweighs the good it could accomplish and the bill should be defeated."[24] Nevertheless, the 1949 legislature modified the procedure in the direction of protecting the voter.* Now the ballot bears a number and carries a detachable stub, also bearing the number. At the time of casting the ballot, the stub is removed, the voter's name written on it, and then locked up, to be examined only in case of contest.[25] Alabama, the other southern state with a modified secret ballot, bases its procedure on the same principle. The ballot bears a number, but a black sticker is pasted over the number, to be removed for official investigation.[26]

Many localities in the South maintain honest voting without infringing on the secrecy of the ballot. The insistence on numbered ballots manifests a primitive conception of the electoral process and makes its motives suspect. In the broad sweep, however, the effects on the Republican party since 1900 have probably been few. Unquestionably, nonsecret balloting, arising from whatever cause, gives pause to some voters who might count in scattered local races. To that extent the gradual accretion of Republican ranks may have been retarded. When compared with other factors, however, nonsecret voting would seem a minor cause of stunted Republican growth in the South.

Republican leaders are justifiably perplexed by the problems of electoral reform. Where can they turn to right the wrongs of the gerrymander, to obtain a fair role in election administration, to correct abuses of procedure? Where can they turn when the legislatures and the courts and most of the vehicles of public opinion are controlled by their opponents?

Too many Republican leaders have answered "nowhere." The

* The Texas legislature enacted an omnibus election law at its 1951 session, but the text could not be obtained before this book went to press.

history of southern politics makes their apathy understandable. But it is futile, and sometimes not quite admirable, to remain forever at the wailing wall. And one sometimes senses in the laments against electoral conditions a convenient rationalization for lassitude that has its roots in other causes. It would be foolish to minimize the enormous legal obstacles that stand in the way of Republican growth. It would be equally unrealistic to conclude that there is no hope. After all, the integrity of the democratic process itself is involved, and that is a matter that concerns all citizens, regardless of party. In a showdown, voting citizens get mightily aroused about those principles of government that seem so lofty in their enunciation but are so direct in their effect. And voting citizens outnumber unconscionable politicians. The recourse, as always, is to the people. To inform the people, to arouse them, to channel their concern into effective action, requires skillful and unflagging leadership, and leadership possessed of the resources and the incentive to stay with the problem until it is partially or fully overcome.

7

BIG FISH IN LITTLE PONDS

H. L. MENCKEN, A PENETRATING IF SOMEWHAT CONTENTIOUS OBserver of American affairs, records some of his views on political parties in a book called *Making a President*. He explains why United States Senator Charles Curtis did not corral more delegates before the 1928 Republican convention. Among other reasons, it seems that old Charlie ("the Kansas comic character, who is half Indian and half windmill") "lacked Lord Hoover's bar'l, could not find an angel to finance him, and hence had to keep out of the Southern states, where only cash money counts." [1]

The fondness of southern Republican delegates for cash money has long been part of the trade talk of our politics, and the talk has contributed mightily to the low esteem in which southern Republican leadership is held. Investigations, not the least of which followed the 1928 convention,[2] have lent credence to the talk. Republicans in most of the South do not win public office and the only posts of significance they can hope to hold are party posts, mostly as delegates and alternates to their own national convention. Year in and year out their eyes focus on the fight over the presidential nomination, where their votes count as much as anybody else's. In the politics of the convention, hopes of patronage and prestige (more often than cash money, be it said) have had their share in attracting southern delegates to nonsouthern presidential aspirants. Delegates from other states do not differ in these regards, but southerners enjoy an advantage. They are not restrained, even indirectly, by what Republican voters want. Neither are they required, for the most part, to answer to the coterie of politicians who make up the real constituency of delegates from other states.

Even before 1900, southern Republican officials suffered the contempt of commentators and fellow politicians; in addition to the corruption, incompetence has been commonplace. The most signal characteristic of the party's southern "leadership," however, has been a lack of interest in winning elections. There are exceptions to all rules, and some to this one, but Republican officials in the South by and large have not wanted to build a party worthy of the name. They have been big fish in little ponds and they have liked it. A nationally prominent businessman visiting a southern state before the 1948 election observed that if a Republican became president the party's chairman and national committeeman in that state "would be equivalent to two senators and half a dozen representatives." In saying that, he went far to explain the nature of the party in the South. Republican officials have not sought to disrupt their closed corporation by electing local candidates. Instead, they have played a game of hide-and-seek for control of the party machinery and its perquisites. They have been "patronage referees" or "palace politicians" but not candidates or campaign managers.

Honorable men have served and still serve Republicanism in the South. In recent years they have increasingly prevailed in party councils. But, though possessing honor, they lack the incentive or acumen to overcome the dragnet of handicaps under which their party labors. A few men of spine have tried to shake loose. They have looked to the national party for aid, counsel, recognition, in developing an aggressive party. But the chiefs in the nation have given scant help. The national leaders are individuals uncertain in their transient positions of power. Their interest in southern state leaders centers on the next convention rather than on the next election, or on elections four, eight, sixteen years away. If they do business with the moguls currently in power in a state they may earn for their favorite candidate five votes on the first ballot or ten on the second in the next convention.

The political ability and vision needed for Republican leadership in the South exceed the needs for party leadership anywhere else in the nation. The numerical superiority of the Democrats, the handicaps of history and rigged election laws, the inevitability of long periods of defeat, and the indifference of the national party must be accepted and overcome if the party is to grow. The obstacles can be overcome only when shifts occur in the economic and social and emotional foundations of southern politics. To take advantage of the changes that are under way, as we shall see later, the party requires a new quality in Republican leadership. To a greater or lesser degree in every southern state there must be changes in the high command if the party is to grow. The quality of its leadership is as important as the size of its membership. A dynamic and skillful leadership with an eye on victory and faith in itself can make much of small beginnings in any good cause. The most preponderant of political majorities can collapse in confusion when inadequately led.

What, in detail, are the characteristics of Republican leaders in the South?

When chided for their lack of aggressiveness, almost to a man they reply: "What is the use?" The answer is so ready on some tongues, that one senses a hint of satisfaction in it. Nevertheless, the counsel of despair is rooted in painful experience. The South has many stout-hearted Republicans who once were fired with enthusiasm and determined to revive their party. Sooner or later they concluded that the odds were too great, that life was too short to spend it butting against a stone wall. The frustration may be greatest where the party is strongest. A conscientious North Carolina party officer noted that in a state like Alabama party leaders can relax and catch what votes happen to come their way: They know at the outset they don't have a chance. In North Carolina, however, the size of the party imposes an obligation. The dutiful officer labors to do the best he can. His reward is failure; he never quite gets into the winning bracket.

Enthusiasm has been dampened, too, by the view held—at least until very recently—by Republicans both North and South, that Republican national victory does not depend on the South. A tidal wave of public sentiment strong enough to carry a southern state for the party would easily sweep the rest of the country and capture Congress and the presidency without southern help. Moreover, southern Republican leaders see little reason to change the kind of government provided by the Democrats in the individual states. Conservative, "safe" government customarily results from the one-party politics of the South. "Democratic state government has been for the most part excellent in North Carolina," a top Republican official privately averred. Republicans constitute a significant section of the Byrd faction in Virginia. After all, it would be difficult to imagine a Republican more Republican than Senator Byrd. In Tennessee it is an open secret that certain Republicans have been eminently satisfied with the governmental arrangements of Democratic administrations. In all states of the South, the conservatives, the economic and social groups generally represented by Republicans nationally, have full representation in the Democratic party. These circumstances limit the incentives of Republican leadership to undertake the Herculean task of revamping and enlarging their party.

Several generations under these conditions have made it respectable for Republican leaders to think almost wholly in terms of controlling the state party machinery. Control of the party organization assures recognition at the national convention and that in turn attracts the flattery and promises of presidential aspirants. For this reason, in so far as the internal operations of the parties are concerned, Republican party organization in the South is far more important than that of the Democratic party, whose vitality is found in the contests for office in the primaries. Control of the Republican party organization depends upon outmaneuvering rivals, and it is usually easier to outmaneuver few rivals than many. Besides, the prospects for mutually advantageous agreements improve when the negotiators are few in number. Moreover, as Republican bosses sometimes frankly admit, the fewer there are to divide the pie the more there is to go around.

The party "organization" that leaders seek to control is distinguished chiefly by its numerical weakness. With the partial exceptions of Virginia, North Carolina, and Tennessee, the party apparatus exists only on paper and in the heads of the state leaders. The neat hierarchies of committees and conventions prescribed by law or party rules often have little relation to the conduct of party affairs.* Sometimes there is careful adherence to the formalities required by law, because convention delegations have been contested on their failure to follow the legal prescriptions. Party officials can produce a list of county chairmen, or a list of state committee members, as one did in Arkansas a few months before the 1948 convention. A county-by-county discussion of the Arkansas list revealed that in about 55 per cent of the counties there existed an "active" organization—that is, one to which a letter could be written and an answer expected. A check in Florida by an informed party official about the same time showed that county organizations with chairmen existed in 39 of the state's 67 counties. About three-fourths of the places on the state committee were filled. After presenting a list of county chairmen and secretaries, the Mississippi state chairman readily acknowledged that the affairs of the party were run exclusively from his own office. Even the Executive Director of the Republican National Committee conceded at the close of 1950 that in 1,220 counties in twelve southern states there were 113 vacancies among county chairmen and 840 among the women vice chairmen.[3] The local party units, save in exceptional localities, have no importance unless jobs are available for distribution. In counties with Republican majorities, of course, or near-majorities, they play an important factional role within the party and in conducting the party's external relations.

All in all, when no patronage is flowing, local Republican po-

* States vary in the degree to which they regulate party procedures. The manner of holding conventions is stipulated in greatest detail by Texas, South Carolina, and Mississippi statutes. In some states the party's "call" for the state convention sets out details of the party structure. The only states in which rules or a plan of organization could be obtained from Republican officials were Virginia, North Carolina, and South Carolina.

tentates are chiefly concerned with rounding up people to attend periodic mass meetings and conventions. For the most part, these meetings function only to select delegates to higher level conventions, culminating in a state convention that in most states adopts a party platform, selects delegates to the national convention, names presidential electors, and sometimes nominates candidates. In theory, the convention system gives the party followers a chance to participate in the government of the party by attendance at precinct and county conventions. Usually such gatherings are of the character of the "office mass meetings" Republican leaders in parts of Virginia are accused of holding. The county leader calls his cronies to his office and they go through the form of a meeting. As a rule there are not enough Republicans in the area to object, but the procedure is hardly designed to stimulate popular interest in the party's affairs. Even in Virginia counties of substantial Republican sentiment, the practice has been employed to perpetuate in office a small group of old-line leaders. In the most populous county in another state the county convention is publicly advertised and all comers are welcome, sometimes as many as 125 showing up. "We," a county leader assured, make a special effort to get certain of the party faithful to attend by writing letters and telephoning them in advance. "We" draw up in advance a list of delegates to the state convention that is voted on by the county meeting. The state convention, usually meeting in the same county, generally attracts about four hundred persons, many of whom are present to hear a speaker of national prominence who dignifies the occasion. "We" get our way in that convention, too.

North Carolina's 1948 state convention got rough treatment when reported in the state's leading Democratic newspaper, but the description has a ring of authenticity:

Hope of national victory in November today brought 1,200 Republicans to their State convention here, but by the time proceedings had dragged out for seven hours, less than 50 were left to adopt a platform.... Before the convention ended, confusion and disorder reigned and the bulk of the delegates had departed. In the confusion, four electors at large were nominated, although there are only two places to be filled. But, it was arranged for only two of them to qualify and the convention went back to nominate candidates for State Treasurer and Insurance Commissioner, two offices that had been overlooked when a State ticket was being named. ... The enthusiasm, which was genuine enough at the outset, seemed to center almost entirely around the national election and selection of spokesmen for the party in national affairs.[4]

This behavior is typical of conventions generally, but to southern Republicans it is of particular significance because the convention hierarchy is pretty nearly the sole source of power in the party. The infrequency of Republican primaries, candidates, and campaigns leaves little means to acquire influence except through the scheme of party conventions. That the participants in the convention process are few does not make it harmonious. Factional fights rooted in personal ambition are forever cropping up. They constitute, in fact, most that is virile in the party's affairs. The skilled and wily operators remain on top; the others, out-generalled, are reduced to snapping at the victors' heels with hurt protestations and challenges for convention seats.

The easiest way to keep a political party small is to fail to put up candidates. In the fall of 1947, Louisiana's Republican national committeeman, speaking before the state executive committee, urged Republicans not to offer themselves as candidates in state and local races. "There is little chance of any Republican being elected in Louisiana." He recommended that all Louisiana's campaign funds and efforts be concentrated on the election of Republicans in doubtful states.[5] Yet, one year later, a Republican candidate for United States senator in his state polled 25.0 per cent of 408,667 votes cast, and a Republican candidate for Congress in the third district received 33.4 per cent of the votes.

No Republican had offered for the Senate in at least thirty years. The only other Republican to run in the third district in thirty years had done so in 1940, when he demonstrated that 34.0 per cent of the voters were willing to vote for his label. One wonders what would happen if the Louisiana party regularly contested elections, regularly capitalized on factional dissensions among the Democrats.

BIG FISH IN LITTLE PONDS

The failure to encourage candidacies looks like a great lost opportunity of southern Republican leadership. When this suggestion is made to Republican leaders, ennui descends. Conscientious workers point to the overwhelming difficulties. Top Virginia officials reported, for example, that they simply can't get anybody to run in most of the counties where the party competes on uneven terms with the Democrats. Urgent appeals to party loyalty will succeed with a few stalwarts who have the time to make the race. They campaign in a spirit of solemn dedication to a public service. Lacking subventions from national headquarters, the state parties have little money to place at the disposal of their candidates. Often the donors of the funds are themselves the only ones who can be induced to make a race. A Republican candidacy then becomes not only a hopeless but also an expensive undertaking.

Nevertheless, contest for office is the backbone of party politics, and the greatest stimulus to party growth lies in a continuous stream of serious candidates. Only the enthusiasm created by torrid political campaigning fires the voters' loyalty to a party and forges the hard core of partisan opinion needed to sustain the party in poor years and to serve as the nucleus of victory in good ones. A more telling measure of the failure of Republican leadership in the South than the low Republican vote is this failure of the party to offer candidates. And the index has been falling. There were Republican candidates in 65 per cent of the southern Congressional races of 1920; in 51 per cent in 1948.*

---

* See Table 11 on page 72. For the frequency of candidacies for governor and United States senator, see Table 6 on page 58. The prevailing situation can be sensed from these scattered reports: In Arkansas in 1948 the party ran candidates for governor and two Congressional seats, for no other state or Congressional offices. In Florida, the same year, Republicans offered for 22 of the 133 seats in the legislature.—*Florida Times-Union* (Jacksonville), May 28, 1948. Thirty-three Virginia Republicans ran for the 120 seats in the general assembly in 1947. In the same election Republican candidates contested for local offices in 31 counties and two independent cities. "Counting all contests—both Assembly and local offices—the GOP has aspirants on the ballot in 42 counties and nine cities." Virginia had 100 counties and 24 independent cities.—*Richmond Times-Dispatch*, October 19, 1947.

When candidates do run for district and state offices, the campaigns are generally perfunctory affairs except in those counties with a real contest over local offices. In 1948, Republican campaign headquarters were opened "for the first time" in eastern North Carolina, the section of Democratic strongholds.[6] A recent Republican candidate for governor of Tennessee found when he started his campaign that the state headquarters did not have a list of all the party's county chairmen. He tried to make an appearance in every county in the state; in many counties, including some with a heavy party vote, he could find no Republican to arrange a meeting and introduce him. Tennessee consistently has a stronger Republican vote than any other state in the South. Yet another of its Republican candidates for governor (radio and screen entertainer Roy Acuff), nominated by primary in 1948, said at the outset of his campaign: "If I have to criticize my opponent, I'll withdraw. Gordon Browning [the Democratic nominee] is my friend." The press reported: "A few weeks ago Browning took a week-end's rest as a guest of Acuff at the entertainer's Dunbar Caves near Clarksville."[7]

The pusillanimous campaigns of Republican candidates reveal the reluctance of the party hierarchy to have its hegemony of party affairs upset. Especially in Tennessee, Republican candidates recite the shoddy treatment they have received at the hands of party officials. They speak as though they had two fights, one within their own party and one against the Democrats. Candidacy for state office, asserts one venerable Tennessee Republican, is used as a sidetrack by the professionals to take care of overambitious upstarts. "The gubernatorial nomination is a position the professional politicians are very happy to honor somebody else with." The ultimate has been reached in Texas where on several occasions the Republicans have turned to the Democrats in search of suitable candidates. "Texas Republicans Seek Democrat Who Is Willing" read the headline of a story reporting the party's search for a 1948 gubernatorial candidate.[8] In selecting a candidate for senator the same year, the party offered the nomination unsuccessfully to W. Lee O'Daniel and Martin Dies, Democrats.[9] Some argued that the way to woo votes from the

Democratic party was to put up a Democratic candidate. All of this had something to do with the nature of Texas Democrats as well as Texas Republicans. But the same thing has happened elsewhere in the South, and it does not connote a militant leadership intent on partisan victory, the necessary objective of a major American political party.

There is, however, a wing of Republican leadership in almost every southern state that wants to win elections. These mavericks generally favor party primaries and aggressive general election campaigns. Sometimes they show up as candidates for office, like the late John Wesley Kilgo of Tennessee, who ran for governor in 1944 as though he were interested in winning.[10] In late years the most vigorous exponent of a militant southern Republicanism has been Wilson Williams, Georgia member of the national committee from 1940 to 1948. Mr. Williams has advocated the unpopular doctrine of abnegation. He has felt, in a word, that the South ought to put up a real effort to win electoral votes or shut up in national party councils. He opposed the election of southerner Carroll Reece as chairman of the Republican National Committee, charging the South and the territories had no business choosing the most important official in the party, an official whose important work lay in other parts of the country. Following the Republican victories of 1946, Mr. Williams issued a call urging that presidential primaries be held in every southern state prior to the 1948 convention.[11] He recommended that delegates be denied seats in the convention unless selected by presidential preference primaries, arguing that his plan would mitigate the unhealthy bargaining over delegates and thereby aid in destroying the prime motivation for keeping the party weak. His colleagues all over the South denounced the suggestion "to a man" and he failed to get a primary even in Georgia.

Republicans of the Williams disposition would like their party to nominate by direct primary whenever possible. Through the primaries they see a way to develop party spirit, to build party allegiance. Actually, very few Republican nominations are made by primary in the South. In a few areas where the party is relatively strong, primaries are held. They are employed most widely in the counties of eastern Tennessee and western North Carolina. They are found in scattered counties in other states, principally three or four in the Ozarks of Arkansas and in northern Alabama. Fannin County, Georgia, seems to have nominated Republican candidates by primary until 1932.[12] State-wide Republican primaries are occasionally held, like those for governor in Tennessee and Florida in 1944 and 1948, governor of North Carolina in 1940, United States senator from Florida in 1944, and lieutenant governor of Virginia in 1949. They attract a small vote (in part because "Republicans" prefer to vote in the primaries of the Democratic party). For example:

	Gov. of Fla. 1944	Gov. of N.C. 1940	Lt. Gov. of Va. 1949
Republican primary, total vote	9,720	27,750	8,565
Percentage this total primary vote was of the nominee's vote in the general election	10.1	14.2	13.0
Democratic primary, total vote	406,077	469,396	284,262
Percentage this total primary vote was of the nominee's vote in the general election	112.5	77.1	157.5

Party leaders usually disagree with the eager-beavers who advocate use of the primaries. In states with mandatory primary laws applicable to the Republicans—Florida, Louisiana, Mississippi, North Carolina and Tennessee—[13] a candidate often enters the primary unopposed and is declared the nominee without contest. This practice should not be charged exclusively to a plot to keep the party weak. As an aggressive Virginia leader put it, it's hard enough in some places to find one candidate to run in the general election; it's virtually impossible to find two to run in a primary! Moreover, the cost of holding primaries poses an obstacle. In 1950 the South contained the only states that still required the parties to finance the primaries: Arkansas, Georgia,

South Carolina, and Texas. In those states party officials would have to raise the money, as well as the candidates, to hold a primary.[14] Furthermore, the statutes are so drawn in some of the other states that only the Democratic party can qualify to have its primaries publicly financed.*

Nevertheless, Republican leadership has been something less than alert to encourage the use of primaries. Not until 1947 were Republican rules in Virginia modified to permit local Republican committees to use the primary to nominate for county, city, and certain district offices.[15] In another state, legislation that would have facilitated the holding of Republican primaries was killed by the intercession of the Republican state chairman and national committeeman who used favors at their disposal to influence the critical vote. The play has been most visible in Texas. Under the law at one time in effect, a party whose candidate for governor received more than 100,000 votes in the previous election was subject to the mandatory primary act. In 1926, 1930, and 1934, Republican primaries were held pursuant to this law. After their gubernatorial candidate polled 100,287 votes in 1944, it looked as though the Republicans would be forced to nominate by primary again in 1946. Quickly, however, "the Republicans besieged the Legislature to make that law read 200,000 instead of 100,000," [16] and, the Democratic legislators gracefully obliging, the danger was averted. Two days after the 1948 election the late R. B. Creager, Texas Republican boss, announced, it seemed in triumph, that the "GOP would not have to hold primaries" in the next election.[17]

The aversion of some Republican leaders in the South to steps that might strengthen the party, a sort of negative corruption, has been accompanied by more positive forms of coöperation with

* The requirement in Mississippi that a party must have received one-third of the total vote in the last presidential election automatically limits the privilege to the Democratic party.—*Code of 1930*, sec. 5887. In Alabama the party must have cast 20 per cent of the votes in the last general election for state and county offices.—*Code of 1940*, title 17, sec. 337. In Virginia, the requirement is 25 per cent in the last presidential election.—Virginia *Code of 1950*, title 24, sec. 346. In other states, mandatory primaries are publicly financed.

the enemy. Trading across party lines has been notorious in Tennessee where, indeed, Republican nabobs have failed more dismally to fulfill the obligations of party leadership than anywhere else in the South. Despite a large bloc of assured votes, the majority of Republican officeholders and party officials has seemingly wanted to confine the party's triumphs to the first and second Congressional districts. The state's political sophisticates take it for granted that agreements exist between Democratic and Republican leaders to minimize political strife—to create, in effect, two one-party systems, one for the Republicans in the first and second Congressional districts and one for the Democrats in the rest of the state. It was widely believed when Mr. Crump was state boss that local Republican chiefs received favors from the Democratic administration. Many allege, though less convincingly, that Republicans have benefited by Federal favors from Senator McKellar, long influential in the eastern "grand division" of the state. The Democrats have pretty generally stayed out of the eastern county and district elections. In return, Republican bosses are said to have vetoed hell-for-leather Republican campaigns in state-wide races and to have aided the Crump-McKellar organization by ordering Republican voters into the Democratic primaries to support the organization's candidates. Crump candidates have traditionally found their greatest majorities, outside of Memphis, in the counties of the east. Nobody denies that conspiracies among Democrats and Republicans have existed. Minute questioning of Tennessee politicians, however, suggests that the conspiracy is less grandly organized than is usually pictured. Probably most trades are made with politicians below the level of the county. A general pattern of inter-party communication and trading has, nevertheless, clearly prevailed, and to such an extent as to compromise in the minds of most the good faith of those who have directed Republican affairs in the state.

Though trading across party lines is by no means confined to Tennessee, nor to the South, in no other southern state does it prevail to such an extent.[18] Brazilla Carroll Reece, in Congress most of three decades from Tennessee's first district (Johnson City), has long been accused of being the devil, or the head devil, in the plot. A story on the 1948 state convention, under the headline, "It was Reece, Reece, Reece at GOP Meet," reported:

> The Reece organization has also managed to kill the prospects of a state Republican primary, by discouraging John Kilgo of Greenville, who has been wanting to run again for governor. He probably will not run, however ... The GOP organization doesn't want a state primary contest, as it would prevent or make difficult a possible trade with the Democrats in the First and Second congressional races and in East Tennessee contests for seats in the state Legislature.[19]

Some Republicans oppose the ways of Reece (so much so, in fact, that Tennessee is sometimes said to have two Republican parties). John Jennings, Jr., first sent to Congress by the second (Knoxville) district in 1939, looked for awhile as though he might come out on top. At Philadelphia in 1948 he backed Dewey while Reece supported Taft, who had been responsible for the latter's selection as chairman of the national committee. After the nomination, but before the election, Jennings proclaimed that "The nomination and assured election of Governor Dewey will usher in a new day in Tennessee for the Republican party.... The present corrupt alliance between certain Republican Party leaders in Tennessee and Crumpism in Memphis will end."[20] Many thought the defeat in the Democratic primaries during the same year of Crump candidates for senator and governor, by Estes Kefauver and Gordon Browning, would help. But Dewey was defeated, and in 1950 Senator Taft reached a new ascendancy through his overwhelming victory in Ohio. More than that, after bitter intraparty fights, in 1950 Reece recaptured his old Congressional seat from Dayton Phillips, a young insurgent elected in 1946 and 1948, and Reece's "personal friend," Howard H. Baker, Sr., unseated Jennings in the other Republican district.[21]

The Tennessee experience makes one wonder whether changes are taking place in the nature of Republican leadership elsewhere in the South. After all, granting all the obstacles, if the party is to grow, much depends on the integrity, skill, and incentives of those who run it in each state. They cannot lift the party by its own bootstraps, but they can use or leave idle the opportunities that grow from social, economic, and political alterations in the South and in the country.

A shift in the character of Republican leadership has taken place since the 1920's. The old-style patronage farmers have given way in several quarters to successful businessmen and lawyers. Lack of patronage has dampened the ardor and weakened the influence of some of the old-timers while Democratic heresies have stirred up persons with a financial stake in government policies. Some of the new Republican leaders were once Democrats, a matter we shall discuss in more detail in chapters 10 and 11.

To varying degrees there has been a decline of Negro influence, described in chapter 17, and an increase in what Republicans call the "respectability" of their party. Men of standing, solvency, and integrity run the party's affairs in numerous southern states. They expound happily to visitors on the business success and economic eminence of themselves and their colleagues. They relish their contacts with the party's national leaders and derive considerable satisfaction from hobnobbing at conventions with those in the front line of attack on the New and Fair Deals. They are no less concerned for the perquisites of victory than the old patronage referees, but they would have no truck with the bribes that tempted convention delegations in earlier days. They are men of larger affairs and put their store in prestige and power rather than in petty bribes. Some of them look upon politics as a hobby, "an expensive hobby" one state chairman said, and entertain no foolish notions about winning local elections. A national committeeman said with satisfaction that Republican leaders in his state were honest, sound, reputable citizens; they were not politicians and did not aspire to office.

The transfer of top party posts to new individuals has not meant radical changes in the party following. The bulk of the membership and the scanty lower echelons of party officers remain, in most areas, about as before. An anomalous condition still prevails in the states where the party is weakest. Republicans in the mountain strongholds of the party, where the votes are, play second fiddle to more aggressive colleagues in the cities. Thus, in Alabama, the Republicans of Winston County, the one county in the state that regularly votes Republican, make hardly a ripple in the affairs of the state party. In Virginia, North Carolina, and Tennessee, by contrast, conservatives from the populous lowland or piedmont centers share leadership with politicians from the mountains.

Despite the general trend in party affairs just noted, the type of leaders in ascendancy during the 1940's and the beginning of the 1950's varied from state to state. The minuscule party in Mississippi has continued under the thumb of its national committeeman, Perry Howard, a Negro residing in Washington, D. C., famed as an old-fashioned patronage referee. Equally famed in this regard is R. B. Creager, until his death in 1950 the perennial national committeeman from Texas, whose tight oligarchy for a generation rebuffed all attempts to unseat him. Mr. Creager described his party as "one of the best and most closely knit organizations in any State in the Union." [22] The party in Arkansas has rested in the hands of the same small group almost since anyone can remember.* Leadership of more recent origin prevails in the other states. There have been sharp divergencies in parts of the South from the complacency of Republican leaders so often noted in this chapter. The case of Wilson Williams of Georgia has been mentioned. The 1948 presidential campaign saw "revitalization" efforts in several other states. Virginia Republicans employed a full-time executive director who set about, eighteen months before the contest, to reactivate the party organization. Observers said the newer, progressive element in the party caused his appointment. The press was full of his activities and to all appearances

* The national committeeman selected in 1916, 1920, and 1924 was Col. H. L. Remmel. Col. Remmel's brother was state chairman prior to his death in 1920. Col. Remmel's sister-in-law, wife of the deceased, was elected national committeewoman in 1928, 1932, 1936, 1940, 1944, and 1948. Col. Remmel's nephew, son of the committeewoman, has been president of the Arkansas Young Republicans, vice chairman of the national Young Republicans, chairman of the Pulaski County (Little Rock) Republican committee, and in 1951 was elected mayor of Little Rock. Another Remmel has been a member of the state committee from Pulaski County. The national committeeman since Col. Remmel's last election in 1924 has been Wallace Townsend.

Virginia Republicans made their most serious effort to win votes in twenty years.

In Florida, certain Republican state officials have exhibited remarkable initiative. C. C. Spades, former state chairman who was elected to the national committee in 1948, over a period of years devoted time and energy to the conduct of party affairs almost unknown among his southern counterparts. He had the advantage of numerous migrants accustomed to taking their Republicanism seriously—including some who were able and willing to help out with funds. He systematically raised money, distributed literature, analyzed election figures, and kept up a flow of pep letters to party officials. Characteristic was a circular to members of his state committee dated December 12, 1947. Contrast it with the attitude remarked on earlier that most southern Republicans hold toward Republican candidacies. Mr. Spades wrote:

In just over six weeks time the full slate of Republican candidates . . . must be on file with the proper authorities.

The Republican Party during the elections of 1946 attained more success, more publicity and more recognition within our state than at any previous time in our political history. This was primarily because of our having the biggest slate of Republican candidates ever offered the electorate of our state during an "off year." . . .

We need candidates for every position—candidates to head the ticket, candidates in every county for all of the positions to be voted for.

Efforts to revamp the party in Texas brought about quite a fight. Texans pride themselves on doing things on a grand scale and they have not failed in the factionalism of their Republican party. The fight for party control in Texas is as complex as a Latin American revolution. The party has split into factions and the factions have split within themselves. It all revolved around the late Rentfro Banton Creager, national committeeman from 1923 to 1950. Creager held patronage posts under Presidents Theodore Roosevelt and Taft and remained a power in the party ever after. In later years he *was* the party and a staunch supporter of Taft's son Robert. As such he warded off with no little skill the attacks of Dewey followers. Despite Dewey's nomination in 1948 Creager emerged in charge of his Texas campaign and kept on top of the state organization.[23]

A deep division among Texas Republicans developed in 1947 from the conviction that the party under Creager had not been seeking victory at the polls.[24] The "Republican Club of Texas," independent of the official party organization, was created under the leadership of Captain J. F. Lucey, a Dallas oil man with experience in national Republican affairs. "One of the known but unannounced purposes of the Republican Club is to get rid of R. B. Creager... together with others of the Old Guard." [25] Gerald Cullinan, a club official, explained that

> ... conservative citizens in Texas have traditionally talked about introducing the two party system to the Lone Star State but have failed to do anything constructive about it. Now, at long last, a group of progressive Republicans and anti-New Deal Democrats have come forward with a practicable plan to make two-partyism a reality. The plan is embodied in a new organization... It is a Statewide group, made up of men and women from every walk of life and from every age group, and it intends to build its strength where strength is needed most, in the precincts.[26]

The club seemed to start off well financed, but the effort soon collapsed and when the 1948 election was over Creager was still intrenched as the Republican boss of Texas. Even after Creager's death the "never say win boys"—as their Republican opponents call them—continued to dominate the party. In the spring of 1950 Republican Ben Guill won a special Congressional election in the eighteenth district against a handful of Democrats—the first Texas Republican to go to Congress in twenty years. Guill won although he "received no help at all from either the national or state party." He lost the seat by a narrow margin in the subsequent regular election. One of the few prominent Republicans to help Guill was Jack Porter who had capitalized on a split in the Democratic party to pile up a substantial vote for United States senator in 1948. But Porter and Guill could make no headway in the state organization, and Porter's efforts to gain Creager's vacated seat on the national committee were thwarted. Despite the official Republican attitude, the party increased its share of the presidential vote by 5.6 per cent between 1940 and 1948, and by 7.8 per cent between 1944 and 1948. Even allowing that the 1948 increase is deceptive because the Texas Regulars depressed the 1944 Republican percentage, these figures suggest that Texas offers a serious potential for a united, aggressive Republican party.

It is worth noting that the two other southern states where Dewey gained most in 1948 were Virginia and Florida—the two states where, to all appearances, the Republicans campaigned hardest. Political success grows from a compound of fortuitous and controlled circumstances. While determined and skilled leadership alone cannot assure Republican victory in the South, it is at least a minimum essential. The capacity of southern Republican leadership has increased, but it still is not sufficient for the needs of the party.

8

ROTTEN-BOROUGH POLITICS

LIKE SCOTLAND'S LOCH NESS MONSTER, A REPUBLICAN DRIVE TO ORganize the South makes its appearance every three or four years. And like the legendary Monster, the southern drives have lived only in the imagination of a few persons unable to convince others of what they saw.

True to form, as the parties began to square away for the 1952 presidential elections, out came an announcement from Republican national headquarters. The national executive committee voted "to make the most determined drive in history" to crack the solid South; "they are ready for a 20-year fight if necessary." [1] A negative prognosis became obvious, however, when the committee appointed to spark the drive was weighted with old-line southern chieftains. The seriousness of the effort would become known as the campaign advanced, and if it proved aggressive a revolution in the attitude of Republican national leadership would have taken place. For, like most of the state leadership, most of the national leadership has done little to build a strong party in the South.

The official explanation for this passiveness has been alluded to already. Presidential campaign managers judge it wasteful to divert resources from hot campaigns in doubtful states to hopeless campaigns in southern states. Their candidate can win more easily with electoral votes gathered outside the South than within it—so why bother about building the party in the South?

The record between 1880 and 1948, set forth in Table 14, supports the argument. None of the nine successful Republican candidates for president depended on the South. On four occasions when the Democrat won, a shift of southern votes to the Republicans could have changed the outcome. For Republicans to have captured southern votes in those elections, however, would have required infinitely more effort than to pick up additional votes in nonsouthern states. The size of the pluralities by which the Democrats won reflects the obverse of this condition. Under the electoral college system, the factors that influence the margin of victory in one state are likely to influence it in others; as a consequence, relatively slight shifts in popular preferences are usually compounded into much larger changes in electoral votes. In five of the seven Democratic victories this century, including all of the Roosevelt elections, the margin of victory was so wide that the outcome would have remained the same had all eleven southern states voted for the Republican candidate.

Under these conditions, the disinclination of the Republican National Committee and its adjuncts to support a series of foreign missions in the South seems reasonable. The natives report unanimously that they send more money out of the region than they get back. It is difficult to learn the amounts, but the national committee sets up annual quotas for each state committee. The Florida quota in 1946, for example, was $14,000; in 1947, $6,500; and in 1948, $28,000. The Georgia quota for 1946 was $7,000. The South Carolina, Mississippi, and Alabama quotas in 1947 were $2,000 each. These funds are supplemented by direct contributions from individual Republicans, who send much more to national collection committees than to their state committees. A Senate report on the 1944 election listed individuals who had contributed $500 or more, and the amounts of their contributions, to various campaign committees. The amount going out of Texas to oppose F.D.R. was $220,915.[2]

Grants from national headquarters to the South have for the most part been confined to an occasional $1,000 or so for a close

TABLE 14

THE SOUTHERN ELECTORAL VOTE AND THE MARGIN OF VICTORY IN PRESIDENTIAL ELECTIONS, 1880-1948

Year	Southern votes for Dem.	Southern votes for Rep.	Plurality of winner Dem.	Plurality of winner Rep.	South could have affected outcome
1880	95			59	
1884	107		37		1884
1888	107			65	
1892	112		110		1892
1896	112			95	
1900	112			137	
1904	120			196	
1908	120			159	
1912	126		347		
1916	126		23		1916
1920	114	12		277	
1924	126			246	
1928	64	62		357	
1932	124		413		
1936	124		515		
1940	124		367		
1944	127		333		
1948	88	39[a]	75		1948

[a] Cast for Thurmond, States' Rights Democrat.

Congressional race in a border state. Probably the largest in recent years were made in 1948. The Republican senatorial campaign committee put at least $6,000 into North Carolina and $5,000 into Tennessee to help the party's senatorial candidates.[3] Candidates who futilely sweat through a campaign are wont to resent the lack of help. The Republican running for Congress from North Carolina's tenth district in 1946 cut loose with a blast after his defeat by 3,518 votes out of 45,710 cast. Explaining the outcome, he said, "I had definite promises of financial help from national headquarters, but they let me down."[4]

The phantom nature of the southern party offers national leaders few incentives to pour energy and money into the South. Conservative northern funds have found their way into Democratic primaries with infinitely greater ease. The smallness of the Republican party has created another condition, however, that probably has even greater bearing on the lack of interest by the national leadership in building a strong party. The South enjoys rotten-borough representation in the Republican National Convention: it sends a goodly share of the delegates who choose the party nominees but it has provided few votes of the kind that count on election day. Most of the world's political assemblies, beginning with the House of Commons, have suffered from some degree of rotten-borough representation. Constituencies decline in numerical importance, but their representation in the assembly is not correspondingly adjusted. As the process goes on, the constituents who remain ascend in importance because of the disproportionately large share of votes—delegates—they can influence. Southern Republican politicians thus have become a peculiarly important focus of interest and maneuver inside their own party. The votes of their delegates are crucial and the importance of those votes to presidential aspirants produces a considerable respect in national councils for the status quo in each southern state.

We shall see presently how this works, but first a note on the size of southern delegations. Until 1916, moves to reduce southern representation in the national convention were successfully resisted.[5] In the convention of that year, southern delegates occupied 348 of 987 seats, or 35.3 per cent. Their states had not given the Republican candidate an electoral vote since 1876 and their Republican popular vote had been on a toboggan for twenty years. Moreover, they were charged with all sorts of nefarious activities at the 1912 meeting. (See pages 222-24, below.) As a result, the apportionment of delegates was altered to penalize states with a low popular vote. In the 1920 convention southern delegates comprised 17 per cent of the membership, and they have made up approximately that proportion of each convention since.[6]

The membership rules adopted by the 1948 convention[7] illustrate the way in which states with heavy Republican balloting have been favored. In the old days, a state was given two delegates for each representative in Congress. Under the 1948 formula, two delegates-at-large were awarded for each representative-at-large, and then a district delegate was given for each Congressional district casting a thousand or more votes for the Republican candidate in the previous presidential election or for the Republican candidate in the latest Congressional race. If a district cast ten thousand votes or more for either of those candidates it was given another extra delegate. In the South these bonus delegates provide the chief incentive to local leaders to get out the Republican vote. Furthermore, a state was awarded six delegates-at-large if it gave a majority of its electoral votes to the Republican in the previous presidential race, or if it elected a Republican governor or United States senator at the next election (or at the latest one if there was no subsequent senatorial election). The membership of each delegation was completed by giving every state four delegates-at-large. The detailed formulas for apportioning seats in the conventions have varied from time to time, and in their application some states have been affected more than others. South Carolina's representation dropped from 22 in 1916 to 6 in 1948; Virginia's from 30 to 21. Mississippi's fell from 24 to 8; North Carolina's from 42 to 26. Though the South's importance has been whittled away, it still goes to the conventions with about one-sixth of the ballots, which is about one-third of those needed to nominate for president. The competition for these ballots is hot; in that fact rests a reason for the attitude of national Republicans toward the party in the South. Thus confided one member of the Republican national committee: "The practical politician always prefers to do business with as small a group of people as possible. The competition for delegates is so keen that Republican organization leaders want the present 'closed club' arrangement to continue whereby the marshalling of delegates can be handled through a small clique of friends well known from past experience and able to deliver the votes with some degree of assurance." A live and kicking party, he went on, would mean new state leaders, and more of them, in place of the existing oligarchies. Most representatives of important presidential candidates have established contacts with the southern potentates.[8] They may not have in prospect a clean sweep of southern delegates, or even of one delegation, but they hesitate to offend those in the saddle or to exchange what prospects they do have for the uncertainties that a turnover in leadership would bring.

A further aspect of convention politics discourages revolution in the South. Aggressive Republicans who are interested in candidates and campaigns as well as in delegates and conventions not only must capture the party machinery in their state but also must gain recognition from the national party. Factional fights in the states usually shape up into a contest for seats in the national convention. Republican leaders report that in such contests the attitudes of the competing delegations toward the presidential nomination become important. The merits of the claims are weighed, of course, such as the legality of the way in which the delegates were selected. When the technical issues are hazy, however, the fight becomes one of what presidential aspirant is to get the state's votes. Under these circumstances the long-run welfare of the party fades before the urgent business of nominating a president. The character of the deliberations is suggested by the unwillingness of many delegate-aspirants to disclose their presidential preferences until seated. In this vein, one state chairman asserted that an instructed delegation would be an absurdity in his state where there is a contest at every convention.

The story of the Georgia delegation in 1948 conveys the atmosphere of these contests. Several months before the convention, the press detected a fight coming up and recalled by way of background that "Two Georgia delegations went to the GOP convention in 1944. The group headed by Roscoe Tucker, of Dawsonville, favored Tom Dewey for President. Dewey forces were in control of the convention, and [the] Tucker group was seated." [9] As the 1948 convention loomed closer, the Tucker group and a group headed by Roy Foster, of Wadley, that had been unsuccessful in 1944, jockeyed for position. In a sheath of Georgia press reports covering more than six months, the only basis suggested for the contest was that Tucker favored Dewey and Foster favored Taft. In Philadelphia, two delegations claimed Georgia's seats. The dispatches read:

> With Governor Dewey's supporters on one side and Senator Taft's on the other, Georgia's two opposing Republican political factions took their bitterly contested struggle for national convention seats before the credentials committee Monday. Last Friday the Republican national committee overruled Chairman Carrol Reece by voting 48-to-44 to seat the Georgia group identified with ... W. R. Tucker. ... That meant 16 convention votes, perhaps a few less, for Dewey. ... Over the weekend leaders of both factions, aided by strategists in the Dewey and Taft high commands, were busy trying to corral a majority of the credentials committee's 51 votes.[10]
>
> In ruling 26 to 24 for the W. R. Tucker faction Monday, the credentials committee threw out the Taft-dominated faction headed by Roy Foster, of Wadley, which twice had won legal recognition from the Georgia secretary of the state ... What brought national attention to the Georgia decision was the fact that supporters of Taft, Stassen, and Vandenberg had reportedly joined forces in a 'stop-Dewey' movement to unseat the Georgia Dewey adherents ...[11] *

Southern delegations probably enjoy greater independence on the convention floor than do delegates from other states. There are no hierarchies back home to send them orders and their selection depends on no popular approval. They are not advised by presidential preference primaries—the Republicans hold none in the South—and the conventions by which they are generally

---

* The same credentials committee recommended that contested delegations favoring Taft from Mississippi and South Carolina be seated. In both states, the contest was the projection of a factional feud that national conventions had been arbitrating for years. The Mississippi black-and-tan delegation was seated over its lily-white rival, the traditional outcome of the contest. It is noted at each convention that the party would be damaged in the North if a group openly professing white supremacy were seated. The South Carolina case involved the remains of a faction formerly headed by the late, unbelievable "Tieless Joe" Tolbert and a far more respectable black-and-tan rival that had been recognized since 1940.

chosen[12] leave them free of formal instructions. Personal loyalties and bandwagon tactics flourish.

The endless competition for convention delegates, and the vested interests created thereby, explain in large part why Republican leadership is content with a weak southern party. The significance of this convention politics, and of the low state of southern Republicanism in which it is rooted, has been enormous for the South and for the rest of the United States. The southern oligarchies have greatly bolstered the conservative wing of the Republican party. Jasper Shannon has pointed to the influence of the South on Republican national leadership and hence on the nation[13]—southern support of William Howard Taft in 1912, of Harding in 1920, of Coolidge in 1924, and so on. In the 1940's and early 1950's southern Republicans continued to bulwark the Right wing of the party by their preference for Senator Robert A. Taft.

It has even become fashionable to speak of southern Republicans as though they were the personal property of the Ohio Senator. Drew Pearson writes of Taft's "well-oiled political machine in the South." [14] Headlines read "Dewey Backers Plan Drive to Break Taft's Hold on South." [15] Marquis Childs pointed to the selection in 1946 of a southerner, Carroll Reece of Tennessee, to be the party's national chairman, as a Taft victory. This "remarkable departure from custom ... served to underscore Taft's assiduous efforts in recent years to line up Southern delegates behind his candidacy." [16]

Taft did not rely solely on his political viewpoint to ingratiate himself with southern party chiefs. The foothold he gained prior to the 1940 convention undoubtedly attracted additional strength to him. The gossip circulated that he, along with other candidates, resorted to the tested methods of wooing southern delegates. From the 1948 convention Drew Pearson wrote an historical note:

> The Republican Party has always flirted with the idea of breaking the Solid South....
>
> Yet when it comes to nominating the most coveted prize in the Republican Party, it treats Southern delegates as so many pawns to

be bartered back and forth across the counter. These are the delegates traditionally bought and paid for, who can tip the scales for or against the leading candidate.

Once back in 1928 enough Republicans got so indignant about the barter of delegates that they held a Senate investigation of Herbert Hoover's Southern purchases. According to the sworn testimony before the Senate committee, Ben Davis, colored GOP national committeeman for Georgia, received $2,200 of Hoover money to pay the expenses of Georgia Republicans.

Prior to this payment Ben Davis was not for Hoover. Afterward he was.

Perry Howard, colored GOP national committeeman for Mississippi, also received $2,000 of Hoover money. The Mississippi delegates voted for Hoover.

Rush Holland, former assistant attorney general for Harry Dougherty, was the Hoover bagman who toured the South and paid off the Southern delegates.

Today, Perry Howard, the same GOP potentate of Mississippi, is vigorously in the corner of Senator Taft. Taft has used a technique different from Hoover's. Some time ago he gave Howard's son a job in the Senate post office.

John E. Jackson, chief Republican mogul of Louisiana, is also a Taft man. He is reported to handle some of the law business forwarded by the Taft family law firm in Cincinnati.

This year, however, Dewey has a slice of the Southern Republicans, and the battle to carve them up is the chief backstage battle now being fought in Philadelphia.[17]

A close look at national convention balloting will delineate Taft's relationship to the South. In 1944, and in 1932 and 1936 as well, the Republican convention selected a nominee on the first ballot. The strength of the leading contender overwhelmed the opposition and the behind-the-scenes contest is not reflected in the balloting. For 1940 and 1948, however, it is possible through the convention voting to compare the performance of southern delegates with that of the whole convention. Table 15 shows the percentage of southern delegates and the percentage of total delegates in the 1940 convention who voted for each major candidate for the presidential nomination on the first, fourth, and fifth ballots. The fifth ballot constituted something of a break, and Willkie was nominated before the sixth roll call was completed. On the first ballot, the southerners favored Taft with more than twice the percentage of the votes that the whole convention did.* They gave Dewey about the same relative support as the convention, and threw a handful of votes to Willkie, fewer proportionately than the convention. By the fourth ballot, Taft had

TABLE 15

SOUTHERN VOTING FOR PRESIDENTIAL NOMINEES:
1940 REPUBLICAN NATIONAL CONVENTION

	Percentage of delegates favoring candidates					
	On 1st ballot		On 4th ballot		On 5th ballot	
	Whole convention	Southern delegates	Whole convention	Southern delegates	Whole convention	Southern delegates
---	---	---	---	---	---	---
Taft	18.9	44.4	25.5	45.8	37.8	61.3
Willkie	10.5	6.5	30.7	19.0	43.0	34.5
Dewey	36.0	34.9	25.1	31.0	5.7	1.8
Gannett	3.3	2.95	0.4	0.6	0.1	0.6
Hoover	1.7	0.6	3.1	0.6	2.0	0.6
James	7.4	1.8	5.6	0.6	5.9	0.6
Vandenberg	7.6	5.3	6.1	2.4	4.2	0.6
Bridges	2.8	0.6	0.1	0.0	0.0	0.0
MacNider	3.4	2.95	2.6	0.0	0.4	0.0
Others	8.4	0.0	0.8	0.0	0.9	0.0
TOTAL	100.0	100.0	100.0	100.0	100.0	100.0

* In Tables 15 and 16 sharper contrast would have resulted from using the percentages of nonsouthern delegates voting for the candidates instead of the percentage of all the delegates. The vote in the whole convention was employed, however, to show the progress of the candidates toward the nomination, an important influence on uncommitted delegations intent upon winding up with the winner.

gained slightly in the South, Dewey had lost a little, and Willkie had picked up votes from Dewey and from the scattering that had gone to minor candidates the first time around. In the convention as a whole Dewey lost more heavily than he did in the South. By the fifth ballot, Dewey's following disintegrated, both among southern delegates and in the whole convention, in both cases going about half to Taft and half to Willkie.

In this balloting, southern delegates were clearly less enthusiastic about Willkie—the maverick, the amateur politician, the dark horse—than were those from other states. The original preference of southern delegates for Senator Taft held firm, though on the sixth ballot they started to shift to Willkie. The southern delegates seemed less responsive, however, to the tide of feeling that nominated Willkie than were their fellow delegates. Willkie gained roughly 33 per cent of the convention delegates between the first and fifth ballots. He gained 28 per cent of the southern delegates during the same period. On the sixth and final ballot it was the bolt to him of delegates from nonsouthern states that determined the outcome.[18]

In the 1948 convention, as in 1940, the voting opened with Taft more than twice as strong among southern delegates as in the whole convention. (See Table 16.) The Dewey percentages among southerners and in the whole convention were about even. On the second ballot Taft gained in the South, as he did in the convention. Dewey also gained in the South, but not so much as outside the South. The shift of favorite son votes from Carroll Reece of Tennessee to Taft on the second ballot largely accounted for the latter's increase. Dewey's opposition capitulated after the second ballot.

The preference of southern Republican delegates for the conservative, Taft, can be better understood by examining the voting of the individual delegations, though a warning against reading convention votes too literally should be put on record. As a Virginia Republican who was a veteran of several conventions noted, many factors influence delegates. Virginia stands near the end of the alphabetical roll, for example, and her delegates are inevitably affected by the actions of the preceding states.

TABLE 16
Southern Voting for Presidential Nominees: 1948 Republican National Convention

	Percentage of delegates favoring candidates			
	On 1st ballot		On 2nd ballot	
	Whole convention	Southern delegates	Whole convention	Southern delegates
Taft	20.5	44.7	25.1	48.7
Dewey	39.8	37.2	47.1	40.8
Stassen	14.4	6.4	13.6	6.9
J. W. Martin	1.7	3.2	0.9	2.6
Reece	1.4	8.0	0.1	0.5
Warren	5.4	0.5	5.2	0.5
Others	16.8	0.0	8.0	0.0
TOTAL	100.0	100.0	100.0	100.0

A representative ballot is the second 1948 ballot. The vote of each southern state for each candidate is contained in Table 17. Four state delegations maintained a high degree of unity in their voting. Almost one-third of Taft's 1948 southern votes came from Texas. The Texas delegation was controlled, as usual, by R. B. Creager. In 1940 Creager had served as Taft's floor manager and his entire delegation had then voted for Taft on every ballot. The 1948 Mississippi delegation, controlled by Perry Howard as in many previous conventions, cast its eight votes for Taft. The South Carolina delegates, six strong, comprised the other group that also voted together for Taft. They were tightly knit under the leadership of J. Bates Gerald, state chairman, who had gained recognition for his faction in 1940. Almost half of Taft's southern votes, then, 43 out of 92, came from three states where the party was dominated by a single leader. In the other eight states, with the exception of Georgia, whose contested delegation has been discussed previously, the delegates were divided more evenly among the leading contenders. Dewey claimed 62; Taft, 49; Stassen, 10; Martin, 4; and Reece, 1.[19]

TABLE 17

THE VOTE OF SOUTHERN STATE DELEGATIONS ON SECOND BALLOT FOR NOMINATION OF PRESIDENT: 1948 REPUBLICAN NATIONAL CONVENTION

State	Total delegates	Dewey	J. W. Martin	Reece	Stassen	Taft	Warren	3 others
Alabama	14	9				5		
Arkansas	14	3			4	7		
Florida	16	6			4	6		
Georgia	16	13	1		1		1	
Louisiana	13	6				7		
Mississippi	8					8		
North Carolina	26	17	3		2	4		
South Carolina	6					6		
Tennessee	22	8		1		13		
Texas	33	2			2	29		
Virginia	21	13	1			7		
SOUTH	189	77	5	1	13	92	1	
CONVENTION	1094	515	10	1	149	274	57	88

The splits within the delegations reveal that some of the state oligarchies tolerate, or cannot prevent, internal disagreement. These differences in the nature of the oligarchies from state to state point again to the variety in southern Republicanism. And it is clear that the variety extends to the most critical area of southern Republican activity, the national convention. The convention votes also demonstrate the importance of fixed allegiances between presidential aspirants and southern leaders which has been referred to. The details of the second ballot in 1940, shown in Table 18, reveal much the same internal division in the delegations as prevailed in 1948. South Carolina and Texas voted as units, though this time South Carolina went for Dewey. Mississippi's delegation was, as later, overwhelmingly for Taft. In the Alabama, Arkansas, and Louisiana delegations, the division be-

TABLE 18

The Vote of Southern State Delegations on Second Ballot for Nomination of President: 1940 Republican National Convention

State	Delegates	Dewey	Gannett	Hoover	James	MacNider	Taft	Vandenberg	Willkie	Bridges	4 others
Alabama	13	7					6				
Arkansas	12	3	1				6		2		
Florida	12	9	1				1	1			
Georgia	14	7	2	2			2	1			
Louisiana	12	6					6				
Mississippi	11	3					8				
North Carolina	23	8					7	2	6		
South Carolina	10	10									
Tennessee	18	7			1	1	4		5		
Texas	26						26				
Virginia	18	5					7		5	1	
SOUTH	169	65	4	2	1	1	73	4	18	1	
CONVENTION	1000	338	30	21	66	34	203	73	171	9	55

tween Dewey and Taft was remarkably similar in the two conventions. In the Georgia, North Carolina, and Virginia delegations, Taft carried about the same strength both times.

The dependence of candidates for the Republican presidential nomination on leaders in the southern states who are in the saddle at the moment greatly stabilizes the positions of those leaders. They become, in effect, insulated against outside interference which otherwise might, in efforts to strengthen the party, upset their control of the state organizations. This fact, coupled with the fiscal realities of a presidential campaign that require money to be put where it can do the most immediate good, means that serious, sustained efforts to develop a southern Republican party will not be made by the party's national leaders.

The sources of southern Republican growth lie outside such personalities. The sources will be found in social and economic changes that alter, no matter how indirectly, the incentives that guide personalities.

a gradual revolution

9

PRESIDENTIAL REPUBLICANS

WHEN ALL THE OBSTACLES TO SOUTHERN REPUBLICAN GROWTH ARE viewed together, the effect is overwhelming. One wonders how the party can become a serious force in any southern state. The dynamic feature of American politics that opens such a possibility is the change in the character of political interests, and therefore ultimately in the character of political issues. New issues may divide the South whereas the old issues solidified it.

The issues we speak about and whose origins and effects we shall examine in the next two chapters are increasingly nationwide in scope and of increasing concern to the Federal government. That fact requires examination of the relationship between national and state politics. It is relevant to ask, for example, whether two-party politics might not grow up in Virginia around state controversies through the well-defined factions that have fought each other election after election in the Democratic primaries. Senator Byrd's organization might evolve into a powerful state party, and the liberal wing of the Democratic party might form another. In Louisiana, might not the Long and anti-Long factions in the Democratic party project themselves into a real party politics revolving around state issues?

The development of two-party politics around purely state issues, however, appears unlikely. Rather, it seems that the *motive force* for two-party politics in the South must come from interests and issues treated in the national arena. The separation of state from national issues is, of course, often slight, and we find that the lines which divide southern Democrats among themselves in state affairs frequently parallel disagreements within or between the parties in national affairs. But rivalry for the presidency and control of the Congress promises to be the chief prod to Republican growth. It is not merely that the energies and emotions of state politics are exhausted in the primaries, and that results of the primaries have seldom been questioned in general elections. It is the nature of the American party system that the predominant controversies in party competition have stemmed historically from the national sphere. Lord Bryce, in the first edition of *The American Commonwealth* published in 1888, noted this fact out of a century of American experience. What, he asked, is the relationship between the state parties and the national parties?

There are three kinds of relations possible, viz.—

Each State might have a party of its own, entirely unconnected with the national parties, but created by state issues—i.e., advocating or opposing measures which fall within the exclusive competence of the State.

Each State might have parties which, while based upon State issues, were influenced by the national parties, and in some sort of affiliation with the latter.

The parties in each State might be merely local subdivisions of the national parties, the national issues and organizations swallowing up, or rather pushing aside, the State issues and the organizations formed to deal with them.[1]

The third of these possibilities, he concluded, had happened. "The national parties have engulfed the State parties....The national issues have thrown matters of State competence entirely into the shade, and have done so almost from the foundation of the Republic."[2] National issues have increasingly overshadowed state concerns since Lord Bryce wrote, as vital functions of government have been transferred to the Federal sphere or have been initiated there.

Be it acknowledged, with regard to the party organizations,

that the national units have far from engulfed the state parties. On the contrary, the nationalization of issues has proceeded in a party system noted for its decentralized nature. The major American political parties are federal in character, like the government. Unlike the government, however, the preponderant power in the parties lies in the states.³ Party power rests with state, county, and city leaders, and these politicians are more interested in patronage—broadly conceived—than in issues, except to the important extent that issues must be taken into account to win elections. This discrepancy, incidentally, between the locus of major government action and the locus of party power weakens, in the eyes of many observers, the effectiveness of the American party system.

The pulling power of the presidential elections on both southern and nonsouthern voters bespeaks the greater dramatic quality, and importance to the voters, of national politics. The number of persons who vote in presidential elections in parts of the South often exceeds the number who vote in Democratic primaries.⁴ More significantly, charts of voter participation in state elections all over the country invariably have a saw-tooth profile: the peaks are the years in which a presidential election was held simultaneously with the state election and the valleys are the nonpresidential years.⁵ A similar pattern prevails in elections of United States representatives. Between 1928 and 1946, for example, the total vote cast for House candidates in nonpresidential years was consistently lower than the comparable vote cast in the preceding presidential year. The percentage that the former was of the latter follows: 1930, 72.6; 1934, 87.2; 1938, 84.1; 1942, 59.8; 1946, 76.3.⁶

This pulling power of the presidential race is particularly useful to southern Republicans in the states that elect their governor at the time the president is elected: Arkansas, Florida, North Carolina, Tennessee, and Texas. Figure 7 reveals the special attraction of the presidential contest for Republicans in Texas, a state where the party is weak in numbers, and weaker in leadership. Not only did the number of Republican voters for governor of Texas go up in the years of a national campaign, but the Re-

136   A GRADUAL REVOLUTION

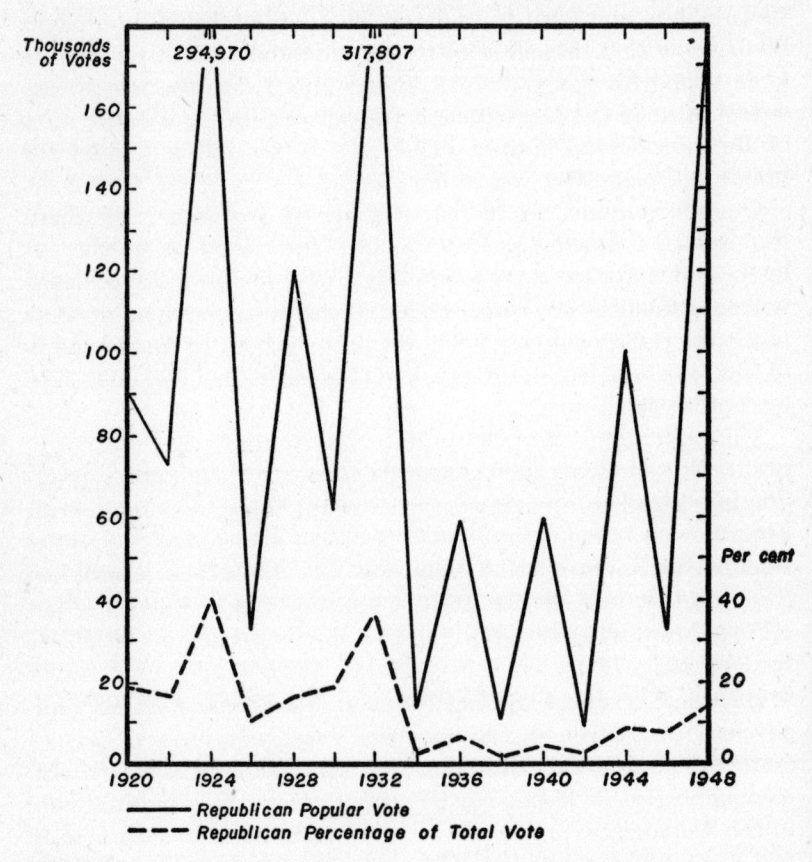

FIGURE 7: THE PRESIDENTIAL CAMPAIGN IN TEXAS AND THE REPUBLICAN VOTE FOR GOVERNOR, 1920-1948

publican percentage of the gubernatorial vote followed roughly the same pattern. (The large Republican showing in 1924 and 1932 was not connected with the presidential campaign: the Democratic party split when unhappy members bolted their party's nominee, "Ma" Ferguson.) In addition to attracting more Republicans to the polls, the presence of the Republican presidential nominee on the ballot probably stiffened party loyalty toward state and local candidates. The data in Table 9 on pages 66-67 show that the effect of the presidential contest on Republican voting for governor in Arkansas and Tennessee is not consistent as in Texas. Nevertheless, the personalities and battle cries of the presidential contest make it a better rallying point for building a party than any other.

Other conditions argue that the key to building a southern Republican following lies in the race for president. Sooner or later, if they are to create a winning party, southern Republicans will need financial aid from outside. If the party's national leaders reach the point of giving such aid, they will do so more readily to win electoral votes for president, or seats in Congress, than to capture state offices.

Moreover, legal and party rules in the South have increasingly been adjusted to permit Democrats to desert their party's presidential candidate more easily than candidates for other offices. The rules encourage, therefore, the group known as presidential Republicans—persons who vote for the Republican candidate for president but not for the Republican candidates for other offices. Presidential Republicans have, in effect, been given official recognition.

Historically, one of the legal bulwarks to Democratic supremacy has been party loyalty tests that required voters in Democratic primaries to support the nominees of the party in the general election. Since in most areas the politically active persons vote in the Democratic primaries—in order to "have a voice" in state and local government—an effective loyalty test would materially handicap efforts to build a Republican party. Toward this end, over most of the South, voters are "required" by one means or another to support the nominees of the primary in which they vote. Some states theoretically exclude from the primary those who have not supported the party for a specified period. Others exact a pledge to support the nominee in the forthcoming election. On occasions when a bolt threatens, party chiefs sound off in pious tones on the fate that awaits those who are disloyal. In fact, however, as soon as an election is over, the instincts of self-preservation prompt the party to lure back into the fold any voters who have strayed. As a consequence, in all sections of the South where there are Republicans, crossing party lines to vote in the primary of another party is a familiar occurrence, and generally goes without punishment.

More stringent sanctions, however, may be employed against candidates than against voters who flaunt party regularity. Statements under oath made at the time of declaring candidacy give moral force to the formal requirements and an opportunity to enforce them. Candidates have influence with the voters. Defections among them could destroy a party. It is important, therefore, that prominent Democrats in some states can be and have been excluded as candidates from Democratic primaries for refusing to promise support for nominees of the party, or for having actively opposed them in the past. Perhaps the best known case is that of the late Senator "Tom-Tom" Heflin of Alabama who was forced to run for re-election as an independent in the general election of 1930. He ran against the nominee of a Democratic primary from which he was barred because of his support of Hoover in 1928. These restraints have tied politically ambitious persons to the Democratic party and made the Democratic primaries the sole ladder of political success.[7]

A growing distinction, however, between loyalty to the "state Democratic party" and loyalty to the "national Democratic party" makes presidential Republicans important. Unhappy Democrats in most southern states could in 1948 support the Republican national ticket without prejudice to their status as Democrats. The change in the rules of the Democratic party in Georgia illustrates the trend. The rules adopted in state convention at Macon on October 9, 1946, admitted as voters only those "who in good faith will pledge themselves to support the Democratic candidates for all offices to be voted on during the year." The rules the state convention adopted at Macon two years later, on July 2, 1948, required a voter to "pledge himself or herself to support in the general election ... all candidates nominated by the Democratic Party of Georgia in this primary ... for the nomination of county, district or state offices ... " In Arkansas and South Carolina changes in a similar spirit were made, with the obligation of can-

TABLE 19

Presidential Republicans, 1948, Selected Southern States [a]

State	Republican vote for president Number	Per cent of total	Republican vote for governor Number	Per cent of total	Excess of president's over governor's vote Number	Per cent of total	Excess as per cent of vote for governor Number	Per cent of total
Alabama[b]	40,930	19.0	35,341	16.0	5,589	3.0	15.8	18.8
Arkansas	50,959	21.0	26,500	10.8	24,459	10.2	92.3	94.4
Florida	194,280	33.6	76,153	16.6	118,127	17.0	155.1	102.4
Louisiana[b]	72,657	17.5	102,331	25.0	−29,674	−7.5	40.8[c]	42.9[c]
North Carolina	258,572	32.7	206,166	26.4	52,406	6.3	25.4	23.9
South Carolina[b]	5,386	3.8	5,008	3.6	378	0.2	7.5	5.6
Tennessee	202,914	36.9	179,957	33.1	22,957	3.8	12.8	11.5
Texas	282,240	24.6	177,399	14.7	104,841	9.9	59.1	67.3
			349,665[b]	32.9	−67,425	−8.3	23.9[c]	33.7[c]
Virginia[b]	172,070	41.0	119,366	32.0	52,704	9.0	44.2	28.1

[a] There was no Republican candidate for either governor or senator in Georgia and Mississippi to provide comparable figures.
[b] Vote for senator rather than governor.
[c] Excess as percentage of vote for president.

didates to support party nominees restricted to nominees of the state primary.[8]

By 1948, only in Alabama and Florida were candidates or voters restrained by party rules or law from voting as they wished in the presidential race. And at the last minute in 1948 the Florida legislature lifted any obligation to vote for a party's nominees in the presidential race of that year, a concession to the situation created by the Dixiecrats. Alabama Democrats, voters and candidates, continued technically obligated to support in the general election all nominees of the primaries, including presidential electors.[9]

Since new Republican voters and leaders must of necessity be recruited among Democrats (or among newly enfranchised persons—see chapters 13-18, below, on Negro politics), presidential Republicans demonstrate a way by which Democrats may be weaned from their party. To increase the number of presidential Republicans would seem an essential step in building a second party in the South.

Table 19 shows the proportion, in nine southern states, of Dewey's 1948 vote coming from voters who did not support the rest of the Republican ticket. The Republican vote for governor (in some cases United States senator) is compared with the Republican vote for president, cast on the same day. Of those voting for Dewey, a fifth in North Carolina, over a third in Texas, and almost a half in Arkansas did not support the Republican nominee for governor. This practice, of course, is by no means confined to the South,[10] and Table 20 testifies that in the South it is of long standing. Republicans regularly run a candidate for governor in the five southern states that elect a governor at the time of the presidential election. In Table 20, the excess of the presidential vote as a percentage of the gubernatorial vote is set forth for each election from 1920 to 1948. In addition, senatorial voting is compared with presidential voting in Alabama, the only state other than the five where the senatorial figures are useful.

Three comments should be made about Table 20. First, contests for senator or governor occasionally attract more Republican votes than the presidential race. These contests usually

TABLE 20

PRESIDENTIAL REPUBLICANS, 1920-1948, SELECTED SOUTHERN STATES

The excess of Republican votes for president over Republican votes for governor figured as a percentage of the gubernatorial votes[a]

State	1920	1924	1928	1932	1936	1940	1944	1948	Median
Texas	−1.4	−126.5	204.8	−225.6	74.9	253.5	91.4	67.3	71.1
Arkansas	52.0	61.3	74.5	39.3	19.3	153.7	108.8	92.3	67.9
Florida	69.6	75.1	51.7	−34.9	30.8	[b]	48.7	155.1	51.7
Tennessee	−45.2	7.9	56.6	4.4	87.8	35.0	26.2	12.8	19.5
North Carolina	1.1	2.8	20.6	−2.0	−21.3	9.3	13.9	25.4	6.1
Alabama[c]	−3.5	7.5		3.7	0.0		6.1	15.8	4.9

[a] In cases where the gubernatorial vote exceeded that for president, the difference is figured as a percentage of the presidential vote and the result is preceded by a minus sign in the table.
[b] Republican candidate for governor withdrew.
[c] The Alabama figures are based on the vote for senator instead of governor.

reflect temporary dissensions among Democrats and not increased vitality in the Republican organization. As the case of Texas illustrates, the aberrations have had no lasting effect.[11] Fluctuations in the percentages from year to year have depended also on the personalities of the Republican state candidates and their enthusiasm for the campaign.

Second, trends in the proportion of voters who are presidential Republicans have no significance in themselves unless they account for significant trends in the total Republican vote. In 1928, for instance, presidential Republicans did bring victory in several states. At first glance, Table 20 might seem to indicate that presidential Republicans are of increasing importance. Such an inference can only be tentative, however, if the fluctuations in Republican strength discussed in chapter 4 are borne in mind.

Finally, the variations from state to state, revealed in the two tables, indicate variations in the character of both the Republican and Democratic parties. In the rim states of Texas, Arkansas, and Florida, where presidential Republicans appear most important, Democratic loyalties are not so deeply imbedded as in the Deep South. Neither is the Republican party in those states a majority party in a large section of the state, as is true in North Carolina and Tennessee, both states where presidential Republicans are less important. In states where Republicans have substantial strength, the proportion who are presidential Republicans goes up in counties of slight total Republican strength. Note, for example, on the opposite page, the 1944 performance of ten North Carolina counties, the five in which Dewey ran weakest and the five in which he ran strongest.

The relatively high figures for presidential Republicans in Virginia that appear in Table 19 do not, it should be remarked, modify these observations. The Byrd organization is so strong outside as well as inside the Democratic party that Republican candidates for senator (governors are not elected in presidential years) operate under an abnormal handicap, whereas the organization is not so enthusiastic in working for Democratic presidential nominees.

Per cent major party vote for Dewey	Republican vote: Pres.	Gov.	Excess of vote for pres. over vote for gov.	The excess as percentage of the vote for gov.
2.9	133	108	25	23.1
3.8	124	64	60	93.8
4.3	113	83	30	36.1
4.7	172	96	76	79.2
5.5	495	274	221	80.7
62.1	9121	9012	109	1.2
64.0	4392	4393	−1	−0.0
65.7	4388	4206	182	4.3
75.7	3192	3146	46	1.5
79.1	3178	2990	188	6.3

Southern voters who split the ticket, and hence become presidential Republicans, fall into two categories. Some have long favored the Republican party but have concluded that there is no future in bucking the Democrats in state politics. They may refrain from supporting Republican state candidates because of having voted in the Democratic primaries or because they are contemptuous of the candidates offered by the Republican party. More important for the future of southern politics are disaffected Democrats who more recently have taken to voting Republican because they don't like the national Democratic administration. From both these groups, Republican leaders report, financial contributions come to state headquarters bearing the stipulation that they must be used only in the race for president, at home or in doubtful states, and not for other Republican candidates. There is no way to know how many disaffected Democrats are among the presidential Republicans, but their increase will in large part set the pace at which the South moves toward party politics.[12]

10

THE MATERIALS OF REVOLUTION

DURING THE 1948 PRESIDENTIAL CAMPAIGN, A DISTINGUISHED MISsissippi liberal announced his support of the Republican candidate. Hodding Carter argued in his Greenville newspaper that above all else the South needs independence in its politics. The best of the alternatives to Truman was Dewey, so Mr. Carter struck a blow for a two-party South.[1]

At about the same time, Jesse Jones of Texas came out for Dewey. Mr. Jones, a man of many enterprises and much wealth, held posts of eminence under Franklin Roosevelt and was long a tower in Democratic politics. Some observers may have been surprised at Hodding Carter, but not at Jesse Jones, unless they were surprised because he did not take the step sooner. By economic interest Mr. Jones seemed a natural for the Republican party.

Intelligent criticism and enlightened newspaper leadership alone cannot lift the South out of the one-party mire. The circumstances that stirred Mr. Jones to action, however, might make the materials of a revolution in southern politics. Mr. Jones is the sort of successful, respectable, energetic Democrat whose leadership and resources the Republicans need as much as they need southern votes. Mr. Jones, personally, might not be their man, but he was their type, and defections of many persons like him would presage a serious division in the Democratic party. What could cause these defections? First, what basic conditions perpetuate Democratic rule in the South, and next, are they changing in a way to threaten that rule?

The political story is the more visible one. Southern one-party politics originated in the resolve of white southerners to hold Negroes to a well-defined economic, social, and political place. Whites joined in the Democratic party and made it their weapon in state politics and in national politics. Sensitiveness about the Negro was such, and could be so manipulated, that white southerners never disagreed among themselves sufficiently on nonracial matters to destroy their Democratic unity in state politics. On nonracial matters in national politics, they found their regional economic interests adequately represented by the party. Out of the struggle and all that preceded it an emotional attachment to the Democratic party developed that became independent of the conditions that originally brought it about.

The nonpolitical story is probably more important for the future of southern politics. Any political system lives as part of a community and is intimately entwined with the economic and social conditions of the community. Economic and social systems possess great power because they embody the working and living relationships on which men depend. This power is used by those who prosper under existing conditions to reward and preserve their advantage. The power is used to form and influence the political system of the community. The political system possesses power of its own through its control over the formal rules that govern the community and it can thereby alter economic and social conditions. A dynamic interplay is created in which government is both a product of the economic and social conditions and an agency of community self-consciousness through which the community can preserve or change those conditions.[2]

In the South, the social and economic matrix that has perpetuated one-party politics is dominated by what Jasper Shannon calls the "banker-merchant-farmer-lawyer-doctor-governing class."[3] This class has had its way in much of the South most of the time since Reconstruction, and the political institution through which it has ruled is the one-party system. Once the system became established via political channels, it generated its own self-perpetuating forces. The banker-merchant-farmer-lawyer-doctor-governing class governed not at the expense of Negroes alone, but also at the expense of other whites, the tenant farmers, mill hands, debtors, persons of humble status generally. Lest we be misunderstood, let it be clear that we speak of the consequences of conditions and not of personal motives. Here it matters not whether the actions that created these conditions were taken deliberately or incidentally, benevolently or maliciously.

As in all societies, those who have ruled and prospered in the South naturally want to continue to do so. In the final analysis, however, it matters little to them whether they do so under a one-party system or a two-party system. Which means that economic, social, or political changes of sufficient magnitude to threaten the position of these people would lead them to seek a revision of the one-party system. Correspondingly, they would resist a revision when the alternative appeared unfavorable.

There are, then, in addition to nonrational loyalty, three crucial features that explain the one-party system. First, it originated in the purpose of excluding Negroes from effective political action, and indirectly from economic and social opportunity. If the system can no longer do those things, or if southerners no longer desire it to do them, an obstacle to change is removed, though change is not compelled. Second, the system has benefited some southerners more than others. If it ceased to serve those people in state politics or in national politics they would have incentives to change it. Third, the system has operated in an economic and social context that has nourished its survival. Fundamental changes in that context might force changes in the system.

What has been happening in the South and in the nation at each of these points to cause the Jesse Joneses to vote Republican?

In a long series of decisions culminating in 1948, the Supreme Court of the United States destroyed the white primary. No longer could whites under any pretext exclude Negroes from the Democratic party. They might increase suffrage requirements in general, as Georgia and South Carolina proceeded to do, but Negroes could not be singled out for special restriction. Negroes had been voting in Democratic primaries in a few states for many years, but the Court's decisions prompted some observers to foretell the end of one-party rule. Both parties would now compete for "the Negro vote" and whites would just as soon vote Republican as Democratic. The excuse for the one-party system, they said, was gone. The sudden effect of the Court's actions on Negroes in politics will be the subject of several later chapters. There was no immediate effect on the one-party system. The forces of inertia and self-interest that had made bolting the Democratic primaries futile or dangerous for three-quarters of a century remained. Nevertheless, an historical barrier to the growth of the Republican party had been removed.

Moreover, the way the South received the decisions uncovered a divergence in white attitudes toward Negroes that contrasted sharply with the traditional Democratic unity on the subject. In every southern state, Democratic factions arose to defend Negro political rights with an openness that would have meant political suicide a few years before. True, the motives of those who opposed the Talmadges and the Bilbos were often mixed, and the politicians usually confined their argument to an apologetic plea to "uphold the law and the courts." Some observers asserted that southern acceptance of mixed primaries stemmed solely from the Court's enforceable mandates. Nevertheless, whatever the reasons, by the end of 1950 Negro enfranchisement in much of the South—though not in all parts of all states—rested on growing popular guarantees as well as on judicial decrees.

There were reasons to believe that a general improvement in southern race relations was taking place that would further destroy the old bases of the one-party system. As Negroes achieved economic and educational advantages, their assertiveness increased and sometimes led to more rather than to fewer temporary frictions. It was more difficult, for example, to hold biracial meetings in certain Atlanta and Birmingham hotels in the 1940's than it had been in the 1930's. And in the years following World

War II a series of white brutalities against Negroes shocked the nation—almost as much, it might be said, outside the South as within it.

The evidence pointed undeniably, however, to long-run lessening of race tensions. The number of lynchings declined dramatically, though a tragic few still occurred. The failure of the Dixiecrats in 1948 and 1950 demonstrated that great masses of southerners would no longer be bamboozled by racist appeals. Some of the labor unions could press nonsegregation policies without irretrievably alienating their white membership. Local juries and judges, white, impartially punished crimes committed by whites against Negroes.[4] Under pressure from the courts, state authorities admitted Negroes to the graduate schools and white students accepted them without incident.[5]

Southerners who felt a lessening in the peculiar fear that whites have held of Negroes rested their hopes on two evolving conditions. If Negroes had not been equipped all along for full citizenship, they were obviously more so now than before. It was literally true, as Frank Graham had said at Tuskegee, that never before in all history had a race advanced so much in so short a time as southern Negroes since 1860. Though full equality in educational and economic opportunities was not yet offered, Negroes were increasingly better qualified by training and experience to exercise political rights successfully under the delicate conditions their traditional role in the community makes inevitable. Many indices measure their improved status. Though applying to the whole country, the following percentages of Negroes between the ages of five and twenty in school illustrate the trend in the South:

1900	1910	1920	1930	1940
31.0	44.7	53.5	60.0	64.4

The increasing political experience of Negroes produces an increasingly responsible, though no less determined, conduct that mitigates the fears of whites whose visions of Negroes in public life are limited to stories of Reconstruction. That the roof did not fall in when Negroes began to vote in substantial numbers during the 1940's assuaged the fears of many who viewed the trend with misgivings. The education of whites may have been improving too.

Another fundamental development promised to improve race relations. Opposition to Negro political activity—and race tensions generally—are greatest in the rural areas where Negroes are concentrated in large numbers. Both the Negro proportion of the southern population and the number of areas of Negro concentration are steadily declining. Table 21 shows that in every southern state the Negro percentage of the total population fell importantly between 1900 and 1950. Moreover, the number of southern counties in which Negroes made up 50 per cent or more of the population declined steadily: [6]

1900	1910	1920	1930	1940
284	263	221	191	180

At this writing, complete figures on nonwhite shifts between 1940 and 1950 are not available. The estimates by regions made by the Census Bureau in April, 1947, however, point to the net transfer of Negroes from the South to other parts of the country and from rural to urban places within the South. The changes in the nonwhite population between 1940 and 1947, as percentages of the 1940 nonwhite population, were estimated as follows:

Area	Total	Urban	Rural
United States	+11.6	+39.7	−14.2
West	+67.1	+76.9	+56.6
Northeast	+66.1	+79.5	−51.0
North central	+49.9	+57.7	+5.2
South [7]	−4.8	+16.6	−16.9

The factors that govern prejudice are difficult to weigh. Experience in Europe and the United States with prejudice against religious and ethnic groups testifies that equality of education and income is no cure-all. But on the level of politics, the cardinal fact stands out: Democratic exclusiveness toward the Negro has been breached for once and all by the courts, and it should be remembered that responsible courts do not act in a vacuum. Wise justices have a yen for the feasible and learned justices keep abreast of the times. While the courts were busy, the Democratic

TABLE 21

DECLINE IN THE SOUTHERN NEGRO POPULATION:
1900-1950

State	Negro percentage of the total population		
	1900	1940	1950[a]
Alabama	45.2	34.7	32.1
Arkansas	28.0	24.8	22.4
Florida	43.7	27.1	21.8
Georgia	46.7	34.7	30.9
Louisiana	47.1	35.9	33.1
Mississippi	58.5	49.2	45.5
North Carolina	33.0	27.5	26.6
South Carolina	58.4	42.9	38.9
Tennessee	23.8	17.4	16.1
Texas	20.4	14.4	11.5
Virginia	35.6	24.7	22.2

[a] Computed from preliminary estimates of nonwhite population appearing in the Census Bureau's "1950 Census of Population—Preliminary Reports," Series PC-6 and PC-12.

party also displayed a developing interest in Negro welfare. This interest has weakened the historic role of the party as the weapon of southerners in national politics. Before the Civil War, the Democratic party in the South came under the control of conservatives and planters. Following the war, it became the instrument through which the politically articulate South secured a voice in national affairs. In the nominating conventions, until 1936, a rule required that two-thirds of the delegates approve all nominees, a condition that gave the South great weight in selecting the party's candidates, though not a statistical veto over them.[8] Southerners were repeatedly returned to Congress from their one-party districts and thereby acquired influence beyond their numbers. When the Republicans were in control, they dominated the minority membership. When the Democrats were in control, their seniority assured them a disproportionate share of the posts of influence. Generally, the Democratic party upheld southern viewpoints, in debate if not always in action, most notably on the tariff and on matters affecting Negroes. Negro voters North and South were conceded to the Republicans.

During the administrations of Franklin Roosevelt two developments occurred. By the nature of its economic and social programs, the Democratic party increased its strength outside of the South and became less dependent on southern electoral votes. At the same time, it embarked on a campaign that in its effects wooed the votes of Negroes outside the South. Over the years the chorus of lament from conservative southerners grew. They disapproved of gestures that recognized social equality between whites and Negroes. That the wife of a *Democratic* president should be photographed with Negroes burned many a black-belt planter to the core. When the national administration evinced an interest in the welfare of Negroes inside the South, the boys blew up. Not all of the boys, but most of those accustomed to look upon the Democratic party as their special spokesman in national politics.[9]

The ultimate was reached in 1948. The Democratic President sponsored a "civil rights program." Its contents were not as portentous as some pretended, but it did assert Federal jurisdiction over certain aspects of race relations in the South. Resentful southerners sullenly charged it to a play for Negro votes in close states. With the exception of North Carolina, every southern state delegation unanimously opposed President Truman's nomination in the 1948 convention. But he was nominated and, in the face of southern opposition, the convention adopted a platform that endorsed the civil rights program. The course of the president and the party through all this appealed to voters outside the South and was, it seemed, an important factor in his election. The President then pressed for civil rights legislation in Congress and met the head-on opposition of twenty of the South's twenty-two senators. It would be hard to imagine a more complete reversal of the Democratic party's traditional deference to its southern wing on racial matters. The following passage, opening the weekly letter of March 19, 1949, "Capital Comment," from the chairman of the Democratic National Committee to party officials, indicated the friction:

> *Veto by filibuster* continues as the rule of the Senate.
> *The Republicans got what they wanted*—a long and serious delay in action on the Fair Deal Program.
> *The Southerners got what they wanted*—a cloture rule that is no cloture at all.
> The Northern Democrats and a few liberal Republican Senators were defeated.
> *The People lost.*

This sort of thing produced apoplexy among old-line Democrats.

A wholesale exodus did not occur in 1948. The pronouncements of the Republicans were just as bad and their record was much worse. Desertions of some of its voters to the Dixiecrats, moreover, did not force the Democratic party to retreat from its official position. In addition, the 1948 election suggested that the country is no longer "normally Republican," a fact that would increase the difficulty of making the Democratic party again the party of the South. The effect of it all was to remove another obstacle to a change in one-party rule.

The New Deal and Fair Deal not only created disharmony between the southern wing and the rest of the Democratic party on matters affecting Negroes; they also created sharp disagreements over economic and social policies. The spirit of the conflict was caught in an editorial appearing on November 1, 1947, in *The Southern Weekly,* a conservative Texas journal that wants to strengthen the southern units of the Republican party:

> It will be a long time before a majority of the people of most of the Southern States will become out-and-out Republicans. The thing that is needed first, and the thing that is attainable, is for Southern Democrats who have no intention of becoming Republicans and who continue to vote in State and local primaries, to band together to fight the

CIO-Communist-big-city-machine coalition in Presidential elections and to induce other Southern Democrats to do the same. Let them realize that the national Democratic party they supported in the past is no more. The party that masquerades under the Democratic name is a labor-collectivist party, opposed to practically everything for which the historic Democratic Party once stood, and the only organized opposition to it today is the Republican Party.

It serves no purpose here to debate for what the historic Democratic party once stood. Many would contend that a spirit of courageous concern for the common man linked the parties of Truman, Roosevelt, Wilson, Jackson, and Jefferson. Nevertheless, a goodly number of southern Democrats felt like Jesse Jones when he announced his support of Dewey: "This will not be a case of leaving our party, rather our party, as we inherited it from our fathers, and as we would still like to have it, has left us." [10] The New Deal and the Fair Deal added up to a program of national political action so distasteful to many planters and businessmen—who formerly had made the Democratic party their home and their servant—that conservative Democrats began to desert to the Republicans before there were any Dixiecrats.

Briefly, the trouble arose from two things: first, from Democratic policies pointed toward the special needs of plain people, and, second, from the Democratic assertion that the powers of government should be extended and used to ensure a prosperous, stable, and just national life. Everybody might agree vaguely on these objectives, but the way the New and Fair Deals set about to achieve them caused the rub. Certain Democratic bigwigs in the South were as displeased as Republican bigwigs outside the South with such things as the Wagner Act, minimum wages, work relief, public works, public housing, price and rent control, a national health program, higher taxes, Federal control of tidelands oil, and the Farm Security Administration. Most of the programs involved the extension of Federal interest to matters that hitherto had not been handled by government or had been handled in the states. Conservative southerners had the perfect chance to raise the honored cry, states' rights; and they did.

In political terms, Roosevelt and Truman relied upon an uneasy, three-way combination, much noted in the press, of organized labor, which was more and more politically self-conscious; "northern machines," whose jurisdictions included more and more Negroes; and the traditionally loyal southerners, often conservative. In reality, of course, Democratic victories rested on a more complex and subtle set of allegiances, including agricultural and middle-class interests, but these were three important, politically articulate groups that had claims in the formulation of Democratic policies.

The programs of the New Deal were not born full-blown one night in the oval study of the White House. They emerged from the evolving nature of the nation and its problems. They cut two ways in their effect on the relationship of the South to the Democratic party. The party no longer represented the regional interests of the South as that interest was conceived by much of the South's traditional political, economic, and social leadership. New Deal programs also gave political expression to differences among economic and social interests within the South itself, a closely related result. Such programs as those launched by the Farm Security Administration received hearty applause from some southerners and bitter condemnation from others.

These things happened as a profound transformation was taking place in the economic and social matrix of the one-party South.[11] The transformation was achieving two things that seemed to have direct political consequences. First, regional homogeneity, economic and otherwise, that demanded political expression, was being destroyed. In simplest terms, the old agricultural realm, where cotton reigned, was disappearing, and the South was left without a clear regional economic interest that set it apart from the rest of the nation.[12] Second, the changes increased the capacity for political action of groups in the population who had traditionally supported the political regime of the banker-merchant-farmer-lawyer-doctor-governing class despite the fact that their interests did not always coincide.

When speaking in these terms, prudence requires the utmost caution. One of the most famous analysts of the American party system made this statement, relevant to the thesis being advanced here: "In the South itself economic changes are tending to unsettle parties, the 'Solid South' is breaking." [13] M. Ostrogorski made the statement in 1910, and four decades later his prophesy had not been fulfilled. Moreover, political behavior, like human behavior in general, is only partly rational, and reasonable expectations often never develop.

Nevertheless, by the 1950's, the regional economic unity of the South, vis-a-vis the rest of the nation, was being diluted by increasing industrialization and increasing diversification of agricultural production.[14] The increased industry created organizable labor. Drives by the AF of L and the CIO, though not fulfilling their hopes, increased the number of organized laborers [15] and, especially among the membership of the CIO, gave them a start toward political cohesiveness hitherto unknown in the South. The new industrialization also contributed to a class of business, commercial, and industrial managers, some of them from outside the region, who inclined toward the national policies of the Republican party as the new proletariat inclined toward those of the Democratic party.[16] Technological developments in agriculture, like the flame cultivator and the cotton picker and all the equipment that hitched behind H. C. Nixon's steel mules,[17] began to revolutionize the social structure of the rural South, the seed bed of southern one-party politics. The relationships between farm managers and farm workers were changing and the number of rural inhabitants declined as population shifted to the cities.[18] Southern politics was slowly changing from rural to urban politics (retarded always, of course, by state legislative apportionment favorable to rural areas, and in Georgia by the county-unit system of nominations). The ultimate meaning of these and other economic developments—like the discovery of oil in Mississippi—could not be perceived in detail. Yet they would tend to create classes within the South more nearly approximating those of eastern and northern two-party states.[19] These developments, slow in the making and slow in their political consequences, would affect the ability of the one-party system to serve those who had benefited most under the old economic and social conditions.

These changes would inevitably contribute, it seemed, to political alertness among persons of lower incomes in the cities and in the rural sections, a result of leadership and organization and a rise in economic status. The lowering of suffrage barriers, chiefly the poll tax and the white primary, would increase the vote among southerners who were customarily the pawns of southern politics.[20]

The effect of these divisive forces would be felt in primary campaigns and might lead to a more rigid factional structure, at least for a while, within the Democratic party in state politics. Efforts to retard the developing political and economic effectiveness of lower income groups would undoubtedly be made, especially in attitudes toward employee organizations. Ultimately, however, the way was being opened for a clearer identification of economic interests with political action. If the liberal wing of the Democratic party achieved increasing ascendancy in the South, especially in the primaries for Congressional posts, as it had in the nation, conservatives would find powerful incentives to junk the traditional party alliance for a party better able to represent them in a politics of economics. In fact, it seemed that some had taken the first step.

11

FISSURES IN THE DEMOCRACY

A STORY, INTENDED TO BE HUMOROUS, IS TOLD ABOUT THEODORE Roosevelt and an "hereditary" Democrat. T.R. was campaigning for president in 1912 on the so-called Bull Moose ticket. As he spoke, a man in the audience kept repeating audibly, "I'm a Democrat. I'm a Democrat."

Suddenly T.R. stopped his speech and asked the man why he was a Democrat. "My grandfather was a Democrat. My father was a Democrat. And I'm a Democrat," was the answer. That was waving a red flag at the Republican bolter.

"If your grandfather had been a Bull Moose, and your father had been a Bull Moose, what would you be?"

"I'd be a damn fool," came the reply.

Somewhere around three-fourths of the voters in the United States inherit their party preference.[1] Political habit probably affects the way people vote more than any other factor. Especially in the South, loyalty to party shows itself decade after decade in the fixed locations of Republican and Democratic majorities. These consistencies may at times rest on continuing geographical interests, but often a political habit persists after the original reason for its existence has disappeared. We have already remarked on Republican enclaves scattered over the South whose presence is explained only by events of five to ten decades before.

Moreover, in individual cases, the politics a person inherits may be a matter of chance, as with Tennessee's famous Taylor brothers. Bob and Alf Taylor grew up together, yet even as boys they held heated political arguments. Alf is said to have acquired his Republican leanings from their father; Bob, his Democracy from an uncle. Each brother was nominated by his party for governor in 1886. Bob won that war of the roses and later went to the United States Senate. Alf was elected governor in the Republican landslide of 1920.[2]

The problem of Republican growth is not only one of overcoming all of the interests vested in the one-party system, but also one of overcoming this political conditioning of people. If, as we tried to show in the previous chapter, the materials of a revolution in southern politics are being made, the decisive question becomes: How rapidly will hereditary preferences give way to other influences over the voters? There is no certain answer; human behavior is not fully understood. But we do know that time can mitigate, as well as intensify, sharp feelings, and that bitter resentment toward the Republicans has given way in some circles to bitter resentment toward the Democrats. Once, in 1928, a crisis in feelings temporarily disrupted old habits.[3] In the 1940's and early 1950's fissures of a more significant kind appeared in the Democracy.[4]

Rumblings were heard as early as 1936. On August 7 of that year, for instance, a number of wealthy southerners joined a large group of anti-New Dealers meeting in Detroit. In the ensuing election the "Constitutional Democrats of Texas" opposed Roosevelt. There were more straws in the wind in 1940,[5] and by 1944 anti-Roosevelt sentiment boiled up into formal political action in three states.

In South Carolina, electors running in 1944 under the name "Southern Democratic" and favoring Senator Byrd for president received 7,799 votes, or 7.5 per cent of those cast. The total Republican vote came to 4.5 per cent. According to a leading spirit, the movement aimed to give South Carolina Democrats a "respectable" way to vote against Roosevelt—that is, a way that did not require them to vote Republican. Those behind the effort opposed

Roosevelt on numerous scores, but concluded that to win the most votes they would have to play on the race issue, and so they did. Prior to the election, South Carolinians consulted Roosevelt foes in several other southern states in an effort to make the protest region-wide. Separate "Southern Democratic" electors did not, however, appear on the ballot elsewhere. The law then existing in South Carolina provided for no general ballot, and therefore imposed no eligibility requirements on candidates for elector. Like the leaders of any political group, the Southern Democrats had merely to print their tickets and leave them at the polling places to be chosen by such voters as wished them.

In Mississippi, in 1944, a quietly laid plan succeeded whereby anti-Roosevelt Democrats captured the state convention and selected Democratic electors among whom were some who would not vote for Roosevelt in the electoral college. Supporters of the President were caught napping and not until the legislature came to the rescue a few days before the election was a slate of electors favorable to Roosevelt placed on the ballot. The insurgent ticket, called "Regular Democrats," received 5.5 per cent of the votes, as compared with a total Republican percentage of 6.4.

Similar actions by the "Texas Regulars" received more publicity. After capturing the May convention of the Texas Democratic party and naming a large number of anti-Roosevelt electors, the Regulars lost control of the September "governor's convention" and the electors unsympathetic to Roosevelt were replaced by a slate pledged to him. A legal tussle ensued. In the end, the Roosevelt electors appeared under the Democratic label and the Regulars ran a separate slate. The latter polled 11.8 per cent of the votes as compared to the Republicans' 16.8 per cent.

The desire to run under the Democratic name electors who would not vote in the electoral college for the nominee of the Democratic National Convention found full expression, as we saw in chapter 2, in the Dixiecratic movement of 1948.

These rebellions against the national Democratic leadership were led by those whose political views in the modern parlance are dubbed reactionary. Across the whole South the leaders of the 1944 agitations and the leaders of the later Dixiecrats fell almost invariably into the conservative wing of the party. Corporation lawyers, wealthy businessmen, industrial captains, black-belt planters—joined inevitably by a spate of malevolent opportunists—made up the backbone of the leadership of the bolts and revolts.[6] Many of them, especially the planters among them, were closely wed historically to the Democracy. They abhorred joining the Republicans, the party of the hated Reconstruction, now contemptible in its weakness. Unlike Jesse Jones, they tried to have their cake and eat it too: to remain Democrats but to oppose Democracy as it had come to be approved in the rest of the country and in much of the South. Their action assumed enormous significance as the first step in a break that, if carried to its logical conclusion, would land them in the Republican party.

This was true of the prime movers, but what of the one million southern voters who nominally supported the bolt-revolt of 1948? Can they be looked upon as a source of Republican recruits? An analysis appears in Appendix I of the votes received by Thurmond. Quite clearly, appeals to white concern over the Negro told most effectively and accounted for the great bulk of Dixiecratic votes. In state after state, with only occasional exceptions, Thurmond found his highest percentages among the whites in the counties with the largest proportions of Negroes in their population—where white livelihood has been most closely tied up with the plantation economy, with its associated racial and social attitudes, and with the relationships of interdependence between whites and blacks.

The quality of the campaign that Dixiecratic leaders waged to attract these votes requires comment.

Many honest southerners felt deeply all they said in 1948 about the dangers of the Truman policies to the country and to the South. They were particularly exercised over proposals for Federal legislation affecting the Negro. Many individuals expressed their specific grievances against the New Deal and their general opposition to centralized government in a fervid concern for "states' rights." Some Dixiecratic spokesmen, notable among them Governor Thurmond, repeatedly emphasized that what they opposed was not the Negroes or the laborers but a philosophy of social action at variance with the South's most noted slogan.

Zealots, however, are tempted beyond their normal bounds of propriety and integrity. Among the leaders of the Dixiecrats were many zealots. They saw readily that their greatest chance for a sure, if limited, popular appeal lay in the South's ancient fears of race. They translated their whole opposition to the Democratic party's economic and social programs into warnings against civil violence and enforced social intermingling between the races. They brutally agitated racial prejudices, a disservice to the country hard to equal. Some did it blindly in their zeal. Others, the abler and more experienced, did it deliberately, with full awareness of the humbug they purveyed.

Callous misrepresentation was nowhere greater than in Alabama. Prior to that state's 1948 Democratic primary in which delegates to the national convention and candidates for presidential electors were chosen, a full-page advertisement appeared in the *Birmingham News* (May 2, 1948), reading, in part, as follows:

>   DEFEAT TRUMAN'S CIVIL RIGHTS PROGRAM
>   Safeguard Segregation!
>   What "Civil Rights" Means to you:
>
> President Truman has asked Congress to pass his "Civil Rights" Program—aimed at the destruction of the South's segregation laws. Here is what this program calls for:
> 1. Abolishment of segregation in all public schools—both as to children and teachers.
> 2. Abolishment of segregation in all colleges, including church schools, such as Judson, Howard, Birmingham-Southern and Huntingdon.
> 3. Abolishment of segregation in State-supported colleges such as Alabama, Auburn, Montevallo, and the Teacher Colleges.
> 4. Abolishment of segregation in restaurants, hotels, picture shows, street cars, buses, barber shops, beauty shops and swimming pools.
> 5. Compulsory employment of negroes in every business establishment (up to approximately 40% in Jefferson County) and the dis-

charge of present employes where necessary to achieve a ratio of employment in all businesses of 60% white employes and 40% negro employes.

6. Compulsory association of whites and negroes, working side by side in offices and factories, food, drug and department stores.

7. Compulsory upgrading of negro employes to positions of supervision over whites in the same racial ratio.

8. Enforcement of these requirements by fine and jail sentences.

Those who drafted the advertisement must have been bemused. The President's civil rights proposals were contained in a message to Congress that was printed in the *Congressional Record* for February 2, 1948. The only direct reference to segregation concerned interstate transportation: "The Supreme Court has recently declared unconstitutional state laws requiring segregation on public carriers in interstate travel. Company regulations must not be allowed to replace unconstitutional state laws. I urge the Congress to prohibit discrimination and segregation, in the use of interstate transportation facilities, by both public officers and the employees of private companies." There was nothing about the beauty shops, swimming pools, picture shows, church schools, and the rest.

In the message, the President repeated his request "that the Congress enact fair employment practice legislation prohibiting discrimination in employment based on race, color, religion or national origin. The legislation should create a Fair Employment Practice Commission with authority to prevent discrimination by employers and labor unions, trade and professional associations and Government agencies and employment bureaus." None of the bills that had been introduced to create an FEPC called for the extreme action, nor for its application to every business establishment, that was represented in the advertisement.

The inaccurate pictures of the President's recommendations no doubt had diverse origins. Some persons did not know the facts, confusing Truman's recommendations with the contents of *To Secure These Rights*, the report of the committee that he had appointed to inquire into the state of civil rights. The President had, in fact, declined to recommend many of the committee's

FISSURES IN THE DEMOCRACY

proposals to Congress.[7] Other persons no doubt exercised license to convey what they felt would be the ultimate consequences if parts of the program were adopted. As one person put it, "These so-called social reforms always come in broken doses. Their first draft is but an opening wedge.... Remember that the octopus was once an egg ... and kill him in his shell."[8] Whatever the explanations, the result was a series of inflammatory falsifications designed to stir the forebodings of the mildest southerners on the subject of race relations.

One of the prominent campaigners, former governor Frank Dixon of Alabama, persisted in the kind of statement contained in the advertisement, and added other wrinkles. For example, in the published text of his keynote speech to the Dixiecratic conference in Birmingham on July 17, 1948, he charged that according to Truman's recommendations to Congress "the poll tax is to be eliminated, all Negroes to be registered to vote without regard to intelligence or capacity."[9] It was simply untrue that the President had urged that Negroes (or whites, or bright blue Missouri mules for that matter) be permitted to vote without regard to intelligence or capacity. His expressed interest in non-discriminatory suffrage requirements wholly accorded with the Constitution, the spirit of American democracy, and much American practice. To hint that droves of illiterate Negroes of all ages would troop to the polls and swallow up southern government if poll taxes were abolished—they had already been abolished in four southern states—was arrant foolishness. That men of obvious ability and achievement should resort to this sort of thing gave ample evidence of the pathological character of race prejudice.

The Dixiecratic voters were moved by a kind of primitive nativistic anxiety. Those who responded most numerously lived in the areas that had formed the backbone of southern solidarity since the 1850's. Their counties had voted for secession in 1861. Their counties had remained most loyal during the Republican challenge of 1928.[10] They were, in short, the Democrats with the firmest traditional attachment to the Democratic party. That they should lead in the dissent of 1948 dramatized the changed relationship of the South to the Democratic party as nothing else could do. It could not be said of them, however, as it might be said of their leaders, that political interests made them logical recruits for the Republicans. Of some, naturally, this was true, but not all whites who live in close proximity to Negroes are prosperous planters. Many of them have little in common with the leaders of the Dixiecrats except a susceptibility to Negrophobia.[11] In the long run, no national party could adopt an active or passive racial policy acceptable to the diehards of the black belts. One day this fact would gain greater currency than it had in the 1940's. The chances seemed good that many black-belt citizens, smaller and poorer in their operations than their neighbors, would find the over-all programs of a liberal party, buttressed by traditional loyalty to it, preferable to the party of Taft and Dewey.

The formal States' Rights movement declined sharply in prestige after 1948 and in 1950 it was rocked by a series of defeats and rebuffs. In Arkansas, Governor Sid McMath soundly whipped former Governor Ben Laney, chairman of the States' Righters' national committee. Cried McMath: "This will kill the Dixiecrat movement... since Arkansas was definitely a target state..." In Alabama, careful leadership by loyalist Democrats including Senators John Sparkman and Lister Hill reduced the Dixiecrat majority on the Democratic state committee, won two years before, to a 29-43 minority. In South Carolina, Senator Olin Johnston, who had kept his record of technical loyalty clear, in a contest for re-election defeated former presidential candidate Thurmond. James F. Byrnes, at outs with the President, remained aloof from the Dixiecrats in winning the governorship. In Louisiana, Senator Russell Long swept the state, having long before clashed publicly with Leander Perez, the national director of the Dixiecrats. He carried all the parishes in the state except Perez's personal holding, Plaquemines Parish.[12] In Georgia, Herman Talmadge, elected governor in 1948 and 1950, deliberately avoided the label of Dixiecrat. Even in Florida and North Carolina, where candidates avowedly favorable to the Administration were beaten, the victors took care to deny association with the Dixiecrats.[13]

When the third annual south-wide Dixiecratic convention met in Jackson, Mississippi, in May, 1950, many states had only nominal representation and Georgia had none at all. Though the speakers "time and again made references classed as racial and religious bias," they made it clear the group had broadened its interests. It would oppose, now, not only Truman's civil rights proposals, but the Fair Deal and "a national trend to socialism." [14]

As 1952 approached, from several quarters came the suggestion of an alliance between Republicans and Dixiecrats.[15] The Republicans favored limited government, the Dixiecrats cried "states' rights," and it was clear from American history that when the states' rights cry is raised "oftentimes the real question is the question of whether control is to be exercised at all rather than whether the agency of control should be a state or the federal government." [16] Republican National Chairman Guy Gabrielson was reported in the South conferring with some top Dixiecratic leaders about a "trial marriage at the top" between their two groups.[17] Senator Karl Mundt, Republican of South Dakota, proposed that his party and "southern Democrats" get together in an involved strategy that would produce combined backing in 1952 for such a presidential candidate as Senator Byrd or Senator Russell.[18] Senator Russell himself, around whom southern opposition to Truman rallied in the Democratic convention of 1948, had said earlier that he would like to see "a very strong Republican party in the South." He predicted that "conservatives—those who believe in constitutional government"—will eventually get together in the nation.[19] Indications that many persons who supported conservative candidates in the Democratic primaries also voted Republican in the general elections made the proposal an understandable one.[20]

The suggestions found little favor, however, with Republicans concerned about marginal votes in close states,[21] and in the South dissatisfied Democratic politicians continued to hope they could work out their troubles without leaving the traditional party. This sentiment had existed all along among large sections of voters and politicians but a new emphasis was symbolized in the person of Governor James F. Byrnes of South Carolina. In contrast to the

Dixiecrats of 1948, Mr. Byrnes showed some balance as well as determination in his opposition to the Administration. He disappointed many admirers in the South and across the nation by locally attuned declarations on the problem of equal education for Negroes. Nevertheless, he had labored many years in the vineyard of liberal government and in the spring of 1951 he formally declined the leadership of the Dixiecrats when offered by former candidate Thurmond.[22]

Mr. Byrnes, and those of his cast of mind, had two sources of strength. One was regional. In 1946 Hodding Carter had called it "the connecting thread of intensifying sectional unity." In an article called "Chip on Our Shoulder Down South," which discussed how northern attacks on Bilbo had aided the Mississippi senator's re-election earlier that year, Mr. Carter spelled out a simple fact:

> Southern resentment is not all honest by any means. Much of it is artificially expressed in politically calculated outbursts; much arises from the economic fears of industrial and agricultural conservatives; some of it stems from pure emotionalism and a nostalgic clinging to old ways. But some of the resentment is reasonable. And today the connecting thread of intensifying sectional unity is joining these resentments together.[23]

Secondly, Mr. Byrnes would find some approval of his attacks on the national Administration and the socialization, centralization of government power, and wasteful spending for which he charged it was responsible.

He seemed to view his mission as that of reforming the Democratic party, the first step being the retirement of Harry Truman from the presidency. Mr. Byrnes' presence added dignity to the anti-Truman following, but in 1951 his pronouncements presaged the same ambiguities and uncertainties that marked the Dixiecratic strategy in 1948. Though hoping to win his point in the Democratic National Convention, Mr. Byrnes hinted that should he fail he might cast his eyes beyond the old party. He declared: "My earnest hope is that next year, in electing a president, the people will disregard labels of political parties."[24] He was reluctant, however, to commit himself beyond the meeting of the national conventions, and it was likely that the nature of the Republican nominee, as well as the Democratic nominee, would influence his course and that of others sharing his feelings.

In 1951, it appeared probable that, for the immediate future at least, those who dominate the politics of each southern state, with the exception of Mississippi and possibly South Carolina, will continue to work within the Democratic party. After varying degrees of dissension in the 1952 convention they will probably with varying degrees of enthusiasm support the Democratic nominee. Only the nomination of General Eisenhower by the Republicans would be likely to upset the conventional pattern, and only then because he would be viewed by many voters as essentially nonpolitical.

These events would mean that the socio-economic groups and often the personalities who had prevailed in southern politics for several decades would continue to do so. That, in turn, would indicate that the economic and social changes discussed in the previous chapter had not matured sufficiently for full, effective political expression. Specifically, it would reflect the strength of a middle-class outlook—indeed, of a middle class, if we may use that ambiguous term—moderate or uncertain in its political beliefs. It would reflect clearly the absence of effective political organization among lower-income industrial and agricultural groups. Enfranchising the Negroes, tenant farmers, and mill hands would produce no revolution in southern politics unless they saw a class interest and organized around it to modify the established way. As the manager of a plantation of several tens of thousands of acres commented, he didn't care if the Negroes voted: they'd vote as he told 'em. The southerners who have capped the economic and social matrix of southern society since the Civil War have, in instance after instance, opposed the organization of lower-income groups into unions of employees. And they have appealed unconscionably to race prejudice to divide groups that possessed a common interest in liberal government policies. The 1950 second senatorial primary in North Carolina saw the device successfully used to divide labor.[25]

Some southerners have predicted that progressive elements in southern politics will seek political expression outside the Democratic party.[26] Why speak in terms of conservative southerners breaking away to join the Republicans?, they ask. Why not speak of liberal southerners breaking away to help form a new liberal party? But party realignments that have been taking place within the two major parties since 1933 more and more make the Democratic party a labor-liberal party.[27] It seems unlikely that southern laborers and liberals can find a more effective channel for political expression. In a way, they enjoy an advantage over their local opponents. The latter in recent years have been forced by inheritance and circumstances to go along with a national party whose policies in many matters they disapprove.

The South stands at what Shannon calls "the strategic center of the future of the Democratic party."[28] Through its representatives in Congress and in party councils, especially when the party is out of power, southern Democrats can, perhaps, control their party's course—whether it will continue as a broad-based party of the Left, or whether by rejecting the liberal role it will encourage the emergence of a new party of the Left.[29] Whichever occurs, the old-time certainty of southern politics will be out of date.

12

A CHANGE IN THE RULES

THE GREAT GAME OF POLITICS, LIKE ANY GAME, IS PLAYED ACCORDING to rules. If the rules change, the game changes. Our discussion in the previous chapters has assumed that certain legal procedures and institutional practices that have governed American politics for more than a century will continue to do so. But what if they don't?

The constitutional feature that most determines the nature of the American party system is the method of electing the president. If that method, called the electoral college system, were abolished or severely modified, as is often proposed, the effect on southern politics would be immediate and radical. Under most of the proposals, party competition would intensify overnight and the nature of political appeals and party discipline would change. The question is not an idle one. In 1950 the Senate of the United States approved by a vote of 64 to 27 an amendment to the Constitution that would abolish the electoral college. Though not passed that year by the House, the proposal continued to enjoy strong support, much of it in the South.

Whence come the criticisms of the present system?[1] Most of them are ancient, and arise from the practice whereby all the electoral votes of a state are customarily cast for the presidential nominee who receives a plurality of popular votes in the state.

The practice creates the possibility that a candidate receiving the highest number of popular votes may not receive the highest number of electoral votes—as indeed was the case in 1824, 1876, and 1888. Critics note that candidates receive no benefit from votes cast for them in states where they do not obtain a plurality. Such votes are "thrown away," a feature particularly disadvantageous to minor parties. Other persons view unhappily the allotment to states of electoral votes equal in number to their representation in Congress. Small states enjoy equal representation in the Senate with large states, hence receive a share of electoral votes greater than their proportion of the population. These critics look with even less favor on the method of selecting a president and a vice president when no candidate receives a majority of the electoral votes. Under the Twelfth Amendment, the election of president is thrown into the House of Representatives and that of vice president into the Senate. In the balloting, each state, regardless of size, is given one vote. The possibility that this procedure might produce a president and vice president of different parties has been pointed out. Still other critics have feared an occasion when electors would forsake custom and vote in the electoral college contrary to the popular preference of their states.

Since the advent of the New Deal, greatest criticism has stemmed from another feature of the system. A premium is placed on the so-called independent vote in states where the parties battle on relatively even terms. Republicans and Democrats alike have tailored their appeals and chosen their candidates to fit the marginal groups that determine victory or defeat in these close states. Some southern Democrats specifically charge that the traditional attitudes of their party, long cherished in the South, have been abandoned for alien measures designed to win the votes of Negroes and organized laborers in doubtful states. These southerners have looked at their section's record of unparalleled party loyalty and become embittered to realize that this very faithfulness accounts for the alleged lack of consideration they receive in party councils.

Various proposals have been advanced to meet the objections. The most drastic change seriously proposed would have the president elected directly by nation-wide popular vote. Senator Langer of North Dakota has led such a move.[2] Others have proposed that presidential electors be selected by districts rather than by the states-at-large, a practice found in some states before the time of Andrew Jackson.[3] Alterations in special aspects of the procedure have been recommended: for example, to throw contests in which no candidate receives a majority of electoral votes into a joint session of Congress in which members would vote individually, rather than by state delegations, to elect both a president and vice president.[4]

The proposal attracting greatest support is called the Lodge-Gossett Amendment, after Senator Henry Cabot Lodge of Massachusetts and Representative Ed Gossett of Texas. A Gallup poll in August, 1948, found 58 per cent of the general population favoring the change they proposed, while 15 per cent were opposed.[5] When Senator Lodge introduced a resolution incorporating the amendment in 1949 he was joined by ten co-sponsors, five of whom came from the South.[6] When the measure, as amended, was approved by two-thirds of the Senate in 1950, almost all of the southerners favored it. When the House Rules Committee temporarily buried the measure later that year, it was against the votes of the southern members. When the House itself defeated the measure, sixty southern Democrats favored it and thirteen opposed it.[7] Leaders of both parties in Texas endorsed the proposals.[8] Mississippi Democrats as far apart politically as Governor Fielding Wright and editor Hodding Carter approved.[9] Senator Olin Johnston of South Carolina announced his support,[10] as did many newspapers inside and outside the South.

Senator Lodge's resolution, as finally approved by the Senate, called for a constitutional amendment that would make four changes: (a) abolish the electoral college; (b) allot a state's electoral votes (the apportionment of electoral votes among the states not to be changed) among the candidates for president, or vice president, in proportion to the popular votes each received within the state; (c) require that 40 per cent of the electoral votes be necessary for election, rather than a majority as in existing law; and, (d) require, if no candidate received the required amount, that the selection be made by the Senate and House in joint session, from the two persons with the highest numbers of electoral votes, with a majority of the combined membership necessary for a choice.[11]

The advocates of the amendment claim it will remedy the defects of the present system that can be attacked with any chance of success.[12] Opposition has arisen from several sources and on several grounds. As a matter of fact, national leaders of both parties were cool to the proposals at first.[13] President Truman announced his opposition just before his inauguration in 1949, but apparently later changed his mind.[14] The new system, it is claimed, would diminish the political authority of the president by making possible his election without a majority of the electoral votes. Furthermore, critics have viewed with distrust the recognition given to minor candidates in the electoral votes. They fear that splinter parties would be encouraged, leading to demands for proportional representation in Congress. Adoption of proportional representation in state legislatures and Congress would break down the two-party system.[15] Senator Taft believed the changes would weaken the Republican presidential prospects. He charged that Democrats would continue to win most of the electoral votes in the South whereas Republicans would lose large chunks of electoral support in other states—states where the GOP in good years can build national victory by winning all the electoral votes despite the presence of large numbers of Democrats. For example, the GOP might carry Ohio and yet win only thirteen electoral votes while the Democrats hauled in twelve, a net GOP gain of one. At the same time, in South Carolina the Democrats would be assured of virtually all that state's electoral votes, a net GOP loss of eight.[16] The Senator received scholarly support for his position from Ruth C. Silva. After a detailed analysis, Dr. Silva concluded:

More than the fate of the Republican Party is involved. The operation of a democratic party system, in contrast to a Democratic Party system, depends on the existence of an opposition which has a reasonable chance of winning control of the executive. To make it virtually impossible for the Republicans to win the Presidency ... is to render the Republican Party ineffective as a counterpoise.[17]

The Senate vote on the resolution suggested that the Democrats agreed with the Taft-Silva analysis. They voted 46 to 4 in the affirmative. The Republicans, however, divided on the matter, 23 to 18 against it. The problem in the analysis lay in the difficulty of predicting the kinds of campaigns and candidates that would appear if the amendment went into effect. The fact that they would change seemed self-evident; and, incidentally, rendered somewhat futile the practice of computing what the electoral votes of candidates in previous elections might have been had the measure been in effect. It is doubtful that the popular votes would have been the same. In large part, the Republican disagreement over the matter involved what the South would do under the proposed arrangement. Senator Lodge felt that stiff party competition would develop and the Republicans would pick up enough electoral votes to offset their losses outside the South. Others were dubious about the Republican future in the South and indicated that southern Democrats would use all their historic weapons to preserve their monopoly of the electoral votes. What would probably happen?

The national leadership of both parties would look to their knitting in the South as never since Reconstruction. Republicans would be forced to do so by their losses outside the South. Moreover, any vote received would now count. A driving competition in presidential politics would develop. No longer could national party authorities afford to sustain the kind of Republican leadership that has prevailed in most of the South; no longer could they expect to draw off campaign funds in a steady stream without in turn helping out in southern races. To secure the most effective support for presidential campaigns, they would of necessity insist on vigorous state and local organizations, would incite them to make vigorous campaigns for state and local offices. They would select campaign issues and appeals with an eye to the southern constituency. Similarly, party consciousness among the Democrats would intensify. No longer could they automatically garner all the electoral votes by smothering the opposition in a weakly contested election. Democratic leaders would work for a turnout of voters that would create the largest Democratic percentages.

These developments would contribute to a clarification of party attitudes and to an increase in party discipline that seemed likely to strengthen the Republican party in the South.

In at least two ways the existing electoral college encourages incoherent party programs. Both major parties, but especially the Democrats, enjoy traditional superiority in certain parts of the country. Each party therefore has a sectional base, or bases, and the interests and attitudes of those sections are represented by their politicians in party councils, especially in the national conventions and the Congressional caucuses. At the same time, the real presidential campaigns are fought out in the other parts of the country, in the states where neither party is securely based, and precisely for that reason. The managers of the presidential campaigns direct their appeals to the uncertain voters (and to the lethargic among their own followers) in the uncertain states and tend to ignore the areas where they will win or lose regardless of what they do. The political interests and attitudes of the sure and unsure areas need not be the same and, understandably, are often quite different. As a result, each party tends to contain a potpourri of policies and attitudes, a condition not without advantages in a country as large and diverse as the United States.

The electoral college encourages confusion in party policies in another way, closely related to the first. A party wants to win a plurality of the votes in as many states as possible.[18] States fall by characteristics and interests into sections. Generally, it has been easier to win the necessary pluralities by appealing to the sectional interests of the voters, the interests that all the voters in the states of the section are likely to feel in common, than by appealing only to what may be called the class interests of the voters within each of the states. The party's state managers favor this sort of local chauvinism as the handiest way to fight their local wars. Class lines are not sufficiently clear, and classes are not sufficiently large, for sharpened appeals to economic and social interests alone to attract pluralities. In consequence, both sectional and class appeals are made, sometimes coinciding, often contradicting each other, and always producing an incredible complexity of planks, platforms, and pledges.

Abolition of the electoral college would force the parties to campaign in every state, thereby eliminating the first of these sources of confusion in party attitudes. The change would also confer a premium for winning as many votes as possible in each state and section, rather than merely for winning a plurality, and would thereby mitigate the clash between sectional and class appeals. Sectional appeals would still be stimulated, of course, for there are sectional interests. And it must be remembered that the number of electoral votes a state enjoys would remain unchanged, regardless of how many people voted. But a party's sectional appeals would now have to be designed not to alienate important groups of voters in states that now can be ignored because of the foregone preference of a plurality of voters in them. As commented earlier, the relatively simple, historic, American sectionalism resting on an agricultural economy is giving way to the growing urban nature of the nation. The opportunity for a nonsectional emphasis in politics thus increases.[19]

In still another way the Lodge-Gossett amendment would contribute to the clarification of party doctrines. The amendment would seem to encourage greater party discipline. The interest of presidential politicians in state and Congressional races would heighten, for they would have a more direct effect on the winning of electoral votes than now, especially in the South. In two-party states under the existing system tickets for state and local offices often are chosen with an eye to their effect on the presidential race. Not so in the South. If a Congressional candidate in the South were forced to campaign with the outcome of the presidential contest in his district as a major consideration, his independence would be curtailed and the interest of the party's national officials in his conduct would be increased. They would be induced more than at present to use the disciplinary weapons at their command—such things as campaign aid, official endorsement, committee assignments, and that grand catch-all of jobs and influence called patronage. Outside the South the party's national leaders would become less dependent on the state "bosses" who now often offer the most expeditious approach to the vital margin of voters who determine total victory or total defeat. The margin would cease to be vital and would become merely a fraction of the state's electoral votes. While state control over the nominating process would continue to restrict the disciplinary channels open to national party leaders, and would continue to guarantee considerable independence to Congressional and other candidates, the slack-rein relationship between the top leadership of the party and its fighting corps would be reduced. In turn, these factors would conduce toward greater homogeneity of party policies and programs.

It should be noted that various proposals to reform the American party system by increasing party discipline and responsibility have been made by the Committee on Political Parties of the American Political Science Association. In so far as they were successful, they would affect the South much as we have been discussing. The committee deemed the development of party competition in the South essential to the development of a responsible national party system.[20]

Several modifications in American politics, then, would appear to result from adoption of the Lodge-Gossett proposal: extension of the party battle to all states, intensification of presidential interest in the elections to other offices, sharpening of party programs, and increase in party discipline. These changes, though they can not be fully predicted in degree and detail, would profoundly alter southern politics. With clearer lines of demarcation between the policies of the parties—though they need not and would not be rigid or neat—and with every popular vote reflecting itself in the electoral vote, many present Democrats who are variously dissatisfied about their party would lose their current apathy. A more disciplined party system would reduce cross-party dealings in and out of Congress. Southern Democrats presently content with the one-party arrangement because "they get what they want" via the informal alliances of Democrats with Republicans and via the frustrations of the Democratic party, would move over to the Republicans to fight in the open. The number of Republican voters would mount abruptly. The number of Democratic voters might also increase. But if the basic changes in the nature of the South that we have discussed are going on, the destruction of the Democratic party's ability to monopolize a state's voice in presidential politics would produce net Republican increases. We hear all the time of southern Democrats who would like to cast an effective Republican vote for president. We do not hear of southern Republicans who nurse a frustrated desire to vote Democratic.

Contrary to the views of some,[21] one of the most important effects of the new arrangement would be a likely rise in voter participation. Heated competition between organized parties is one of the causes of high voter participation all over the world.[22] One of the reasons for the low level of southern voting in the primaries and general elections is the absence of intensive, continuing, organized party competition.[23] To bring into the southern electorate large numbers of persons of low income whose votes were sought by organized parties would further sharpen economic and social issues in state and national policy and contribute to the development of a divisive politics of economics. One may wonder whether formal suffrage restrictions would be brought into play. Suffrage requirements purely discriminatory against persons of color, no. Requirements to discourage voting in general, perhaps. But it is hard to see how such requirements would work to the advantage of Democrats now in power. They would probably find a greater source of recruits among the politically unalert, those persons of low educational and economic status most affected by burdensome suffrage requirements, than the Republicans.

A greater source of Republican frustration would be the partisan administration of suffrage requirements and elections. The election machinery is in the hands of the Democrats. But that problem confronts parties in all two-party areas, and if it cannot be met there is no hope for democracy anyway. Suffrage restrictions or their discriminatory administration would directly concern party members elsewhere in the nation and conceivably could lead to an interest by the Federal government in state conduct of elections.

More probably, the Federal government might seek to establish rules uniform for all states governing admission of candidates to a place on the ballot. After all, each candidate by law would be entitled to his share of a state's electoral votes. These last thoughts, incidentally, may give pause to some in their consideration of the amendment.

The way would be open, too, under the Lodge-Gossett proposal, for a special group with an overriding concern—that no major party would recognize—to express itself election after election with a degree of effectiveness. Such a group would not, however, when formally dissociated from the major parties, achieve Congressional, Federal, or state office, elective or appointive, to sustain a continuing organization. The inducement to such groups, like the Dixiecrats in the South, to work for proportional representation in the Congress and the state legislatures constitutes the chief danger of the whole Lodge-Gossett proposal.

It is probable, however, so far as the Dixiecrats are concerned, that the change in the electoral system would remove much of the political frustration that spurs the movement. The leading Dixiecrats could make their influence and resources as well as their votes felt by wholeheartedly turning Republican. Furthermore, the campaign strategy of both major parties might well undergo modifications that would undercut the campaign oratory, the appeal to worries about race, of the Dixiecrats. It would seem that the opportunities of the Republican party to recruit among those Democrats who were disgruntled over economic and social policies would be greatly enhanced, and party competition correspondingly strengthened.

Whatever its other consequences for the national party system, the revision of the method of electing the president along the lines of the Lodge-Gossett amendment would constitute a fast and sure path to increased party competition in the South.

the new negro politics

13
THE NAACP

Up to this point, we have focused our attention on white southerners as a potential source of voters for a revitalized Republican party. Our speculations on the future of southern politics have ignored Negroes as a politically articulate group except in so far as the abolition of the white primary weakened the understructure of the one-party system. Yet Negroes make up one-fourth of the southern population, and Negro political activity jumped by leaps and bounds in the 1940's. By tradition, in and out of the South, Negroes had looked to the Republican party as their champion. Might they offer a grand new source of Republican recruits? The answer, for the moment, is negative, but no one can look into the future of the South without a keen curiosity about Negro politics, new style.

Even the most recalcitrant of Dixiecrats concede that southern Negroes will take an increasing part in politics. The estimated number qualified to vote in the eleven southern states rose from 151,000 in 1940 to 595,000 in 1947 and to 900,000 in 1950.[1] In a section where Negroes had been largely confined to the Republican party, approximately 290,000 of them voted in the Democratic primaries of 1946,[2] and more did so in 1948 and 1950. Those voting in 1946 comprised 6 per cent of the primary voters. They were only one-sixteenth of the potential Negro electorate, and the legal barriers to the ballot that had most restrained them in the past were being swept away.

The influx of Negroes into the electorate—sudden in some states, gradual in others—would inevitably affect the candidates and the issues of state campaigns. Whether the new voters in the long run would alter party relationships within individual states, or in the region as a whole, is quite another question. The prophets might learn that Negroes would affect the balance of southern party power only if certain unlikely developments take place. We shall examine in detail the impact of these new voters on the relative strength of the parties. To understand their significance, however, we must know the nature of the new Negro politics—its form, its motivation, its leadership. Is it a return to the old days of "black Republicanism" when "Goose Neck Bill" McDonald, "Tieless Joe" Tolbert, and Benjamin Jefferson Davis held sway? Or are Negroes developing an organized politics along entirely different lines? In the 1940's more Negroes were qualified by education and experience to exercise effectively the rights of full citizenship, individually and in group action, than ever before. In nation-wide organizations they possessed a national civic consciousness militantly concerned about their right to political action and the benefits that could flow therefrom. Many changes had taken place among Negroes, and among whites as well, since Reconstruction, since the nineties, since the twenties. It seemed axiomatic that changes in the political potential of Negroes had also taken place.

Negro political activities in the South fall into three phases convenient for our story. Establishing the right to vote and encouraging its use are essentially impartial matters of good citizenship. This first phase, noted in the present chapter, has proceeded under the leadership of the National Association for the Advancement of Colored People. The next chapter treats the second phase: the kinds of associations Negroes have organized for partisan political action, their relationship to the NAACP, and their size and vitality. In several states they bear the name Progressive Voters' League. The third phase concerns the political campaigns the leagues conduct and the tactics they employ.

In the South, the National Association for the Advancement of Colored People has played a greater role in modern Negro politics than any other organization. The NAACP has been the driving force behind the awakening Negro political consciousness. It has led in most of the Negro's legal battles for equal rights, the most important among them, the right to vote in party primaries. For this right to mean anything, however, Negroes must meet the suffrage requirements, intricate and baffling in many states, and go to the polls and vote. Like the Junior Chamber of Commerce or the Civitans, the NAACP sponsors better-citizenship drives to increase citizen-participation in government through exercise of the ballot. A Negro's decision on *how* he should vote is inevitably bound up with the struggle he has gone through to get the right to vote. To "educate" him to vote his obvious interests is the logical step after getting him qualified and to the polls. The NAACP, as an organization, remains officially nonpartisan, but it exerts profound influence on when Negroes vote, why they vote, and also on how they vote.

Its influence varies from place to place. It is likely to be less in the cities of North Carolina, Tennessee, and Virginia, where Negroes have been voting for many years, than in Georgia, Florida, and Alabama, where the privilege is newly acquired. It constitutes, nevertheless, a force of regional and national importance that must be understood if Negro politics is to be understood.

The organization was founded in 1909 by a group of whites and Negroes interested in securing for colored people justice in the courts and equality of social, economic, and political opportunity.[3] With headquarters in New York, it has accepted memberships and has sought its aims in all parts of the country. Its local units are called "branches," each containing fifty or more members. In most states these branches are organized into a state "conference." By 1940, NAACP membership totalled 200,000 organized in 550 branches. The war intensified its activities all over the country; by 1948 membership had risen to 500,000 organized in 1,139 active branches and in the South to 206,000 in 601 branches. Two years later, however, membership in the nation was down to 250,000 and 935 branches, and in the South to 99,065 members organized in 537 branches. The decline was attributed by one official of the organization to an increase in dues from one to two dollars per year and to intimidating activity. All but 5 to 10 per cent of the membership is Negro.[4]

The NAACP enjoys great prestige among Negroes who favor an aggressive demand for equal rights. Among these Negroes are most articulate young people and many of the older generation. It has done most of its fighting in the courts and has remained an uncompromising advocate of "full citizenship" for the Negro. The NAACP's approach veers sharply from the recommendations of Booker T. Washington, famed Negro gradualist. Dr. Washington's advice is considered outdated by many modern members of his race. He counselled that Negroes eschew political demands and concentrate on vocational education and economic productiveness.

The general secretary and moving spirit of the NAACP since 1931 has been Walter White, a Negro and a native of Atlanta.[5] The association's funds come primarily from membership fees and from contributions by private citizens.

The NAACP has had four principal concerns in the South in recent years. It has pressed for the admission of Negroes to state institutions of higher learning on a basis of equality with whites. It has sought the equalization of pay schedules for white and Negro school teachers. It has continued its efforts to reduce mob violence and to obtain fair treatment for Negroes in the courts. And it has persisted in its demands for the free exercise of the ballot by Negroes in primaries and general elections. The NAACP has pursued its ends by stimulating local leadership and by aiding with legal counsel in the recurring court battles.

In 1946 the Board of Directors of the association adopted a political action program which included the following resolutions:

(1) That the Association go on record as not endorsing any political party or any individual because of party connections or affiliation.

(2) That the policy of the NAACP shall be that branches are urged to examine proposals, purely non-partisan in character as listed below, affecting local or state public issues and which require electorate approval; to take a position for or against such proposals within the Constitutional limits of the Association, unless good cause be presented why a position not be taken; and give active support to a position taken thereon.
To include such issues as:
   (a) Proposals arising locally or statewide by and through initiative and referendum.
   (b) Bond issues.
   (c) Charter and Constitutional Amendments. Where proposal is state-wide, state conferences of branches, where they exist, are urged to determine and announce a position to be binding on all branches. Otherwise, some workable intra-state method should be devised for unified coordinated action after consultation with the National Office.
(3) That the National Board call a meeting of all representative Negro organizations to consider the question of focusing attention on issues that will come up for decision in the election of candidates in the fall and the importance of Negroes participating actively by registering and voting. Further recommended that advertisements and other material be carried in the press.
(4) That the Board call upon every branch to conduct a registration and voting drive.
(5) That an entire issue of the Bulletin be devoted to registration and voting.
(6) That the Board consider the use of staff assistants and preparation of material that would be of assistance to the local branches in the conducting of registration and turning-out-the-vote drives.[6]

A note was added that a concentrated drive was planned to increase registration in the areas where Negroes had only recently been given the right to vote.

Many southern branches before and after the adoption of these resolutions undertook to increase the number of Negroes voting.

They waged local fights to hustle officials into admitting Negroes to the invalidated white primaries. In Florida, in 1947, for instance, efforts made by the St. Petersburg, Tampa, and Brevard County branches of the NAACP broke down the bars to the municipal primaries.[7] In many places, such as Baton Rouge and New Orleans, "registration schools" were held at which registration procedures were explained and instructions were given in subjects on which applicants might be questioned. Such a program was conducted in Birmingham during 1945-46. There, the NAACP branch held classes and sent "quotas" of applicants before the Board of Registration. Representatives went with the applicants to assist them and to record the disposition of the cases. In Richmond, the *Times-Dispatch* reported on May 3, 1947, that Negroes were qualifying to vote in larger numbers than whites and headed the story: "Drive by NAACP Exhibits Results."

A Negro man wearing a NAACP badge on his coat lapel was supervising the poll tax payments and registrations of many Negroes yesterday. He patrolled the first floor of the City Hall and directed Negroes to the line outside Mr. Hulce's office. As soon as each Negro paid his poll tax, he told him: "Now go to the fourth floor, Room 414; that's where you register." Meanwhile a truck equipped with loud speakers continued to make the rounds of old Jackson Ward and other Negro residential areas urging them to pay their poll taxes and to register.

These efforts were logically extended to getting out the vote on election day. In Mobile, for illustration, the NAACP branch sent out post cards before one of the primaries to "just about every qualified Negro voter" urging him to vote. The cards also reminded the recipients of the Alabama law against selling and buying votes. All over the South, NAACP officials exhort their fellow Negroes through the Negro press to turn out and vote. A thin line separates actions of this kind, getting a person to vote, and the suggestion that he vote a certain way. Throughout, the NAACP has proclaimed its nonpartisan status. Its Executive Secretary, in the March 1948 *NAACP Bulletin,* took a column to remind NAACP officers and members of the rule against action that could be interpreted as support of a political party. "The NAACP has its particular job which must be done and neither its time nor energies should be diverted from its basic program."

The determination to avoid alliance with a political party naturally has greater significance among Negroes outside the South than within it,[8] where party preference is not at issue in the primaries. The interests of Negroes *per se* have sometimes lain so obviously on one side in the primary fights that a policy of neutrality has in effect been impossible. To meet the need for political action without compromising its traditional position, the NAACP encouraged the development of Negro voters' leagues in all the southern states. The types of organizations created and the ways in which they developed have differed from state to state, but in all the states they have given Negro voters a channel of organized political expression independent of the political parties.

14

THE PROGRESSIVE VOTERS' LEAGUES

THE MODERN MOLD OF SOUTHERN NEGRO POLITICS WAS CAST BEtween 1944 and 1948. In the former year, the United States Supreme Court started it all by opening Democratic primaries to Negroes, and in the latter year the Court blocked attempts to circumvent the earlier decision. The following presentation rests on developments during those years.

The close connection between the NAACP and what have been called its "political arms" is illustrated by the way the Progressive Voters' League of Florida was created. On May 24, 1947, the president and executive secretary of the league addressed a letter to their fellow citizens telling the story:

In April, 1944, the United States Supreme Court rendered its famous decision in the Texas Primary Case, thus establishing the principle that Negro citizens have a right to vote in all elections in the South. It then became apparent that golden political opportunities were within our grasp and that a state organization was needed to help arouse Florida Negro citizens to a fuller realization of this fact. Therefore, a state-wide meeting was called in Lake Wales in August, 1944, under the auspices of the Florida State Conference, NAACP, and the Progressive Voters' League of Florida was organized. In 1946 the Progressive Voters' League was chartered under the laws of Florida.

PROGRESSIVE VOTERS' LEAGUES

On July 26 of the next year, following the Democratic primaries, the secretary further reminded his readers:

> The Voters' League stands for a full program of civil rights for Negro citizens. In fact, the Progressive Voters' League was organized by the Florida State Conference, NAACP, and through political action the League is fighting for those same fundamental objectives that have been advocated by the NAACP for nearly 40 years.

The league's executive secretary, a native of Florida named Harry T. Moore, served also as paid secretary and organizer for the NAACP state conference.*

In American experience generally, political clubs making formal demands on the time and funds of their adherents attract limited membership. Frequently the active members of these clubs work formally and informally through existing groups having related interests. So it proved with the new political leagues. Three years after the formation of the Florida league, its president (a school teacher) reported the existence of twenty-two city chapters, county organizations in nine of the state's sixty-seven counties, and "district committees" in four of the six Congressional districts. Total membership was unknown, though the league considered as members all Negroes registered to vote in counties where there were chapters. Dues were one dollar per year, half to the state organization and half to the local chapter, but collections were few. In several instances, new organizations had been formed, but "a goodly number" of the local units were Negro civic clubs that had voted to affiliate with the state league. The state president of the NAACP (a groceryman) reported that in one area where no voters' league had been formed persons who were members and officials of the local NAACP branch occasionally investigated candidates and published their findings, equivalent to recommendations. At the time, the NAACP had about seventy active branches in the state with over ten thousand paid-up members.

---

* Mr. Moore was one of several Negro leaders particularly helpful to the author in supplying information for these chapters. He was murdered the night of December 25, 1951, by an explosion beneath his home near Mims, Florida.

The leaders, it is fair to suppose, used the branches informally as channels of communication when the voters' leagues would not serve.

Overlapping organizations and interlocking directorates characterize American society, and this is especially true of southern Negro communities. Negroes sufficiently secure financially to lead in the so-called "protest" activities, and in political action, and who are inclined to do so, are few. The same individuals frequently appear in all organizations concerned with the Negro's status.[1] Something of an oligarchic leadership prevails, producing intimate communication among Negro political leaders, sometimes resulting in harmonious and integrated activities, sometimes not. In areas where the right to vote has been most hotly contested, the concentration of leadership is greatest. Educators, newspapermen, businessmen, and lawyers, forming a sort of elite corps, have most often taken the lead in the new Negro politics. In this connection, one white Mississippi editor, friendly to the aspirations of Negroes, expressed a common concern of thoughtful southerners. Does a sufficiently numerous, competent, and mature Negro leadership exist to cope with the problems that face their group? Perhaps yes, perhaps no, but one thing seems plain. Leadership ability can only be developed through leadership opportunity and leadership responsibility. The surest way to broaden Negro political capacities is to impose the full responsibilities of citizenship.

In Alabama, in contrast to Florida, no state-wide political league developed during the years immediately after the 1944 Court decision. Local NAACP leaders, however, stimulated the growth of political organizations in several cities. Active groups appeared in Birmingham, Montgomery, Mobile, and a number of smaller cities. In Birmingham the Progressive Democratic Council devoted itself exclusively to political affairs. In Anniston, political cohesiveness was achieved through several organizations, but primarily through the Model City Improvement League, a civic group dominated by businessmen. A leader of the Anniston group (the owner of a tailor shop) noted that the NAACP offered the only formal state-wide channel for coördinating the activities of the various political clubs.

NAACP national officials need not appear on the scene to have influence in the formation and activation of local political groups. Through its *Bulletin* and its monthly magazine, *Crisis*, the NAACP has done much to set the tone of Negro political thinking throughout the country. In Mississippi, in fact, Negro leaders asserted that they found such hostility among "our white friends" to the NAACP that they refrained from driving vigorously to expand its membership. They recalled with some amusement an incident of a few years before. The Jackson branch announced a membership drive. The choleric editor of a white daily took the news to mean a branch was to be formed. In a bitter editorial he denounced the NAACP and warned of the dire consequences should it be allowed to come to Jackson. The branch was then eighteen years old.

In a few places in Mississippi a political club preceded an NAACP branch. By 1947 there were a dozen branches as compared with a slightly larger number of local political clubs affiliated with the state Progressive Voters' League, founded in 1946. In one delta town a surprisingly active political league was found. Its leader told with some satisfaction of the tolerance of local whites, but said he had consistently opposed the formation of an NAACP branch. Visitors from Jackson and New York had tried to get one going but he opposed it. "We cannot handle it yet." The attitude of Mississippi whites (arising from the large proportion of Negroes in the population) has retarded the development of voters' leagues as well as of the NAACP. In 1947 the leagues were confined to the larger towns. The state president (an insurance agent) estimated state membership at around 4,000 but conceded the figure might be wide of the mark. Dues were a dollar a year but collections were irregular. Quite understandably in the setting, the president emphasized that local political clubs operated independently of other Negro organizations.

The most highly organized of all the political leagues developed in Georgia. The Georgia Association of Citizens' Democratic

Clubs arose during 1944-46 while the NAACP was conducting a registration drive. The association grew rapidly, largely on the impetus of the 1946 gubernatorial campaign. In that year Negroes voted in numbers in the Democratic primaries for the first time—about 90,000 strong. They were incited by the campaign of Eugene Talmadge who made their participation the principal issue of the campaign. Approximately 75 groups scattered in towns and counties over the state were affiliated in the association, with total membership somewhere between 15,000 and 20,000. A Negro lawyer of Atlanta, A. T. Walden,[2] served as the state president. Mr. Walden served also as state secretary of the NAACP and chairman of the board of directors of the Atlanta Urban League. He ran the association with the aid of an executive committee composed of the state officers and a representative from each Congressional district. As with the political leagues in all the states, the Georgia Association's plan of organization called for an annual convention and for the selection of the governing committees by popular means.

Negro political organization in South Carolina took the form of an independent political party. Until 1948, Negroes were barred from South Carolina Democratic primaries, so the editor of a Columbia newspaper, the *Lighthouse and Informer,* took the initiative in forming the "Progressive Democratic party." To its first state convention, held in May of 1944, went 172 delegates from 39 of the state's 46 counties. The convention adopted party rules closely akin to those of the state's Democratic party, even making provisions to hold primaries. Rule No. 1 read:

This organization shall operate as the Progressive DEMOCRATIC Party of South Carolina, subject to the rules of the National Democratic Party, and the rules herein set forth. The adjective "Progressive" shall distinguish it from all other "Democratic" organizations that exist, and may exist within the state.

There were local units of the party in approximately three-fourths of the counties and there were "district organizations" in each of the Congressional districts, though the state chairman could not estimate the total membership. The local units, he declared, enjoyed considerable independence of state headquarters.

Something of the functioning of the party can be learned from the "STATE TREASURER'S REPORT OF FUNDS HANDLED BY THE PROGRESSIVE DEMOCRATIC PARTY FROM MAY 24, 1944 THROUGH MAY 8, 1946." Income of $5,781.50 was shown as follows:

Counties, from 30 of the state's 46 and miscellaneous	$5,166.89
Pre-organization gifts	77.11
At first convention	260.00
Held for paid worker	40.00
Counties paid in 1946, from 11 of the state's 46	237.50

Expenses of $5,585.55 were shown, as follows:

Phone and telegrams	$ 80.89
Office Equipment	77.75
Supplies, postage	459.61
Printing (the party distributed bulletins such as "How to Register in South Carolina" and "Register to Vote—and—Vote")	246.10
Travels	567.41
Advertisements	609.76
Radio Programs	437.38
Clerks' salaries	634.07
1944 delegates (all) to national Democratic convention (not seated)	2,250.00
1944 attorneys' fees	125.00
Rents	65.58
Miscellaneous	32.00

The party focused its attention on gaining admittance to the Democratic primaries, and when that aim was achieved in 1948 about 35,000 Negroes voted. The leadership held no plans for the continuance of a separate "party." In fact, both before and after Negroes were admitted to the primaries, the Progressive Democratic party behaved almost identically with the voters' leagues in other states. As might be expected, the Columbia editor who headed the party had taken a leading part in drives to expand the membership and activities of the NAACP. He was a close associate of the state president and of the state secretary of the NAACP, and, in actuality, the trio led South Carolina's Negro politics.

These developments in Florida, Alabama, Mississippi, Georgia, and South Carolina—making up most of the Deep South—show similarity because they occurred in states where Negroes had least access to the ballot prior to 1944. In two rim states, Arkansas and Texas, and in the Upper South, the story is somewhat different.

Generally, the NAACP played a less important role. In Arkansas, for instance, the Arkansas Negro Democratic Association was first formed in 1928 by a Negro physician of Little Rock, Dr. J. M. Robinson. That year the organization supported a native son, Senator Joseph T. Robinson, for the vice presidency, a fact not unconnected with its formation. Subsequently it became relatively inactive, when Democrats declined to admit Negroes to the primaries. In the spring of 1947, in the spirit of the times, Dr. Robinson launched a membership drive that quickly extended his organization to seventeen counties and a membership of about 2,500. In a printed letter dated May, 1947 he intimated he had supplemented the court decisions by an agreement with Democratic officials: "An official receipt will be sent to you identifying your affiliation in the event of a challenge at the polls." Organizers were given incentives. A minimum of twenty-five members was required to form a club. Organizers were permitted to retain half of the dues, one dollar per person, collected before a club was organized. After it was formed, the club received half the membership fees and half went to state headquarters. Dr. Robinson claimed that his groups operated independently of other Negro organizations, but admitted the usual overlapping of memberships and occasional duplication of programs.

Younger Arkansas Negroes criticized the doctor and the leaders of his clubs as old, complacent, and ineffective. They charged that the association was a one-man show, and with apparent cause, for the doctor nodded assent to the assertion. In these days an important rival for the political leadership of Arkansas arose in Harold Flowers, a Pine Bluff lawyer and sometime president of the state NAACP conference. In 1947 the NAACP had about forty branches with six to seven thousand members and conducted a "political education" program to increase the number of Negro voters. It proved a good deal more active than the old association. Feelings ran deep, between and within the two groups, presaging a bitter wrangle to come among the state's Negro politicians.

In Texas, Negroes also organized themselves for political action earlier than in the Deep South. For a number of years prior to 1944 they participated in municipal elections in cities like Dallas, Fort Worth, San Antonio, Galveston, Port Arthur, and Houston, and in some of these cities organizations of Negro voters pre-date the 1944 Court decision. The Bellingers in San Antonio controlled the best known organization. First the father and later the son allied a large portion of the Negro vote with a white machine. The Bellingers were reportedly more concerned with their own business interests, however, including gambling, than the rights of Negroes as a group. Two Texas organizations, more familiar in type, claimed membership in the years after 1944—the Progressive Voters' League, of some forty chapters, and the Texas Club of Democratic Voters, with chapters in several cities. The NAACP apparently did not play the leading role in their formation.[3]

Tennessee, North Carolina, and Virginia offer signs of Negro politics in transition. At the time the white primary was abolished elsewhere, Negroes had been voting in the Democratic primaries and general elections in parts of Tennessee and North Carolina for several decades. They had participated in Virginia's general elections for an equally long time and had been admitted to the Democratic primaries since 1930. Ralph Bunche estimated Negro voting in general elections prior to 1940 at about fifty thousand both in Tennessee and North Carolina and at about twenty thousand in Virginia.[4] Luther P. Jackson, until his death the best informed person on Negro voting in Virginia, wrote of his race's affairs in 1946: "This year found the states of the Upper South doing precisely as they have been doing for the past fifteen years, and that is to allow colored citizens to vote with practically the same freedom as white citizens." [5]

Although conditions were not uniform, the bulk of voting Negroes lived in the cities. In their preferences they followed much the pattern of white voters. In Memphis, Negroes along with whites supported Crump. In Nashville, deep divisions marked the Negro community, with petty bosses competing against each other to deliver Negro votes to white candidates. In the North Carolina cities of Charlotte, Raleigh, and Durham, white politicians solicited Negro votes, usually through Negro ward heelers and on behalf of white machines. In Virginia, Negro voters in many places lined up with local units of the Byrd organization. It is reported, probably with truth, that in some areas Negroes chose their local affiliations in a way to buttress their right to the ballot.

In the Upper South, and in other parts of the South where Negroes were permitted to vote in one kind of election or another, such as bond referenda, Negro politics had a personal orientation resembling that of the whites. Negro politicians usually used their influence for conventional personal advantage. Outright buying of votes was not uncommon. Negro politicians sometimes interested themselves primarily in the protection of business operations, some of them of questionable legality. Some were satisfied with the prestige they received as political big shots. In this type of politics, which was usually municipal politics, Negroes were seldom organized in support of a program to benefit the Negro community as a whole. Rights and privileges of Negroes as such were not the issues. Negroes did not unify their vote and bargain with it in behalf of such community objectives as better street-lighting for Negro residential sections, more Negro policemen, better schools.[6]

The story of Negro politics in Durham, North Carolina, illustrates the kind of change that took place in many cities. Around 1935, the Durham Committee on Negro Affairs was formed. The committee's concern extended to Negro civic matters in general, including political action. In 1947 the organization had over two thousand members and was run by an executive committee of members elected at an annual meeting of the membership, plus the head of the ministerial alliance and any Negro heads of CIO unions. When the committee came into being, political candidates, by accepted practice, paid money to Negro ward heelers in hopes of corraling a portion of the Negro vote. Many were the double crosses. The heeler sometimes pocketed his money and made no effort to deliver the vote; sometimes he worked on behalf of two candidates for the same office. Whatever the shenanigan, the arrangement benefited the professional politicians, white and black, more than the citizens whose votes were the pawns. As an official of the committee tells it, the new organization set out to gain something for Negroes as a group. At first it sought to encourage candidates favorable to Negro interests by contributing to their campaign chests. The traditional subventions continued to flow, however, to the ward leaders. To undercut their power, the committee wrote to candidates it favored beseeching them to withhold payments from such individuals; it would not endorse candidates who did not comply. The committee set up a schedule of assessments against these candidates. The money raised went directly into the committee's treasury to be used in electioneering for the endorsed candidates. By following this procedure in several campaigns, the committee claimed it consolidated all but a "fringe" of the Negro vote. The only independent leader who retained influence over a significant number of voters became a member of the committee, and reportedly went along with its program. The leaders of the committee believed that Negroes received greater consideration from officeholders and party officials than before. They felt, too, that they had "cleaned up" Negro politics, an important contribution to the cause of Negro voting. Organizations of this type, though perhaps not so well operated, sprang up in several cities of North Carolina. An early effort to set up a state organization was not pushed, and failed.

An experienced North Carolina leader pointed out that local initiative played a major part in the development of Negro political action in his state. There was less need for the NAACP, sustained from the outside, than further South. Negroes in North

Carolina (and in Tennessee and Virginia) had enjoyed more political freedom, for a longer period of time, than Negroes in Alabama, Mississippi, and other states where the NAACP was prominent in prodding local leadership. A top NAACP state official stated that his organization might informally take the lead in another attempt to get a state-wide league going. He showed none of the familiarity with state-wide politics, however, that his counterparts in the Deep South exhibited.

Negro political associations existed in some of the cities of Tennessee. One of the most prominent was the Nashville "Solid Block" club, an organization that at first encountered much difficulty in gaining the voters' support. Generally, in the 1940's, Tennessee Negro voters continued as the pawns of politics. Groups of them were allied with various municipal machines and campaign observers reported the need to put substantial sums into Negro politicking. The words of George Fort Milton, written in 1927, still described the practices more accurately than farsighted Negroes liked:

... in the three largest cities,—Memphis, Nashville, and Chattanooga, —a vicious type of boss domination depends upon the purchasable Negro vote to control municipal affairs.... I confess freely that the voting Negro in cities which have come under my observation, has hitherto served merely as a tool for debauching elections, and maintaining corrupt and unfit men in power.[7]

The NAACP had conducted its usual campaigns to increase the number of qualified voters but had not sparkplugged political action groups. When asked in 1947 who might take the lead in forming a state voters' league, a state NAACP leader thought the chances as much in favor of the CIO or the Southern Conference for Human Welfare as his group. Indeed, the CIO Political Action Committee had already tried to create a degree of unity in Negro political activities. Generally, because of the lack of organization, Negroes were perhaps more closely integrated as individuals into the customary political life in Tennessee than in any other southern state.

Negroes were admitted to the Democratic primaries of Virginia, as noted, in the early 1930's.[8] As in North Carolina and Tennessee, no formal means existed in the 1940's to coördinate Negro political activities on a state-wide basis. The Virginia Voters' League, founded in 1941, with only a scattering of chapters, had not been aggressive. It was originally formed to encourage Negroes to qualify to vote, but during and after the war the NAACP assumed the lead, working with the league where it had alert local units. Local political followings were active in some cities and, as elsewhere, Negro civic clubs sometimes assumed a political role. The NAACP often worked closely with these groups in efforts to get out the vote at election time, taking the usual care to protect itself against charges of partisanship. As elsewhere in the Upper South, some old-line Negro politicians allegedly "sold out" to white politicians.

These notes on the structure of Negro political organizations lead to several important questions. What principles of political action guide the new organizations? How do they conduct their campaigns? What of the consequences?

15

CONSOLIDATING THE VOTE

THE NAACP AND THE PROGRESSIVE VOTERS' LEAGUES HAVE SHOT FOR one goal in southern politics: to increase the political power of Negroes. More than bars to the ballot have blocked the way. Historically, white politicians misused Negro voters; and Negro voters misused their votes and in the end dissipated their political potency. A Montgomery educator and politician gave the view held by many of his fellow-members in the voters' leagues: "The Negro lost the vote once because his vote could be bought, and we don't want to give that excuse again." More than that, a corrupted ballot is a weak ballot, and this, too, Negro leaders know. To make Negro votes clean votes not only creates a responsible and respectable Negro politics; it also increases the political power of Negroes. And precisely for that reason, it should be said, opposition to the new Negro politics has arisen in some quarters.

Negroes know better than their critics how much in southern history black votes have been corrupted. In the last century, and more recently, too, white politicians used all the tools of their trade to buy and bargain for black (as well as white) votes wherever Negroes voted. Inducements ranged from police protection for illicit activities through outright bribery to the more subtle forms, like timely contributions to the building fund of a deserving pastor. It was ever thus, even before the Confederacy, when whites connived for the votes of "free men of color."[1]

"Modern" Negroes look with disgust on this old-time politics. They complain that in such places as Daytona Beach, Clearwater, Birmingham, Mobile, and Dallas, Negro political influence has in the past been wasted by self-seeking Negro politicians. Votes were divided and sold to benefit individual politicians, not consolidated to advance Negroes as a group. In the manner of the Durham Committee on Negro Affairs, new organizations arose across the whole South to fight the corruption and political waste. They waged campaigns of political education, and sought to win the support of their communities. With full political rights a growing reality, they set out to clean up and consolidate the vote. How did they go about this?

The Progressive Voters' League in one state adopted the following "general objectives":

1. To carry on extensive campaigns for registration of Negro voters.
2. To solicit the co-operation of other organizations (civic, fraternal, business, and religious) in an effort to get more Negroes registered.
3. To conduct voting schools for Negro citizens, so that all may become familiar with the techniques of voting.
4. To check closely the records and attitudes of all candidates for political office, and to make recommendations to Negro voters on the basis of such records.
5. To oppose vigorously any "lily-white" tendencies in either major political party.
6. To encourage the organization of county and city voters' leagues that will help to carry out these same objectives on a local level.[2]

Expand point four to include campaigning for the recommended candidates, and the statement lists the things most voters' leagues throughout the South want to do. The nature and effectiveness of their methods in part determine the solidarity of Negro voting and its significance in the future of the southern party system.

The top leaders of a voters' league usually fix its official attitude toward candidates and issues. They may ask candidates to answer in writing questions submitted on behalf of the organization. On the basis of their responses, or on what otherwise is known about the candidates, the officers or executive board of the league decide. They are circumspect, however, about publishing their endorsements. Open Negro support may prove the kiss of death for the favored candidate.[3] The decisions are generally passed by word of mouth and private bulletin. In Nashville, the "Solid Block" tried to follow a "democratic" procedure whereby its steering committee submitted recommendations to a mass meeting for approval or rejection. The gesture did not prevent, however, the endorsement of a mayoralty candidate in 1947 who enjoyed the support of only a small minority of Negro voters.

Negroes have long been accustomed to vote in Nashville. Where they have newly begun to vote, large numbers go to the polls only when spurred by aggressive leadership, and those who go are likely to look to the leadership for guidance. An Arkansas Negro politician told a story that points up this condition. Two white candidates, equally favorable to Negroes, offered for office. Our politician told his people that both candidates were good men, to take their choice between them. Immediately his followers protested, "Tell us which one." The leader laid the docility to Negro inexperience in self-government. He recalled a congregation that had long been led by an iron-willed, dictatorial preacher. The preacher made all the decisions, told his deacons what to do. Eventually a less domineering personality succeeded him, one who expected the deacons to accept some responsibility for the church's affairs. After a short time the deacons had an awful row and the church split up. "They were not," said our politician, "trained for running their own affairs."

Granting that the leaders of the Negro political organizations usually agree among themselves on the candidates to favor, the success with which they turn out a large vote depends in significant measure on their skill in electioneering. They must reach beyond their own membership, of course, for not all Negro voters formally ally themselves with the voters' leagues. The Georgia Association of Citizens' Democratic Clubs, for instance, could claim as members in 1946 only about one-seventh of the approximately 125,000 Georgia Negroes registered to vote. Similarly, the

Arkansas Negro Democratic Association in 1947 claimed a paid-up membership equal to only 5 per cent of the estimated number of qualified Negro voters. In areas with a smaller proportion of Negroes qualified to vote, the percentage of voters claimed as members of the political league may be higher. In Mississippi, the president of the state Progressive Voters' League thus claimed a membership somewhat larger than the number of Negroes whom he said actually voted. The concept of "membership," too, is variable. To a Florida leader, as we saw in the last chapter, it meant "all the registered Negroes in the county." In a North Carolina town it meant "every Negro voter." Regardless of who are considered members, the problem remains the same: to rally the voters behind the favored candidates.

Campaign techniques resemble those employed in white politics, and they similarly vary with time and place. The activities of the Citizens' Democratic Club in Savannah, Georgia, during 1946, illustrate well many of the procedures and problems of Negro politics. Because of Negro residential separation, the club achieved marked results from conventional block-by-block, precinct-by-precinct soliciting. Precincts were organized by districts and blocks; volunteer and part-time workers knocked on doors and distributed literature in behalf of a list of state and local candidates endorsed by the executive board of the club. On election day, paid workers electioneered near the polls, assisted voters, checked their names against copies of the voters' list, and performed the other rituals of urban politics.

To provide a continuing structure, precinct organizations were formed, each placing representatives on the executive board of the club, whose jurisdiction extended over the whole county. In an ambitious set of "Recommendations for Precinct Organizations," the club's officers described a system of year-round weekly precinct meetings. The officers and members of each precinct "Will plan interesting and informative meetings so that the people in the precinct will be encouraged to attend regularly and gain needed information for participation in the political program for our city. The parent body will lend any assistance needed in the form of speakers, etc." Topics suggested for discussion included

"How to Vote," "Elections: When they occur, and for whom to vote," and "How to Register." The representatives to the county executive board would report on the progress and needs of the precincts. The precinct organizations would have their own treasuries, independent of the annual dues of one dollar collected by them and turned over to the county club. Certainly a peak of interest could not be maintained between campaigns, but the club's success in the summer of 1946 aroused local opposition forces to intense efforts to woo the Negro vote in later campaigns.

In Savannah, as in other communities, much campaigning was done through fraternal, religious, and civic organizations. Precinct meetings were often held in churches; in fact, preachers were sometimes precinct captains. The president of the Citizens' Democratic Club was also president of the Hub, a businessman's organization. Dependence on established organizations offers hazards as well as aids in creating cohesive political action. Because the leadership of the organizations is drawn from a relatively small and oftentimes well-knit group, integration of political efforts may be achieved. On the other hand, patriarchs may cause divisions among the voters along lines of organizational loyalties if they do not act in unison. Observation of this influence of individual leaders over their respective flocks, religious or otherwise, has frequently led white politicians to feel they could split up the Negro vote by "getting to" individual Negroes of influence. Savannah Negroes noted that the local "administration" forces strove to do this in the municipal elections late in 1946, following the July primaries in which administration candidates received only slight Negro support. Allegedly, administration leaders "spent money right and left" and succeeded in gaining the help of about 65 per cent of the preachers. After this experience, one local politician concluded that the unity of Negro voters could be preserved only through a system of block and precinct organizations.

In the Savannah primaries of 1946 the Citizens' Democratic Club teamed up with the county and city "reform" movement called the Citizens' Progressive League. Negro campaigners at the polls worked for CPL candidates and were paid by the CPL through the Negro organization. Otherwise, the organization's leaders assert, no funds were accepted from candidates or their representatives.

In other urban areas over the South, the Savannah type of campaign has been found with variations. In Atlanta an even more systematic organization in 1946 assigned to volunteer workers responsibility over precincts, census tracts, and blocks. Records were kept, on prescribed forms, of door-to-door calls, return visits, and results of the calls. In most places—as in Anniston, Alabama, where a small but alert group of Negro voters obtained municipal benefits through their political action—the campaigning was more informal, through personal and organizational contacts. In rural areas, active campaigning among Negroes has been rare. Distance creates difficulties, but more important are the factors of intimidation in white-black relations.

Effective action by a Negro political league is almost invariably local action. Depending directly on the quality and interests of local leadership, the intensity of local efforts varies from place to place. The well integrated, centrally directed, state-wide campaign has been almost unknown. The state officers of a league may issue exhortations, may even convene a meeting of representatives from several localities. A person may swing around the state trying to activate his friends. But these are mild gestures. They seldom achieve a degree of state-wide organization and planning equaling that reached in Georgia in the Talmadge campaigns. In Eugene Talmadge's last race for governor, in 1946, the Georgia Association of Citizens' Democratic Clubs led a vigorous campaign in behalf of James V. Carmichael. Special persons were hired to take charge of the campaign in individual counties, or in groups of neighboring counties. Travelling representatives from state headquarters kept tab on these local campaigns. Counsel, especially on legal matters, was dispensed to aid the local efforts. Speakers were sent out. The initiative of the Atlanta headquarters accounted in no small measure for the unusually high degree of political activity shown by Negroes in small towns and rural areas. Advice and encouragement were needed to spruce the morale in sections where Negroes had not customarily asserted themselves.

Following the general policy of accepting subventions from the war chests of candidates it endorsed, the association received aid in this campaign from the Carmichael forces and from other white groups supporting liberal candidates. All over the South white candidates find it wise to make their solicitations to Negro voters through other Negroes. When candidates appeal personally to Negro voters, they sometimes stir resentment. A 1947 resolution of the North Little Rock Democratic City Central Committee read as follows:

It is detrimental to the best interests of society to have white candidates soliciting Negro votes and shaking hands with Negro electors and speaking before Negro gatherings and placing themselves on equal social standings with the Negroes of this community by such actions.

Therefore, be it resolved that candidates for Democratic nomination for city offices refrain from soliciting Negro votes in the city Democratic primary elections; that such action is detrimental, degrading and contemptible to the white Democrats of North Little Rock.[4]

Though later the Southern Conference for Human Welfare became generally inactive over the whole region, for a while it played an important role in Georgia and in several other southern states through its local affiliates. The conference's local affiliates sometimes spent funds, brought Negro and white leaders together for consultation, and supported the Negro in his fight for the vote. The conference's efforts proved most significant in states where no other means existed to coördinate state-wide Negro political activity. It should be noted parenthetically that in Georgia and elsewhere a few labor unions have, on occasion, in limited areas, assisted Negro voters in similar ways.

The activities of white groups in Georgia in 1946 found their greatest significance for Negro politics in the support they gave to the Negro's general right to political action. Hostile warnings had been issued in several parts of the state against Negroes who might dare to try to vote. In many localities the warnings reached the proportions of intimidation. Following a request of Carmichael leaders, the Attorney General of the United States issued a statement early in the campaign that Federal laws (and Court decisions) would be upheld in the forthcoming primary election. According to both Negroes and whites active in the campaign, the effect was electric. Everywhere in the state the courage and enthusiasm of Negroes surged up. The political league in Savannah, according to one of its officers, was formed only after the Attorney General's announcement gave heart to local leaders.

The activities and significance of the Negro voters' leagues vary considerably from state to state in the South. The ability of the organizations to clean up the vote, or simply to activate a small portion of the potential Negro electorate, depends on many variables. Among the most important are the skill and energy of Negro leadership, the suffrage requirements, the attitudes of local whites, and the nature of candidates and campaign issues. As a result, the number of politically active Negroes and the consequences of the new Negro politics will read differently in different places.[5] Allowing for all the variations and imperfections, however, one common consequence seems apparent: Negroes in the late 1940's exhibited in their voters' leagues greater determination and independence than they had ever known before in southern politics. As the new decade began, all signs pointed to the increasing significance of Negroes as a political interest group. In many parts of the South, the voters' leagues will give the impetus and the form to the future Negro politics. The organizations will change, as the conditions in which they arose change, but their existence remains a new fact of southern political life.

16

BLOC VOTING

THERE WAS AN EARLIER TIME, REACHING INTO THE TWENTIETH CENtury, when southern Negroes voted in large numbers, attended party conventions, sat in Congress and state legislatures, won state, county, and city offices.[1] In those days the actions of Negro politicians and voters directly affected the internal management of the two political parties and the relationship between them. The Negro's behavior in politics had much to do with the development of the one-party system, which pretty generally eliminated him from politics.

The preceding chapters described the form taken by the new Negro politics of the 1940's. The present chapter and the two that follow concern its significance for the party balance in the South. The influx of Negro voters need not affect the relative strength of the parties. Or, like any enlargement of an electorate, it might have far-reaching consequences. The facts in the forties were these: southern Negroes entered the Democratic primaries to have a voice in local and state government and in the halls of Congress; they were drawn to the Democratic presidential standard by the policies of Roosevelt and Truman; and the Republican party made no move to woo them. Nevertheless, Negro voters as a whole were not wed to a single party, as once they were wed to the Republicans. In their political leagues they resolved to "vote their interests" regardless of party. Will Negroes ultimately flood back into the Republican party, perhaps restoring the stigma that long marked it as the party of the Negro in the South, or will they serve merely to strengthen Democratic superiority? But first, will Negroes, *as a group,* do anything?

The Negro political leagues strive avowedly in their clean-up-the-vote campaigns to solidify the Negro vote and to use it in bargaining for Negro interests. They naturally wield greatest influence when they vote together, especially where Negro voters are numerous enough to affect the outcome of elections. Many persons, however, question the wisdom of Negro bloc voting. Some of these are Negroes, and not all the whites among them oppose Negro suffrage. The problem encompasses the future position of the Negro in the South.

The line of debate was clearly drawn by the editor of *The Columbia Record*, a paper that approved the Negro's struggle to enter the Democratic primaries of South Carolina. Preceding the primaries of 1948, the first to which Negroes were admitted, mass meetings of Negroes were called in various counties of the state for instruction in preparing their ballots. Negro political leaders also "prepared recommendations and made them available to the members." John H. McCray, head of the Progressive Democratic party (Negro), explained: "It was the only course to avoid confusion and to provide these new voters the opportunity to stand together at the polls, as they have been forced by law, custom and tradition to stand together." In his issue of August 12, 1948, the editor of the *Record* indicted the action as a major blunder.

By this single act ... the Negroes surrendered everything for which they [have] fought ... If the Negro Democrats can hold a caucus and select candidates, then in logic the white Democrats can hold a caucus or even conduct a primary and choose their candidates. They would be justified even in so doing. By this blunder the Negroes, who undertook to segregate themselves instead of allowing themselves to be absorbed into the party as they have been arguing they should be ... have supplied the precedent and the excuse for white "bloc" voting which is all the advocates of the white primary have ever desired.

Blunder or no, a large number of Negro leaders place their faith in concerted political action by members of their race. Attempts to organize bloc voting among Negroes will in all probability loom importantly in southern politics for some time to come.

Voting behavior in the South has not been studied sufficiently to permit conclusive generalizations on the extent of bloc voting and the conditions under which it occurs. The need for detailed analyses of white and Negro voting under current suffrage conditions appears to anyone who contemplates southern politics. We are not prevented, however, from drawing inferences from direct observation and from the testimony of Negro and white politicians. Southern primaries and elections since 1944 provide a variety of examples of Negro voting behavior.

Essentially, Negroes behave like other groups of common origin. Like the Irish in Boston or the French in Quebec or southern senators in Congress, they stick together when their interests as a group are at stake. Because of skin color and practices of discrimination and exclusion against them, Negroes possess a keener sense of group identity than do most minorities. When their political rights are at issue, they oppose with a high degree of solidarity candidates who challenge their right to vote, and they support those who uphold it. "Ninety per cent of the Negroes voted for Carmichael," politicians concluded all over Georgia following the 1946 primaries in which James V. Carmichael ran against Eugene Talmadge and Ed Rivers. Carmichael was backed by Ellis Arnall under whose leadership the state Democratic committee had admitted Negroes to the primary. Talmadge denounced Negro voting. Spot checks of the returns from Negro boxes in various cities confirmed the expectations.[2] In Mississippi, there is little reason to doubt the contention of Negro leaders that few of their race voted for Bilbo, nor in Alabama that Negroes who voted on the discriminatory "Boswell Amendment"[3] were opposed to it, nor in North Carolina that Negroes favored Frank Graham, a candidate whose respect for human beings knew no bounds of color.[4]

Even when the debate revolves around no so-called race issue, however, Negro community interests often are involved. Common concerns appear most frequently in municipal and county politics. Though residential segregation is not as extensive in the South as sometimes is supposed, all cities have sections inhabited principally by Negroes. These sections, like Castle Hill in Tuscaloosa or Yamacraw in Savannah, have traditionally suffered such deficiencies as poor paving, infrequent street lights, scant sewage disposal and water facilities. Negroes find common bond in their desire for more municipal services. The petition of a Negro civic club to the aldermen of Chapel Hill requested the following:

(1) sidewalks on Graham and Church streets;
(2) traffic lights at Church street and Rosemary lane and the Graham street and West Franklin street intersections;
(3) pipes in the open ditch extending from Rosemary lane along the side of Mitchell lane;
(4) enforcement of parking regulations for automobiles along Church street; and
(5) a school attendance officer for Negro children.[5]

Negro voters want improved schools and playgrounds for their children, at least some nonmenial public jobs for Negroes. Many Negroes, like many whites, know their government only through the law enforcement agencies. They are deeply convinced they deserve uniformed policemen of their own race. Moreover, they know the attitude of the sheriff and his deputies affects them more than any group of whites. The president of the Progressive Voters' League of Florida put it this way in an open letter to "Florida Negro Citizens" in 1948:

But as important as the presidential election is, we must not overlook the fact that the election of state and county officials is of equal importance to us. These are the officials who have direct control of our everyday affairs. Most Negroes in Florida today have never seen a president. But practically all of us know our tax collector, our sheriff, and our county judge. We know the circuit judge, the state attorney, and the clerk of the court, because we often have to come in contact with these officials. The safety and welfare of Florida Negro citizens depend very largely upon the attitudes of our sheriffs, judges, and other law-enforcement officials.[6]

Where Negroes organize under group-conscious leadership, they bargain with candidates for city and county offices in an effort to gain civic benefits. The attitudes of Negroes under these circumstances vary from person to person like those of whites. Civic-minded ones favor the candidates most likely to deliver on their commitments to the community. Others may be guided by personal relationships to the candidates, or by special inducements. The voter's leagues have at times undertaken major campaigns to improve their bargaining position by achieving a relatively solid vote. They have not been uniformly successful, but an example or two will illustrate the type of bloc voting found in the forties in some places in the South and will suggest a kind of simple analysis that is helpful in understanding Negro political behavior.

Florida has not had much by way of race politics, and the secretary of the state Progressive Voters' League judged that "probably most Negroes who voted followed the recommendations" of the league. He submitted the results of a race in a small town in his county as evidence. In the municipal "primary" in Titusville, Florida, September 2, 1947, sixteen white candidates offered for five seats on the city council. After investigating the candidates, the local league endorsed five of the sixteen and published the endorsements in the Negro press. The results shown on the opposite page were reported.

The candidates marked with an asterisk were endorsed. The figures show several things. First, no issues were involved that pitted race against race, for Negroes and whites favored several of the same candidates. Second, Negroes showed a higher degree of solidarity than whites. In voting on four of the candidates, between 79.3 and 92.2 per cent of the Negro voters followed the recommendations of the league. The four strongest preferences among white voters received between 61.1 and 65.0 per cent of the white votes. Third, Negroes split their votes between an endorsed candidate, Ramer, and an unendorsed candidate, Bryan. The explanation given indicated something of the limits of the league's influence: a large number of Negroes worked for a company headed by Bryan. Fourth, fewer votes were scattered among

	Votes received			Approximate percentage of voters in each group voting for each candidate	
Candidate	White	Negro	Total	White	Negro
*Day	378	98	476	64.5	84.4
*Boyd	358	107	465	61.1	92.2
*Poe	364	99	463	62.1	85.3
Bryan	348	53	401	59.4	45.7
Matthews	381	16	397	65.0	13.8
*Wager	201	92	293	34.3	79.3
*Ramer	124	50	174	21.2	43.1
9 others	778	64	842	14.7[a]	.6[a]
TOTAL	2932	579	3511		
Approximate number of voters	586	116	702		

[a] Computed on the basis of the average vote cast for each of the nine candidates.

minor candidates by Negroes than by whites, perhaps indicating fewer personal or business ties with the candidates. Generally, Negroes seemed to see a group interest in the voting and pretty much followed it. The returns also indicate, however, that the cohesiveness of the Negro vote was easily disrupted, and by a factor apparently unrelated to the group's welfare as interpreted by the political organization.

The results of two elections in Savannah will serve to follow up the discussion in the last chapter. At the time of the state primaries in July, 1946, two local factions fought for control of the county government. The "administration" had been in power for over twenty years. Its record with the Negro community led the Negro political organization to favor the Citizens' Progressive League, a new group that promised to do something toward employing Negro policemen and providing better school, health, and other civic services. Whereas the administration's officers had at times discouraged Negro registration, the CPL made a show of welcoming Negroes into the electorate. In the legislative race, where the battle lines were drawn most clearly, 81.8 per cent of the 8,032 Negroes voting favored the CPL.[7] The following December the battle was fought over again in the municipal elections, although county voters outside the city limits could not now participate, and the CPL won again. Between July and December, however, administration leaders increased their overtures to the Negro community and reportedly exerted much effort to convert Negro politicians to their support. This time 62.2 per cent of 7,841 Negro voters supported the CPL candidate for mayor.[8] Leaders of the Negro political club attributed the desertions to voters who placed their personal gain above what the club considered to be the welfare of the community. The two elections suggest the important conclusion that cohesiveness among Negro voters lessens when their right to vote is not challenged, and when white candidates solicit their votes with the same impartiality that they solicit white votes. Certainly such is the experience in the Upper South and in northern cities.[9]

While the importance of one basis for bloc voting among Negroes will decline as Negro suffrage becomes better established, another basis for unity in Negro voting exists. Thoughtful Negroes hold a remarkably uniform view: Most Negroes are underprivileged; they should therefore support candidates advocating economic and social policies beneficial to the mass of underprivileged citizens. Some segments of Negro opinion even hold that broad economic philosophy should take precedence over immediate "racial" issues. A North Carolina Negro politician, for instance, pointed out that Negroes in his state usually backed candidates who favored the FEPC. Yet that threw them frequently behind minority candidates with little chance of winning. He thought they would be wiser to back the candidate most favorable to them who had a chance of winning. Our informant argued that if he were a Florida voter he would back Senator Pepper even though the Senator opposed FEPC; Franklin Roosevelt's chief contribution to the Negro was not his personal stand on civil liberties nor his opposition to racial discrimination, it was his programs for the ill-housed, ill-clad, ill-fed.

Some opponents of Negro suffrage hold it poppycock to say that Negroes will vote as a bloc only when an issue of Negro community concern is at stake. Such an opponent pointed to the Muscogee County primary returns for lieutenant governor of Georgia in 1946. One Dr. Huff ran a poor race in the state as a whole. Yet he carried Muscogee County, and its seat, Columbus, where Negroes gave him about ten times the votes they gave to the other candidates combined.[10] He did not receive such support from Negro voters elsewhere in the state. Our informant, a local white politician, nodded knowingly, and hinted the support had been induced by means closely connected with the personal prosperity of certain Negro politicians. It may be significant that officers of the Georgia Association of Citizens' Democratic Clubs, the state-wide voters' league, complained that they had made no headway in getting Columbus Negroes to form a local unit of the state organization. The story suggests that Columbus possessed at the time of the election a Negro political following of the type often found in cities of the border states.[11]

In all quarters, of course, the specter of a "Negro balance of power" is raised. The thought disturbs many whites, who, nevertheless, on principle, uphold the Negro's right to vote. Obviously, in a close race, any group whose members vote alike may constitute a balance of power and be able to affect the outcome. A few examples have cropped up around the South. Negro votes in Conway, South Carolina, are said to have elected an all-white municipal slate that received a minority of the white votes. Negroes reportedly at times have been important in the politics of Pinellas County (St. Petersburg), Florida, because of the closeness in strength between Republicans and Democrats. Wherever people vote there will be many balances of power, and wherever Negro voters are numerous and well organized they will be one of them, like the union members, the prohibitionists, and the fisherfolk. The significance of a balance of power, however, is not always as imagined, as suggested by the title of a chapter in Ralph Bunche's analysis of the political status of the Negro:

"Memphis—Where the Black Balance of Power Fails to Get the Fruits of Victory." [12]

If we may conclude that common political interests conduce to common political action, we may also conclude that the South will see varying degrees of bloc voting in its Negro electorate for many years to come. Men of skill and energy will not always rise to seize the opportunity, and those who do may not always succeed in meeting the competition of others similarly inclined. But the fact remains, practices of segregation in public services and in southern life generally provide a basis in all the southern states for a politics based on Negro welfare. Negroes will continue to share with each other problems of municipal services, education, and equal participation in government.[13] So long as they are affected as a group by public problems, they will react as a group to the problems and to the candidates who seek to solve them. Public policies broader in their effect upon Negroes than "racial" policies may at times supersede the latter in the thinking of some Negroes, but skin color and social exclusion are forces that give the aggressive leader great leverage in organizing for common action.[14]

Of all the forces conducive to bloc voting by Negroes, the greatest is a Negro candidate running against white candidates. Then, Negroes advise, they feel there is something really worth voting for. All over the United States racial and national minorities are given representation on slates of candidates in recognition of this principle. It seems reasonable that Negroes will rally with a high degree of loyalty around Negro candidates until they themselves become more thoroughly integrated into the society than seems probable in the foreseeable future, and until the solicitation of Negro votes extends to the inclusion of Negro candidates on opposing tickets.

It does not seem hazardous to accept the conclusion of Negro politicians that Negro voters generally go wholeheartedly for candidates of their own race.[15] Were their conclusion incorrect, the returns from Negro wards would quickly disabuse them of the notion. The fact remains, however, that no detailed analyses of southern elections after 1944 in which Negroes were candidates have come to hand. Such candidates have generally run for municipal posts and minor positions, the returns of which are not readily available. If the assumption be warranted, however, special attention should be directed to the extent to which Negroes offered as candidates in the South in the 1940's and to the implications for the maintenance of "white rule."

The chances that Negroes will "take over the courthouses" are somewhat less than black-belt planters claim. They are less, too, than the assertions of Negroes themselves. Following the court victories in 1948, for instance, the president of the South Carolina conference of the NAACP announced that Negroes expected to run for office and to hold "many of the jobs in municipal, county, state and federal governments."[16] These claims fail to weigh adequately two forces that retard Negro political participation. Where Negroes are most heavily concentrated, and appear at first to possess the greatest political potential, the mores are least conducive to Negro voting and Negro candidacies. Anyone who has travelled the South knows that in the rural counties where Negroes outnumber whites, and where both are dependent on large-scale agricultural operations, the intangible, extralegal restraints on Negro activities operate with most effect. In those areas, the black belts, most Negroes are depressed economically, socially, and educationally. They have far to travel to acquire the skill, stamina, and leadership to overcome the opposition of their overlords. Wholly aside from factors of social discipline, marked apathy among Negroes retards their political development. All the many conditions that produce low white participation in the South contribute to low participation among Negroes as well. In exaggerated form these conditions combine with the tradition of nonparticipation to create what Negro leaders speak of as the "uphill journey" that lies between their people and civic consciousness. An inquiry sent out in 1950 by an organization concerned with Negro voting asked several important Negro leaders in the South to name the chief obstacles to Negro voting in their states. The replies from the four states seen by this writer included these reasons: "general lethargy of Negroes," "indifference and lack of interest on part of the Negro," "getting local leaders interested in first class citizenship," and "In many cases it is difficult to get Negroes to see the benefits that can be derived from their voting."

Despite these conditions, the frequency with which Negroes offer for office, and the number of them elected, stands a fair chance to increase in the South. The Upper South saw several successful Negro candidacies in the 1940's. Oliver W. Hill was elected to the Richmond city council in 1948. He had previously narrowly missed election to the Virginia House of Delegates.[17] William Lawrence, running as an independent, defeated a white Democratic nominee for the Nansemond County, Virginia, Board of Supervisors in 1947.[18] Rev. Kenneth R. Williams was elected alderman in Winston-Salem, North Carolina, in 1947,[19] and was succeeded by Rev. William R. Crawford in 1951. In the same year Dr. W. M. Hampton was elected to the city council in Greensboro and Dr. W. P. Devane was re-elected to a similar position in Fayetteville. Also in 1951 two Negroes were elected to the city council in Nashville, the first to serve in almost forty years.[20] In the fifth ward, Negroes representing two rival factions ran against each other.[21]

A sign of the times, such news squibs as the following from Burlington, North Carolina, began to appear over the South:

Residents of Graham Tuesday elected J. W. Carter, a 65-year-old Negro of the Haw River Road section as justice of the peace on the Democratic ticket as the first Negro office holder in Alamance County's history.[22]

In other towns, like Augusta in Georgia, and Norfolk and Petersburg in Virginia, and Raleigh, Durham, Washington, and Asheville in North Carolina, Negroes offered as candidates.[23]

In all of these contests, candidates were elected by districts or wards, meaning that Negroes benefited from their concentration in separate residential sections. In some of the cases the Negro candidates received white votes. Such seems to have been true, for instance, in Mr. Hill's election in Richmond, where an agreement was said to exist—not fully carried out—for Negroes to vote for a white labor candidate in addition to Hill in return for labor votes for Hill. There were seven places at stake, and by voting for only two candidates Negroes improved the chances of their election.[24] Minority groups not uncommonly concentrate their votes in this way on one or two candidates in a multi-place race.

In Texas, a trade involving separate offices resulted in the election of a Negro, G. J. Sutton, to the board of the San Antonio Junior College in 1948. The Mexican-Americans constitute a racial minority more important in South Texas than the Negroes. In this contest, Negroes voted for Gus Garcia for a school district post and in return many "Mexicans" voted for Sutton.[25]

Negro candidates offered with increasing frequency in all southern states. Miami, Jacksonville, and even Charleston saw contests in which Negroes offered. A Negro sought the Democratic nomination for Congress in 1950 in South Carolina's first district.[26] The Progressive Democratic party (Negro) had put up candidates, including one for United States senator, in the general elections of South Carolina in earlier years.

Despite these forays into indepedent political action, Negro politicians remain sensitive to the reaction automatically set up among many whites by Negro candidacies. In conversation they propose the wisdom of holding back, of waiting until Negro voting has become commonplace, until Negroes themselves have benefited from greater political experience. Perhaps some who made these suggestions remembered their history.

17

A LESSON FROM HISTORY

COMMENTATORS ON AMERICAN POLITICS TEND TO THINK OF THE Republican party as the traditional benefactor of the Negro. In reality, in the years between Reconstruction and the New Deal, neither major party showed vital concern for the Negro's welfare. In effect, northern Republicans—in power most of the period—as well as northern Democrats, deferred to the views of southerners in matters affecting the Negro, and Negroes disagreed with many of those views.

Out of the experience Negroes learned a lesson they may well remember. They can trust their cause to no party unless their cause goes well supplied with the currency of politics—votes. And they may remember also the ease with which their votes can be frittered away in the absence of skilled and far-sighted leadership. From a reading of these lessons have grown the new political leagues and their efforts to organize Negro voters.

The story of the southern Negro and the Republican party after 1876 has been carefully traced by historians in a number of states. The tales are tortuous and unbelievably complex, and in the end they add up to the most dismal chapter in American political history. One can recall few annals that tell of so much pettiness and futility, and even corruption, in the democratic process. And as we try to view the future of the Negro in party politics, the story illuminates his present relationship to the Republicans and warns of hazards and difficulties that could plague the race and region again.

In essence, the Republicans never found a formula for joining large numbers of whites and Negroes in the same party. Even before the formal disfranchising measures began to go into effect in the last decade of the nineteenth century, the party in several states had suffered crippling splits between "black-and-tan" and "lily-white" factions, enervating schisms that fitted nicely the other events out of which the one-party system was developing. Even allowing for the Populist coalitions, the stigma of blackness in the end deprived the Republicans of any chance for the white support they needed to become a political force. Gradually, the philosophy of lily white-ism caught hold, so that by 1932 the Negro was ready in more ways than one to place his hopes in another party. The drive to rid the southern units of the Republican party of Negro influence arose from various sources: partly from prejudice, partly from jealousy over patronage, partly from the conviction that only under "respectable" white leadership could the party hope to grow.

The story state by state cannot be satisfactorily compressed, because the very details of greed and doctrine and personality and bickering comprise the heart of the troubles. A sketch of the major stages in the story, however, will point up the transition that took place.

At the outset, in the words attributed to the great nineteenth-century Negro, Frederick Douglass, the Republican party was the ship, all else the sea.[1] The party undeniably was the Negro's ship in the first years of storm following 1865, when Republican leaders in Congress feared that resuscitated southern Democrats would join with northern Democrats to put the Republicans out of power. To guarantee the Negro the ballot served the cause of the Republican party as well as the cause of universal suffrage.[2] And after Reconstruction, Negroes naturally continued their loyalty, a fact somewhat encouraged by the Democrats. From Wade Hampton to Joseph T. Robinson, some Democrats received

Negro votes, but the overwhelming number of Negroes who voted did so in the name of Lincoln.[3]

In the seventies and eighties and nineties the Republican party included politicians and voters of both races. And from the beginning in state after state the party was riven by factionalism. The term "lily white" was first used in 1888 in Texas. A Negro Republican leader, Norris Wright Cuney, so dubbed a faction seeking to take control of the party from him. He charged that the "White Republican Clubs" were founded solely on race prejudice.[4] In a similar action, Republican whites in Mississippi sought the aid of President Arthur's administration in wresting the party in that state from Negro control. They charged an alliance between Negro leaders and Democratic Senators Lamar and George. Curiously, Negro leaders allegedly influenced their followers to vote in local and state elections for Democrats and the senators in Washington coöperated in Negro claims for patronage. Not so curiously, it was said that Democratic chieftains were happy to encourage a black Republican party in their state as one way to keep it weak.[5] Elsewhere, the battles went on. In Georgia, in the seventies, the Republican future held great promise. The party won seats in the state legislature and in Congress. A great opportunity arose in the form of an Independent Democratic movement, rising to challenge the Bourbon control of the Democratic party. The Republicans might have joined with the Independents to defeat the Democrats, or they might have maneuvered to take advantage of the split in the Democrats. But blacks and whites within their party fought each other more bitterly than they did the enemy, and in the end the Democrats killed off the Independents and the Republicans as well. The factionalism was accentuated by rivalries for personal leadership and by disharmony among the supporters of Arthur and Blaine, rivals for the Republican presidential nomination. Matters reached a sort of climax when the Republican state convention split wide open in 1882. Rival conventions met in 1884. By 1886 the party had no candidates for state offices and its potency was destroyed.[6]

The inept Republican performance in one state after another in the South was often attended by questionable horse-trading. The conditions led Republicans outside the South to conclude that their southern party was hopeless. Theodore Roosevelt vented the disgust of many in 1901 when he charged that southern Republicans made "not the slightest effort to get any popular votes."[7] This was palpably true, and since most Republicans were Negroes the demand arose to turn the party over to whites. Make the party respectable, northern Republicans argued, and things would right themselves. The idea caught on. President Taft spent several weeks during the winter following his election speaking in conciliatory tones around Georgia. His flattery and jolly nature charmed many a southern white, but no revolution took place.[8] In fact, the real nature of the difficulty in reforming the southern Republican party, then and later, was dramatized in 1912 when delegates from the Negro-dominated organizations in the South accounted in large part for Taft's renomination over former President Roosevelt.[9]

Teddy Roosevelt, no race baiter, set out after this to build his Progressive Movement in the South on white leadership, a decision, one may be sure, based more on the calculations of a politician than on pique over the loss of the Republican nomination. Said the man who had raised a mighty ruckus by insisting on Negro officeholders in the South and by entertaining Booker T. Washington at the White House:

The disruption and destruction of the Republican party ... has been brought about in large part ... by refusing to face the truth, which is that under existing conditions there is not and cannot be in the Southern States a party based primarily upon the Negro vote and under Negro leadership or the leadership of white men who derive their power solely from Negroes.[10]

The miasma of southern Republicanism was infected by acknowledged corruption. The blame was laid by whites at the door of the politically immature Negro. Negroes, and with cause, laid the blame at another door. W. E. Burghardt Du Bois in 1920 quoted the NAACP's publication, *Crisis:*

Every four years the disgrace of buying up certain delegates for the Republican convention is repeated in the Southern South [sic.] ...

They are for sale to the highest bidder. Republican candidates begin their campaign by sending men into the South to buy the support of these men, and the whole Negro race is blamed for this recurring disgrace. But whose is the fault? The fault lies at the doors of the National Republican Party. Not only is the party and its candidates willing and eager to buy up this support, but they have repeatedly refused support or countenance to the better class of colored leaders who seek to oust the thieves.[11]

Nevertheless, the party was corrupt, and because it was corrupt under Negro leadership, the whites who sought to win control of the state organizations received encouragement and sometimes active aid from the outside.

The struggles within several states shaped up decisively after the First World War. In 1920 Florida saw a "Republican, white" candidate for governor running against a regular Republican and a Democrat. In Arkansas, the same year, the lily-white Republicans "discarded" the black-and-tan faction, which then met in rump session and nominated a "Negro Independent" candidate for governor.[12] Perhaps the most dramatic fight took place in Virginia. Since 1865, the Negro had been the traditional source of strength for the party. In 1920 Colonel Henry Anderson led a move whereby Republicans abandoned the direct primary and refused to seat Negroes in the party convention. In the gubernatorial campaign of the next year Anderson, a candidate, declared that the Republicans despised Negroes and did not want their votes. The Negroes put forward a rump candidate under the label "lily-black" (reportedly with the connivance of certain Democrats) and the Republican party thereafter remained lily white.[13]

By 1928 in every southern state lily-white organizations rivaled the "regular" organizations, or organizations traditionally controlled by Negroes. Hoover, the presidential candidate, exhibited open hostility to the black-and-tan factions. He used a campaign committee for southern whites distinct from the black-and-tan state organizations. His encouragement of lily-white factions turned Negroes in several states to support Smith. Among these were "Goose-Neck Bill" McDonald, long-time Negro committeeman from Texas, who joined leaders in other states and denounced the "new" Republicanism. After the election Hoover publicly commended several of the lily-white organizations. He personally dismissed Georgia's veteran Negro Ben Davis from patronage councils. He pledged the "hearty cooperation of the administration" if citizens in Georgia, South Carolina, and Mississippi would clean up the party in their states.[14] Hoover's attitude during and following the election was the culminating influence in the shift to lily-white-ism in the South.[15]

When the shouting was over whites controlled the party in most states, Negroes controlled it in Mississippi, and there was mixed leadership in a few. The successive Democratic victories beginning in 1932 cut into Republican strength in the South as elsewhere and interest in rebuilding the party lagged. The Year of Certain Victory, 1948, found whites in control of the party machinery in Arkansas, Texas, Louisiana, and Florida, though Negroes were not excluded from Republican affairs in those states. In Tennessee, Virginia, and North Carolina, with their large areas of mountain Republicans, and in Alabama, whites were in complete charge. In Mississippi, an all-Negro faction, smaller than its lily-white rival,[16] continued to gain recognition from the national party, and supplied the only Negroes on the Republican National Committee. Perry Howard, the committeeman, always marked because he lives in Washington, D. C., and not Mississippi, and Mary Booze, the committeewoman, a resident of the all-Negro community of Mound Bayou, Mississippi, had held these posts since 1924. In Georgia and South Carolina, whites predominated, but shared their leadership with Negroes to a larger extent than in the other states.[17]

In one sense, the shift of party leadership from blacks to whites tackled a basic problem. No one, white or black, thought that an all-Negro party, or one dominated largely by Negroes, could win in the South. Where shifts to white control were accomplished, however, the party grew no stronger than it had been before. The lily-white movement merely embittered southern Negroes and confirmed their disappointment in the old party. The seeds of disillusionment had been first planted long before by the "compromise" of 1877 when the Republican Hayes was proclaimed president and the last of the occupation troops were withdrawn from the Democratic South.[18] The course of Theodore Roosevelt and William Howard Taft had encouraged the normal tendency of Negroes to follow the liberal New Freedom of Woodrow Wilson, but Wilson's segregation policy and southern background barred the way to a wholesale change of party.[19] In some northern cities, Negroes found their way into Democratic organizations. By 1932, such Negroes as voted in the South were ripe for any Democrat who would give them half a hearing. Their "debt of gratitude," as one leader put it, had long been paid.

From the view of the long-run welfare of the Republican party, the lily-white policy at no time made sense unless it were assumed that Negroes could be eliminated altogether from southern politics. Then a two-party system among whites might develop. Curious is the irony of history. When the courts broke down Democratic bars to Negro suffrage and opened the way to an ancient Republican aim, a vital Negro political life in the South, at the same time they brought a host of pigeons home to roost. Instead of finding the new Negro voters—who would now vote in the general elections as well as the primaries—a source of strength, the Republicans found them one more obstacle to their party's immediate growth. The ultimate consequences, however, were more difficult to perceive. It was not merely that the new Negro voters held out a danger as well as a hope to any party that claimed them, as Republican history had demonstrated. They also stood to strengthen the lower reaches of Democratic voters and in the long run would contribute to the fundamental reconstitution of the southern Democratic party that would in turn revitalize its opposition.

18

SOUTHERN NEGROES AND THE PARTIES

IN THINKING OF FUTURE TIES BETWEEN NEGRO VOTERS AND THE parties, the overriding concern of Negroes for their interests as Negroes should never be ignored. Political habit, economic status, religion, local loyalty, and all the other determinants that interact on each other to produce the way a white citizen votes, condition the party preferences of Negroes as well. But over them all and under them all runs a group consciousness that in the final analysis sets the standards of political judgment for most Negroes. Neither North nor South have Negroes agreed unanimously on candidates, or parties, or issues, but one cannot read half a dozen copies of as many Negro newspapers and talk to half a dozen Negro voters without feeling the deep, unceasing preoccupation with race welfare that permeates the Negro community.

In their southern political leagues, Negro voters possess a means of shifting their support from one political party to another, just as from one primary candidate to another, in accord with group interests. Their maneuverability is enhanced by the fact that only a small minority of Negroes has been exposed to the deepening of party attachments that comes with repeated exercise of the ballot. The attitudes and actions of whites comprise a powerful external compulsion to Negro group identity. Fortified by all the internal compulsions, they produce citizens who think of themselves first as Negroes, and secondarily as brickmasons, or sharecroppers, or Democrats, or Republicans. As the CIO chairman in one southern state observed, his Negro members showed greater allegiance to all-Negro organizations than to the union. "A Negro is more influenced by his lodge than by his membership in the CIO." [1]

This condition will change in the South, as it has been changing outside the South, as Negroes become increasingly assimilated as equal citizens into the community. In the meantime, however, the condition governs importantly the impact on the parties of the new Negro politics.

We do not know for certain what Negroes have voted Democratic and Republican in the South. Analysis of precinct election results would give a line on the question, but adequate returns for units smaller than the county are difficult to obtain. Negroes themselves, however, unvaryingly testify that until the time of Franklin Roosevelt such of their number who voted in the South voted in the main for Republicans, and after 1932—as in states where their votes for president really counted [2]—a marked shift to Democratic ranks took place. In addition, the new Negro voters overwhelmingly tended Democratic, so that by the end of the 1940's the Democratic party had usurped the historic role of the Republican party as the party of the southern Negro.

The same factor that kept many unhappy southern whites hitched to the Democratic party attracted southern Negroes to it: They had to vote in the primaries to have a voice in state and local government. And the government closest to home has special importance for Negroes. Said one Negro leader, under the title, "A Frank Discussion of the Negro's Political Position in Florida":

And we say again that most of the evils that Florida Negroes suffer can be traced directly to these local officials. ... No matter who is elected president, we must go to our school board for better buildings and equipment. No matter who is elected president, we must look to our local officials for better roads, better streets, and better police protection.[3]

A statistical measure of the shift of Negroes to the Democratic party can be found in Florida, the only southern state that compiles registration figures that show party preferences among Negroes. Prior to 1944, Florida Negroes were registered more or less automatically as Republicans. Following the Supreme Court decision of that year, supervisors of registration permitted them, sometimes reluctantly, to register as Democrats. Of the 116,145 Negroes registered in 1950, only 8.4 per cent were listed as Republicans.

Negroes did not, of course, abandon Republican politics entirely. Aside from Mississippi, where they made up the faction recognized by the party's national organization, they participated sufficiently during the 1940's in Georgia, South Carolina, Florida, Louisiana, Tennessee, and Arkansas to earn them places on the state committees or as delegates to the national conventions. Their Republican preference arose principally out of two sources. One was a desire for patronage. An Arkansas Negro, whose political beliefs put him left of most Democrats, in 1947 explained his Republican connection by his thought that the GOP would gain the White House and he might receive some such post as district attorney in the Virgin Islands. A carryover of allegiance from the old days provided the other source. Among those wed by tradition to the party, the oldsters predominated. Younger Negroes reported that many elders sadly shook their heads at the brash, headstrong drive to thrust the Negro into politics, and Democratic politics at that.[4] They were little inclined, or able, however, to fight the trend, and offered a "negative opposition" generally ignored by their juniors and therefore productive on occasion of bitter personal and even family squabbles. In a few localities, usually where whites had competed for the Negro vote for a number of years, there could be found organized factions in the Negro community of which some voted Republican. There were Negro Republican clubs—usually inactive between elections—in places like Miami, Orlando, Little Rock, Nashville, and even Baton Rouge. Something of their effectiveness is suggested by the rueful comment of a white Republican in Nashville who had spent several decades in Tennessee Republican politics: "Nashville Negroes are Republicans up to the time they enter the voting booth and as soon as they leave it; but they vote Democratic while in the booth."

Negroes occupied fewer niches in the hierarchy of the Democratic than the Republican party, though white resistance to their participation in the governing of the party was breaking down. The Democratic party rules of Arkansas even provided that no Negro could be a candidate in a Democratic primary or hold a party office, but the 1950 state convention abandoned the provision, which was of doubtful legality anyway.[5] Negroes participated to a very limited extent in party conventions and party committees in a few states, but not often enough to be significant except as a portent. A handful showed up at the state conventions in North Carolina and Virginia. In 1950, two were elected to the Petersburg, Virginia, Central Democratic Committee, as earlier four were elected to the Columbia, South Carolina, city Democratic executive Committee.[6] A few found a part in the hierarchy of conventions and committees that governed the party in Texas.[7]

In most states the Negro political leagues interested themselves chiefly in the Democratic primaries, though they asserted no formal allegiance to either party. Georgia provided an exception, as the name of the Georgia Association of Citizens' Democratic Clubs implied. To affiliate with the association, members of the local clubs were supposed to subscribe to its principles, which seemed in essence merely an agreement to support the Democratic party. Another exception, the Arkansas Negro Democratic Association was formed in 1928 to support the vice presidential candidacy of Joseph T. Robinson. The by-laws read that "The object of this Association is... to unite Negroes who believe in the principles of the Democratic Party and who will work to promote its best welfare and expansion."[8] Its leader was reported, however, to be willing in later years to drop the "Democratic" if he could thereby lure influential Negro Republicans into the fold. In Texas, in addition to a Progressive Voters' League, Negroes formed a Texas Club of Democratic Voters.[9] In none of these states, however, did anything in the record indicate that these groups would blindly follow the party if their leaders felt the best interests of Negroes would be served otherwise.

The situation in Florida better represented the spirit of independence characteristic of the new Negro politics. Florida had a large enough Republican vote and a large enough Negro vote for the latter to mean something in the general elections of a few localities. Virginia and North Carolina were also states with many Republicans and many Negroes, but Negroes had been offended by exclusion from Republican activities. Not so in Florida, at least not so sufficiently to prejudice them deeply against Republican candidates. "We believe in the principle of 'men and measures', rather than blind allegiance to any one political party," said the officers of the Progressive Voters' League in an open letter dated May 24, 1947. Accordingly, in another open letter of October 21, 1948, the league, again through its officers, recommended for president, a Democrat; for United States representative from the fifth district, a Republican. This spirit of independent action was also clearly expressed in the attitude of South Carolina Negro leaders. Prior to 1948, South Carolina Democrats excluded Negroes from their primaries. Also, the Republican national leadership rebuffed a plea for aid in expanding the number of Negro voters, to the end of upsetting Democratic supremacy in the state, as not being "expedient." Rejected by both major parties, Negroes in the spring of 1944 formed a new party, the Progressive Democratic party, comprised almost entirely of their own race.[10] Republicans, including the chairman of the Richland County (Columbia) Republican Committee, played leading roles in the new party, the chief purpose of which was to gain entrance to the Democratic primaries. A leading Republican, long militant in the causes of her race, had helped draft the first platform of the Progressive Democratic party. Asked if her multiple loyalties were inconsistent, her answer was firm: "Through the years, my philosophy and my strategy in meeting any problem or challenge is 'strike as hard as you can, as fast as you can, in as many ways as you can.'"[11]

The problem, as Negro leaders in South Carolina and elsewhere saw it, was simply to gain for Negroes maximum benefits[12] through the effective exercise of political rights. They would support whatever party offered the greatest progress toward the goal.

In 1948 Negroes disagreed as to which party that was. The *Journal and Guide,* published in Norfolk and often called the most competently edited Negro paper in the country, supported Dewey. So did the *Afro-American,* published in Baltimore, with southern editions. Both papers had endorsed Smith in 1928. Yet Walter White, general secretary of the NAACP, bitterly denounced Dewey.[13] And Truman won many Negro votes by his civil rights recommendations, especially in the South, where the Dixiecrats campaigned.[14]

To anticipate the Negro's future party preferences and their effect on the South's party system is a tricky business. Yet certain reasonable expectations can be identified.

First of all, most Negroes like most whites will continue to ally themselves with one or the other of the two major parties. (The determination of Negroes to work for a redress of grievances through the constitutional framework has been clearly demonstrated by the failure of the Communist party to lure any substantial number of them to it.[15])

Second, there is no place in American national politics for the race issue as such. Wholly aside from questions of historic American principle, no major party can afford to bruise the political feelings of Negroes. They hold too many votes in too many places. Moreover, the requirements of United States foreign policy will increasingly spur the nation to document its faith in its own democratic proclamations by ensuring wider justice and greater equality for its citizens of all colors.

Third, the South's one-party system exerts compulsions on southern Negroes as well as whites to fight out their battles within established boundaries, that is, within the Democratic party.

Fourth, the great bulk of Negroes fall into the lower brackets of economic status and would seem the natural recruits of a liberal political party.[16]

Fifth, in the South, Negroes are most likely to vote together when their political rights are at issue, a condition likely to decrease, and when a member of their race is a candidate, a condition likely to increase. They tend to vote together also when their clearly defined economic and social interests are involved in an election.

Sixth, the right of Negroes to vote in primaries and elections free of substantial discrimination because of color will be maintained, and perhaps extended.

These reasonable expectations would seem to destine the bulk of southern Negro voters for the Democratic party. Barring a threat to the national security that disrupted party patterns altogether, most southern Negroes would continue to vote Democratic as long as that party remained generally more liberal than its rival, and as long as the Democratic party did not become marked as an anti-Negro party. The internal realignment of the parties since the 1930's, by which the Democratic party increasingly became a labor-liberal party, made these potentially disrupting influences unlikely. There was, however, a possibility.

When the Republicans once again acquired the responsibilities that go with control of the Federal government, they might push for legislation that posed them as the champions of civil rights, or even, conceivably, as liberals, in opposition to the Democrats, then dominated by their southern members. Such a development is conceivable, despite the inducements to "stay right" on race matters that confront the national conventions, presidential candidates, and northern local candidates of both parties. A shift of support on the part of Negro voters to the Republicans in some northern areas was reported by one observer in 1948, though prior to President Truman's belligerent stand for civil rights legislation. The death of F.D.R., the departure of Eleanor Roosevelt from active politics, the attitudes of southern Democrats, and the failure of the party in power to pass civil rights legislation were given as explanations.[17] That a Republican-Democratic combination might kill such legislation in Republican Congresses as it did in Democratic Congresses might not prevent the blame from falling on the outspoken southerners. Neither might the fact that southern Republicans were just as vociferous as any southern Democrats in opposing the Truman civil rights proposals.[18]

If Negroes lost faith in the desire or ability of the Democratic party as a whole to serve their cause, their votes might at times decide between Republican victory and defeat in the Upper South and some of the border states. If southern Republican whites accepted Negroes into their fold, as they had not in the past, and recognized their political demands as part of the party's program, as seemed unlikely, they could perhaps in the Upper South hold their votes in uneasy combination with the hereditary upland agrarians and the urban conservatives. In the states of the Deep South, where there are few Republicans, a flood of black voters into the Republican party would lead to a Negro-dominated organization, discourage the affiliation of whites, and continue the party as a somewhat larger but nevertheless ineffective minority in presidential politics. Conditions that would lead southern Negroes to vote Republican—a stand-pat attitude by the Democratic party on racial and economic matters—are the same conditions that would satisfy the conservative southerners in the Democratic party and thereby reduce their incentive to desert the party.

These things mean that among Negroes, as among whites, a national Democratic party consistently liberal in economic and racial policy is crucial to the development of two-party politics in the South. A driving liberalism, spearheaded by the northern wing of the party, would insure the loyalty of southern Negroes, at least temporarily swelling the already swollen Democratic ranks. Accommodations to Negroes in the internal management of the party would necessarily follow, but given the numerical superiority of the whites, would probably not produce violent disruptions. At the same time, the Republican party would be spared the revival of the black stigma, and no obstacle would be created to the migration to it of conservative Democrats. Persons who are conservative on economic matters frequently tend to be conservative on all matters, including racial policies, hence the creation of a liberal and a conservative party would be facilitated. Negroes would strengthen the liberal factions in the Democratic primaries, hence aid in wresting state offices and seats in Congress from conservative Democrats. If southern liberal factions captured the party for an extended period, conservatives would feel a powerful incentive to seek a party of their own, one from which they could call on outside support—the existing Republicans—and fight with improved chances of success.

Some might argue that the prospect of creating a Negro "balance of power," of the kind prevailing in several northern states, would deter white southerners in any steps that would bring the parties to more nearly equal strength. A well-organized, maneuverable group of Negro voters would surely wield a balance of power if the opportunity arose. Similar opportunities seem to exist within the Democratic primaries, however, between liberal and conservative coalitions. The question is no longer whether Negroes will wield political influence, but how much and for what purposes.

While retaining group consciousness for some time to come, ultimate assimilation into the Democratic party most probably lies ahead for southern Negroes. The strengthening of the liberal elements in the party would in the long run encourage the shift of conservative Democrats to the Republican party and encourage the growth of competitive party politics.

the future
———————————

19

THE TWO-PARTY SOUTH

IN HIS FAREWELL ADDRESS, WASHINGTON WARNED HIS COUNTRYMEN against the dangers of political parties and especially against parties founded on geographical "discriminations." If he gazes today from a heavenly eminence, he must be struck by the irony of politics in his native South. It would be hard to imagine a party stemming more directly from sectional interests than the Democratic party of the South. Within the South, it would be hard to imagine democratic government conducted with less effective use of political parties.

Since the first president's time, we have come to look upon parties as essential and desirable adjuncts to the constitutional framework that he and his contemporaries created. In contrast to many countries with democratic forms of government, the United States has enjoyed a notable degree of success with its party system. The parties failed to prevent the Civil War, but the crisis was so serious that they could hardly have been expected to do so. With this exception, the party system has provided a peaceful means of reconciling, deflecting, or repressing the ambitions and pressures that create disputes wherever men live together. In doing so, they have contributed to a generally systematic and successful way for men to tackle their common problems.

Many persons do not agree, however, that the South's political health depends on the development of genuine party politics. Some feel the expression and fulfillment of political needs are adequately achieved through the rival factions of the Democratic party.[1] Others are simply satisfied with their place in the present system. Doubtless, some of these approve because they believe that generally the prosperous benefit at the expense of the less prosperous.* Most of those actively averse to a strong second party, however, are governed by the classic reticence of politicians —or indeed of anyone else—to change one situation in which they have a secure position for another in which their position may be inferior, or at best uncertain.

The volition of politicians and sophisticates, who think they know why they do what they do, provides but one source of initiative in the process of politics. The future of southern politics will be shaped in relatively small part by individual acts of will. Rather, the future depends basically on the effects of deep-running social trends on the masses of voters.

In studying politics, students have tried to learn what motivations voters respond to. Why do they vote the way they do? Are they concerned solely about economic welfare, or are their choices affected by such things as ethnic origin, national origin, religious preference, family prejudice, the looks of the candidates, and friendship? If many motivations operate simultaneously, how do they play off against each other to produce a net decision for or against? At the risk of reducing a complex truth to a simple falsehood, we shall say that the study of these questions has revealed the importance of two broad types of influences over voters, one set rational and the other nonrational.[2] Voters not only follow their "logical interests," as New York laborers did when they voted for the author of the Wagner Act; they also vote by prejudice, or habit, or enticement, or in ignorance. The complex combinations of motives that affect political behavior make political predictions extremely hazardous. One hardly knows what factor—or determinant, as the specialists say—most influences a person. To predict with certainty the differing effects of large

---

[2] See chapter 1, above, pp. 10-13.

numbers of determinants on large numbers of voters is hardly possible with our present knowledge of human behavior. To do so may never be possible, given the spirit and will of man.

An attempt must be made, however, if we would glimpse the South's future. We may think of two sets of influences bearing on southerners, one that encourages the growth of a second party and one that retards it. In this book we have sought to identify the two sets, the forces of change and the forces of stability. Both sets include rational and nonrational elements.

The practical importance of conscious and presumably reasonable choices by voters is demonstrated in every election. There is always a group of persons undecided as to how they shall vote, or whether they shall vote. There are enough of them over the nation to make every presidential election a slam-bang affair in which the major parties make fervent appeals to what are conceived to be the immediate interests, and other susceptibilities, of undecided voters. The techniques of analysis employed by students of politics do not yet permit accurate measurement of the response that voters make to the individual appeals extended to them in a party's program. Anyone can plainly see, nevertheless, that dynamic movements such as the New Deal cause identifiable groups, like northern Negroes, to switch their customary allegiances in order to back measures beneficial to them. Moreover, the course of great issues like the free coinage of silver or the tariff reveal that the majority of voters in a geographical area support the party which most favors their views. At the same time, parties tend over the long haul to take stands in accord with the sentiments of the areas where they find their most important strength.

Political analysts have also noted many instances of seemingly nonrational voting behavior, or at least voting behavior in which the rational incentives are so obscure as to make it appear devoid of logic. Traditional party loyalty is one of the political determinants that often appears nonrational.[3] A westerner votes Republican because back East his father and grandfather voted Republican. Large states and tiny precincts prefer the same party, elections on end, without regard to candidates or issues. The origins of such behavior, and the institutional conditions that encourage it, can be identified as we have tried to do in this book with regard to southern politics. But there seems to be an additional, self-perpetuating quality of habitual voting that must be acknowledged in any interpretation of political conduct. Dayton McKean points to little groups of Democrats in New Hampshire who trace their political lineage to Andrew Jackson. Today, their economic interests appear the same as those of neighbors who consistently vote Republican. Individual Democrats have no clear idea what the Jacksonian battles were about, yet they pay them homage every time they vote.[4]

Habitual voting produces strange paradoxes among southern Republicans. At the time Jackson was winning the seemingly imperishable loyalty of Mr. McKean's Democrats in New Hampshire, he found great support among the small farmers and rugged frontiersmen of the Appalachian highlands—the antecedents of the folks who today vote with equally imperishable loyalty for the Republican party. Then as now, these uplanders constituted a yeomanry of small farmers differing in outlook from the large landholders of the lowlands.[5] A strain of protest runs through the history of their politics. As Democrats, they resisted secession; later, as Republicans, they often allied with the Populists. Their Democratic mountain neighbors (often the Republicans themselves voted in Democratic primaries) have supported anti-Bourbon factions of the Democratic party. These mountain Republicans are the sort of people to benefit from government regulation of large businesses, from easy agricultural credit, from public expenditures for education and public welfare. And they turn up voting for the party of Dewey and Taft in preference to the party of Roosevelt and Truman.

The Democratic party holds anomalies, too. Financiers, businessmen, manufacturers, plantation operators, other southerners whom one would suppose hostile to high taxes, public regulation, and the demands of organized industrial and agricultural labor, show up voting for a high-tax party that more closely approximates a labor party than any in the national history.

Anomalies of this kind have characterized major American

parties since the Civil War; they are familiar to all observers. Sometimes they arise from the fact that major parties solicit the same groups of uncommitted voters, hence tend to make appeals that land persons of similar interests in different parties and persons of different interests in the same party.[6] More important, however, is another explanation. The makeup of the two parties grew out of a great national crisis when the decisive issues were slavery, secession, and reunion. The Republican party originated around a single attitude, an attitude toward the place of the Negro in American life. It embraced a wide range of political elements, many of which a short time before had bitterly fought each other in opposing political parties; and those discordant groups, like bankers and midwestern farmers, continued their war-born alliance. The Democratic party provided the Confederate South with a refuge in which unity against a common foe overrode factors that divided the region. The great crisis of civil war, with its attendant cruelties, recriminations, and seared pride, seemed to "fix" party allegiances in the South, and elsewhere in the nation. In a way, the basic composition of the parties froze, or more accurately, the party affiliation of many citizens froze. States and counties, and sub-sections of them, ever after squared off against each other in recurrent patterns of party strength. The composition of a party does evolve, as we have emphasized in this book. But the fidelity to party of large blocs of voters in the face of changing economic and social conditions, and despite changing issues from election to election, makes it possible to predict the political behavior of a large part of the electorate. Louis Bean has documented the consistencies in presidential voting of states and sections outside the South as well as within it, apparently a fundamental of our politics.[7]

The phenomenon is not confined to the United States, nor to Anglo-Saxon nations. In France, the geographical distribution of political tendencies found in the Third Republic had descended unbroken from former times. André Siegfried even traced liberal and conservative attitudes in western France to "patriots" and "aristocrats" of the Revolution. "The pretended fickle Frenchman," said he, "holds to his political opinions just as the Englishman."[8] France had, in the words of another, "a party system based on historical memories rather than on hard economic facts," party formations which were like "luminous rays of those stars whose light only reaches us some hundred years after the star itself is extinguished."[9] The fact that great social traumas like the French Revolution and the American Civil War fix the political outlook and party affiliation of large sections of the public for long periods of time may, incidentally, modify some of the assumptions that underlie our institutions of representative government.

In speculating on the future of southern politics, we cannot measure exactly the force of the habitual Democratic preferences of the region, nor the forces that tend to sustain them or break them down. There is no way, that is, to weigh or quantify the intensity of political tradition and the other determinants of voting behavior. We cannot find a lowest common denominator of the forces of change and stability, add up the values of each, and read a result in the difference between the two totals, like an answer in mathematics.[10] We can, nevertheless, draw on experience and weigh roughly the probabilities.

Professor Arthur N. Holcombe has given a comprehensive interpretation of the American party battle. He discerned a strong tendency toward a geographic sectionalism in politics, gradually modified by rising urbanism.[11] He studied the behavior of sections in presidential and congressional politics and concluded that over a great deal of United States history political parties were made up of combinations of sectional strength. Each section had fairly specific interests growing out of the type of soil, climatic conditions, and agriculture. The political centers of gravity of the parties were found in different sections, and the parties competed for the support of the other sections where the balance of power was more nearly even. With the growth of cities, the preponderant economic and social interests ceased to have simple geographic sectional identifications. At all times, of course, all sections have divided within themselves, so that a sectional sentiment really meant the sentiment of an effective majority within a section. A study of metropolitan voting in presidential elections published in 1949 by Samuel J. Eldersveld seemed to confirm Professor Holcombe's observation of a shift in the balance of political power from the country to the cities.[12]

The evolution of southern politics fits the general contours of this thesis. The South, and the political sub-sections within it, developed stable political affections because of sectional characteristics, chiefly the presence or absence of Negroes, rooted ultimately in the soil and climate and in the types of agriculture they made profitable. Changes in the nature and importance of the historic rural, agricultural society have changed the bases of political controversy in the South—as well as in the nation.

Several layers of causes and effects separate the fundamental underpinnings of political life—like the nature of the economy—from the year-to-year conduct of voters in elections. Basic social and economic changes require time before they work their full political effects. The political lag that results is expressed largely in the traditionalism discussed above, and reflects the failure of voters and politicians to perceive and to react readily to new conditions and to the new issues implicit in them. The lag in the South arises from many sources. Families and friends influence the political views of the young. Prejudices and pressures that induce conformity to group behavior reinforce those views. Pride of difference between adversaries tends to deepen loyalty to the banners under which they fight, in this case party labels. In the confusions of the American two-party system, the frequent inability of voters to see clearly what is involved in party controversies tends to increase the power of the party label. In the South, the procedures and institutions of politics discourage the growth of a party to rival that already in power. Those enjoying superiority draw party rules, election laws, legislative districts—employ any legal device—to stabilize their advantage. Those in the minority party who enjoy privilege seek also to stabilize their advantages, advantages that would be lost were the competitive position of the party radically altered. They ignore opportunities, repress the enthusiasm of insurgents in their own ranks, devote themselves to the exploitation of the status quo. Moreover, concern about the social, economic, and political position of the

Negro, the twentieth-century form of the slavery issue, leads some southerners to desire the maintenance of a political common front vis-a-vis the rest of the country. These obstacles to Republican growth in the South have been spelled out in detail in previous chapters—and they are legion.

A basic institutional modification, for example, in the way of electing the president or the Congress, could change the form of southern politics. Aside from such a prospect, the source of any broad change lies in economic and social developments that underlie southern attitudes. A change in the position of the Democrats might come gradually, or suddenly as a political explosion—as a minor social trauma that would break up and reset political allegiances.

A crisis of a sort occurred in the Dixiecratic fracas of 1948. The national convention and the presidential candidate of the Democratic party defied the wishes of parts of the South; they abandoned passive support for the view that Negro rights should be protected solely by state and local governments. Southern solidarity within the Democratic party had originated in a desire for local autonomy in racial matters, so the bolt-revolt seemed a logical consequence. Two things about the Dixiecratic action, however, qualified its significance. First, the success of the 1948 candidates was relatively mild; and, second, the inability of either major party to adopt the Dixiecrats' ultraconservative attitude toward the Negro would force them to continue as an independent political group. Though racial tensions were tightly drawn, as attested by the fact that Thurmond and Wright attracted popular support chiefly in the black belts, the only states they carried were those in which they appropriated the Democratic name. In more than half the states of the South they trailed the Republicans. In the future, the Dixiecrats might carry on in a few localities and even affect the outcome of a close presidential race. But in the future their local antagonists would guard more alertly the right to the Democratic label.

The nature of Dixiecratic leadership was a more important aspect of the movement than its successes and failures in 1948. Those who spurred the movement were almost invariably adherents of conservative factions in the Democratic politics of their states. Planters, financiers, industrialists—their argument with the New Dealer and his successor did not arise alone from worries about civil rights for Negroes; they disagreed on labor legislation, economic controls, taxation, Federal jurisdiction, and many another domestic issue. Some of them had participated in abortive revolts in 1944 and earlier. In 1948 they found a political tool in the furor over civil rights.

This book expresses the belief that in the long run southern conservatives will find neither in a separatist group nor in the Democratic party an adequate vehicle of political expression. If this is true, they must turn to the Republican party. A separate group cannot reasonably expect to influence the making of national policy more than conservative southerners already do in Congress. It is precisely if and when they lose this avenue of political expression that they will feel greatest compulsion to break away, to seek redress through the Republican party. Such developments depend essentially on the evolving nature of the South and the evolving nature of the American party system.

Developments in the economy and social organization of the South point to an ultimate strengthening of the liberal factions of the Democratic party. The old, relatively homogeneous agricultural South is giving way to a South of diversity. The diversification of agriculture, the growth of industry, the change in agricultural methods, population shifts, the rise of cities and decline of ruralism, the growth of union labor, the political organization of labor and of Negroes, and all the rest, create divisive influences within the South that sharpen differences over economic and social policies and cut into the traditional political domination of the region by the black belts. They also create new relationships and dependencies between plantation owners and plantation laborers, between creditors and debtors, between manufacturers and laborers, between blacks and whites.

The crucial question is whether these changes shake the hold in which conservative politicians and their backers have held the Democratic party in much of the South a good part of the time since Reconstruction. The answer may depend ultimately more on successes in organizing southern laborers and stimulating them to political action than on any other factor. Such groups, joined by lower income groups generally, including Negroes, could form the anchor of a cohesive liberal faction of the Democratic party in every southern state. In several of the states, they could build on existing factional combinations that reflect long-standing political divisions in the electorate. Competing for the large middle-class vote, it would appear that over a period of time the liberal factions might build a stable numerical superiority within the Democratic party. Should they achieve this goal, even in part, in the states where there are important numbers of traditional Republicans, they would give conservative southerners an incentive to seek refuge and allies in the Republican party. Conservative Democrats would carry with them to that party badly needed financial resources, energy, and impetus. The Labor party in Great Britain was much aided in its early years, when victories were slow, by the war chests of the labor unions affiliated with it. Persons of wealth in and out of the South have the means to sustain the Republican party in a long struggle for victory. The development in the South of an urban middle class—in accord with the Holcombe thesis for the nation—susceptible to the blandishments of both a liberal and a conservative party, would give the Republican party a potential source of votes in those states where it could achieve some kind of competitive equality.

These speculations hold, even for the Upper South and the rim states, only if it proves increasingly difficult to divide the expected adherents of liberal factions by appeals to race prejudice. Otherwise, the Populist experience would be repeated. To assume this is optimistic, to say the least, in the face of recent Georgia and North Carolina events. But the prognosis rests on the conviction, elaborated earlier in this book, that the relative decline in the southern Negro population and the increased education of all southerners will continue to moderate ancient prejudices. In part, the suggestion of a liberal Democratic politics in the South depends also on the assumption that lower economic groups, white and black, will vote in increasingly large proportions, with a fair degree of political unity, in response to sustained exertions in political education.

If some of these things come to pass, they will surely come in fragments, with strife, and perhaps in unforeseen ways. Yet there can be little doubt that much of the South is moving closer to competitive party politics. The changes that occur will contribute to more representative, and more responsive, state and local government; and all citizens in the South will have a more straightforward—and more effective—means of influence in national politics.

APPENDICES

Appendix I

SOURCES OF DIXIECRATIC STRENGTH, 1948

The most noticeable evidence that something was afoot in southern politics appeared in the Dixiecratic movement of 1948. In the following pages, the votes received by Governor Thurmond in the presidential election of that year are analyzed.

The general conclusion from the analysis has been expressed several times in the foregoing chapters: The bulk of Dixiecratic votes came from whites who live in close proximity to large numbers of Negroes—that is, from the whites in the black belts. In most parts of the South, a positive correlation existed between the percentage of the total vote received by Thurmond and the percentage of the total population found to be Negro in 1940. It was assumed, from empirical evidence, that only a few Negroes voted (when any at all voted) in the rural areas where they constitute a large share of the population—the rural black belts. All the votes cast in those counties were therefore attributed to whites. It was further assumed that Negroes did not vote in sufficient quantities, even in other areas, to upset the general conclusion drawn regarding the behavior of white voters. Undoubtedly, however, some of the votes cast against Thurmond, especially in urban areas, were cast by Negroes. In these places, his percentage of the total votes was lowered by the Negro ballots. Consequently, the disparity in attitudes among whites in areas of differing racial composition are probably not quite as great as the analyses suggest.

In all of the states, efforts were made to identify relationships between Dixiecratic strength and factors like urbanism, economic status, and a Republican decline. Such correlations as deepen our understanding are reported. More refined methods of correlational analysis, however, might detect other relationships, or at least would measure more sensitively those turned up by the relatively simple statistical procedures used here.[1]

Most of the voters who backed the Dixiecrats—though not necessarily most of the initiators of the movement—are the southerners most firmly wed traditionally to the Democratic party. They live in the areas that favored secession in 1861, that proved most faithful to Al Smith in 1928, that all along have given the Democratic party its greatest majorities. When speculating on potential sources of southern Republican votes, as we have done in this book, this fact should be remembered.

Let us start by comparing Thurmond's vote in each southern state with its Negro population, shown on the opposite page.

The top four states—and they were the ones where the Dixiecrats used the Democratic label—lie in the Deep South. Mississippi, with the largest percentage of Negroes, headed the list by giving Thurmond 87.2 per cent of its votes. South Carolina, next

[1] In a senior thesis for the Department of Social Relations of Harvard University, David M. Heer studied Thurmond's 1948 South Carolina vote by means of partial correlation. He concluded: "... the percentage vote for Thurmond in the various South Carolina counties, all other relevant factors being equal, varied in direct proportion to the percent of Negro population present in the county." Also, he confirmed the difference in sensitivity on racial matters between whites in urban and farming areas: "... the percentage vote for Thurmond among the various South Carolina counties varied inversely, all other relevant factors being equal, with the percentage of urban and rural non-farm persons to the total White population among the various counties."—Caste, Class, and Local Loyalty as Determining Factors in South Carolina Politics (1950), pp. 93-94.

DIXIECRATIC VOTING, 1948

	Estimated percentage Negro, 1950[a]	Percentage of vote for Thurmond, 1948
Mississippi	45.5	87.2
South Carolina	38.9	72.0
Louisiana	33.1	49.1
Alabama	32.1	79.8
Georgia	30.9	20.3
North Carolina	26.6	8.8
Arkansas	22.4	16.5
Virginia	22.2	10.3
Florida	21.8	15.6
Tennessee	16.1	13.4
Texas	11.5	9.3[b]

[a] Based on preliminary estimates of nonwhite population. See Table 21, p. 150.
[b] Incomplete official returns.

in black population, gave him 72.0 per cent. In Alabama, the only state in which Truman did not appear on the ballot, Thurmond drew 79.8 per cent; in Louisiana, he polled 49.1 per cent. In the other states, the Thurmond vote descended roughly in accord with the decrease in Negro population. In North Carolina and Virginia, where something resembling genuine party competition takes place and the parties exhibit something like a corporate spirit, major party rivalry squeezed down the number of dissenters, to account at least partially for the lower Dixiecratic vote than might otherwise have been expected. Analysis of the county-by-county vote in each southern state confirms the over-all conclusion drawn from the comparison of states.

Texas. This state provides a particularly useful analysis. In 1944, an anti-Roosevelt slate of "Democratic" electors, the Texas Regulars, appeared on the ballot. The Regulars represented a dissent from the national Democratic party on matters of general policy that was found in other states as well. Analytical comparison of the 1944 and 1948 presidential contests reveals the different bases of the two protest movements and provides a chance for close analysis of Democratic dissatisfactions.

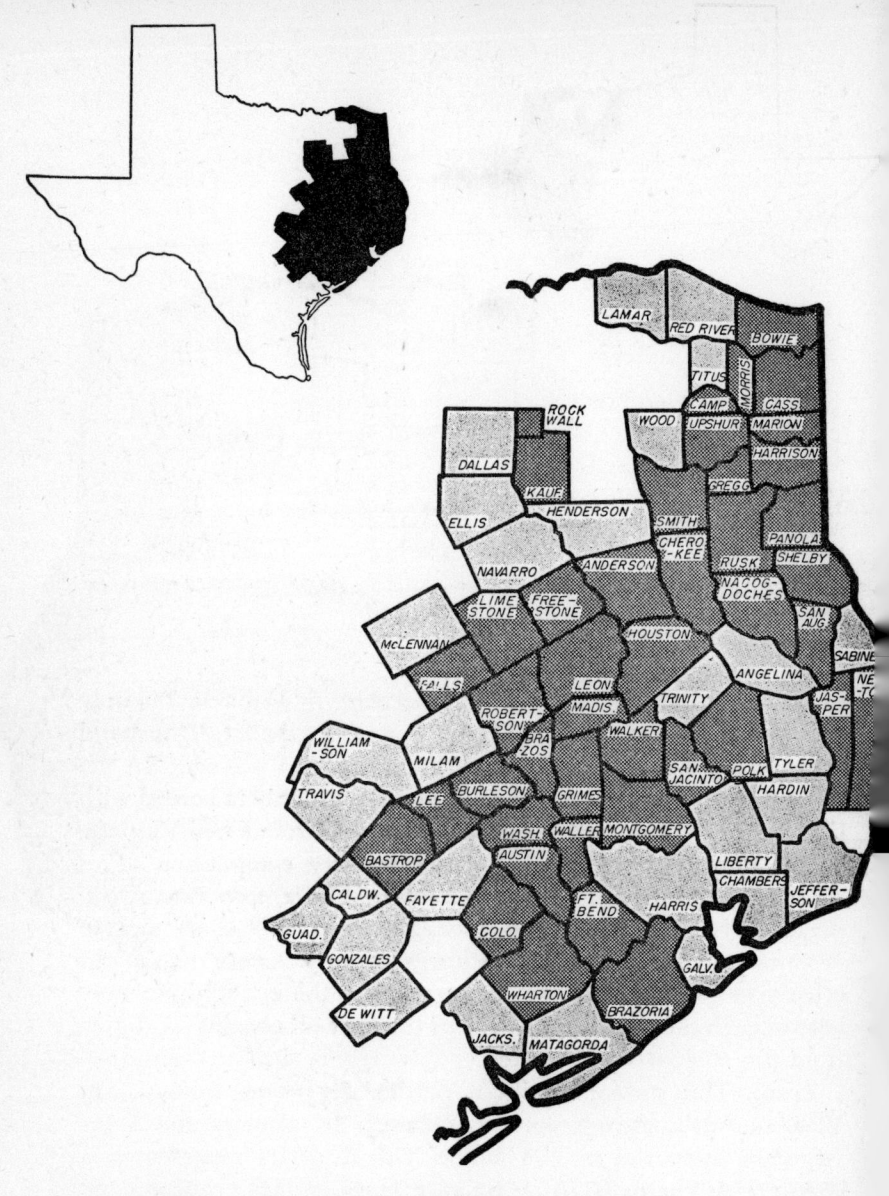

PERCENTAGE OF POPULATION NEGRO, 1940

■ 25 per cent and over

▨ 15-24.9 per cent

FIGURE 8: Texas Dixiecr

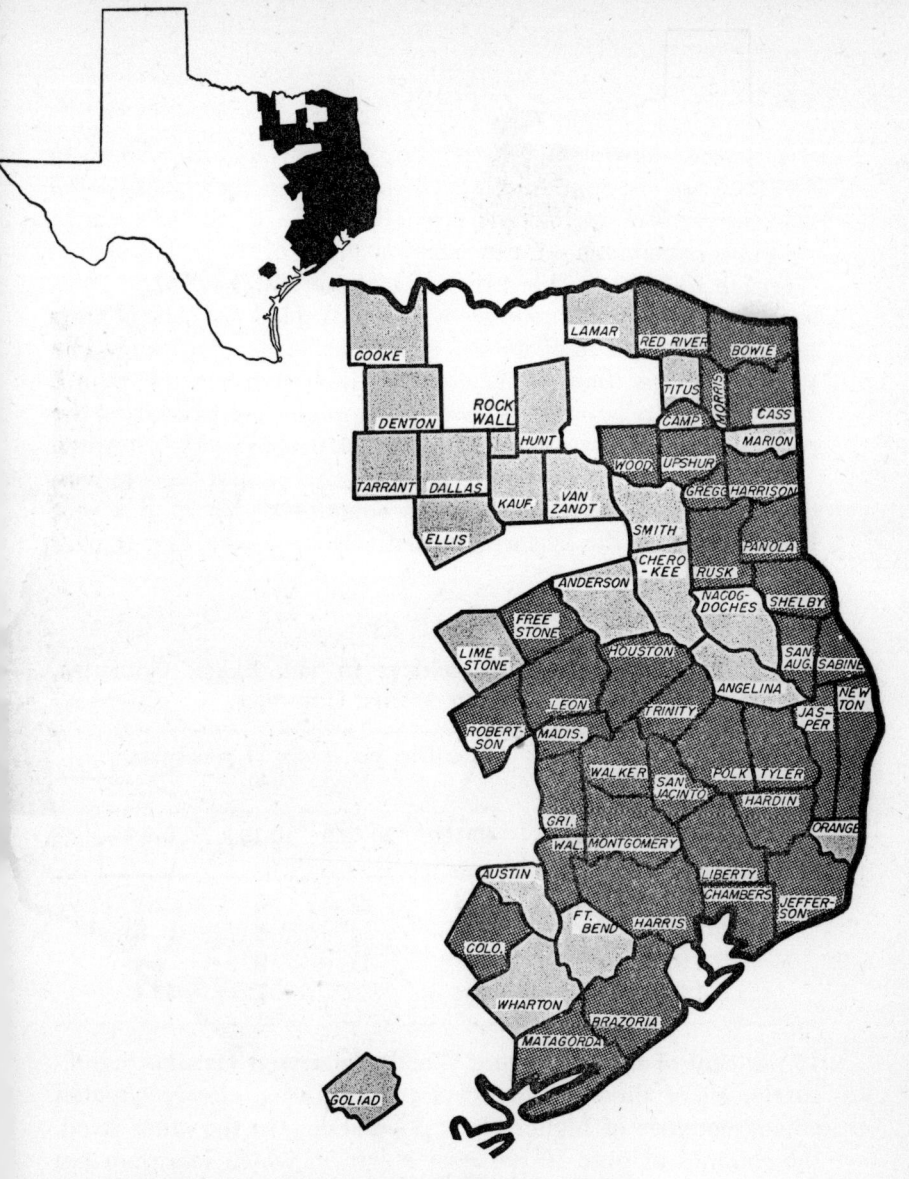

PERCENTAGE OF TOTAL PRESIDENTIAL VOTE
FOR THURMOND, 1948

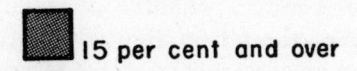

- 15 per cent and over
- 10-14.9 per cent

AME FROM THE BLACK BELT

APPENDIX I

Figure 8, showing the distribution of the Negro population in 1940 and the distribution of Thurmond's vote in 1948, displays the concentration of Dixiecratic strength in the black belt. Of 13 counties containing 40 per cent or more of their population Negro in 1940, 12 gave a relatively high percentage of their votes to Thurmond. Of 170 counties with less than 10 per cent of their population Negro in 1940, 167 gave Thurmond a relatively low percentage, less than 10 per cent, and 114 gave him less than 5 per cent. The relationship between the presence of blacks and the presence of Dixiecrats was relatively sensitive, as Table 22 shows.

The aberrations, however, bear examination, and tend to confirm the general thesis. The three counties under 20 per cent Negro that gave the Dixiecrat a relatively large vote, that is, over

TABLE 22

TEXAS DIXIECRATS WERE STRONGEST IN THE BLACK COUNTIES, WEAKEST IN THE WHITE COUNTIES

Percentage of total vote Dixiecratic, 1948	Counties: percentage of population Negro, 1940			
	40-100	20-39.9	10-19.9	0-9.9
15-100	12	22	3	
10-14.9	1	11	8	3
5-9.9		11	9	53
0-4.9			7	114

15 per cent of the total, were Wood, Tyler, and Hardin. Significantly, all of these lie in extreme east Texas, closely situated among counties of higher black population. On the other hand, the counties of over 10 per cent Negro in which less than ten voters out of a hundred voted for Thurmond lay almost invariably along the western edge of the black belt. More than a fourth of them were found among the "German" counties of traditionally Republican inclination. Most of the others abutted the German areas or had their race consciousness softened by closeness to

the great white expanse of west Texas to which they were joined. One of these counties in the north, Navarro, was the home of the late Governor Beaufort Jester, who opposed the revolt. Another was Hill County, home of Jester's loyal cohort who served as chairman of the state Democratic executive committee, Robert W. Calvert.

In 1948, at the biennial September convention of the Texas Democratic party—called the "governor's convention" as distinguished from the "May convention" held every presidential year—the delegations from the counties containing Houston, Dallas, and Fort Worth attracted much attention by their anti-Truman sympathies. In the process by which liberal forces captured the convention, these delegations were ejected and became the symbols of the revolt against Truman. At the same time, many prominent and articulate Dixiecratic leaders hailed from the large cities. The two conditions suggested that concern over civil rights and Harry Truman might run along with concentrations of urban population. Inspection of the vote reveals, however, that vocal urban conservatives rather than numerous urban voters generally led the Dixiecratic movement. Meaningful variations did not appear in the strength registered by Thurmond in counties of varying degrees of urbanism when the Negro population was similar.[2] Counties wholly rural and counties varying widely in degrees of urbanism appeared seemingly at random among the strongest and weakest Dixiecratic counties.

Dissensions among Texas Democrats appeared in the three presidential campaigns prior to 1948. The "Constitutional Democrats of Texas" were formed in August, 1936, under the leadership

[2] For instance, the 1940 Negro population of Harris, Galveston, and Jefferson counties was 20.2, 21.8, and 23.3 per cent, respectively. The population of each of these counties was 70 per cent or more urban in 1940. There were no others of corresponding urbanism and Negro population. They gave Thurmond 16.3, 6.7, and 15.2 per cent of their votes. There were eight other counties between 20.2 and 23.3 per cent Negro. They were, with their percentage for Thurmond and with their 1940 urban percentage: Ellis, 10.2 (33.0 urban); Gonzales, 8.5 (18.1 urban); Milam, 8.4 (15.2 urban); Red River, 16.1 (13.8 urban); Fayette, 8.1 (8.7 urban); Sabine, 16.6 (wholly rural); Trinity, 19.0 (wholly rural); Chambers, 21.5 (wholly rural).

of W. B. Hamblen. John Henry Kirby, sometime lumber baron, and Joseph Bailey, Jr., son of a United States senator famed in an earlier day for allegedly close relations with financial interests, took active parts in anti-New Deal movements outside the Democratic party. In Roosevelt's heyday, however, with Cactus Jack Garner on the ballot, there was little chance of revolt in Texas. More serious motions of dissatisfaction were forestalled in 1940 when leaders of the Roosevelt and opposition groups agreed that Texas should give favorite son support to Garner for the presidential nomination, while the May convention of Texas Democrats endorsed the Administration. But in 1944 matters came to a showdown. Conservative forces, among them the leaders of the earlier defections, dominated the May Democratic convention which names delegates to the national convention and which traditionally has named the party's presidential electors. Before the September convention it became apparent that Democratic electors selected in May would not vote for Roosevelt in the electoral college though he be the party's nominee. The September convention named a new slate and before the squabble was unravelled there appeared on the ballot a slate of Democratic electors pledged to the President and a slate of "Texas Regular" electors unpledged but bound to oppose Roosevelt.[3]

There were references in the 1944 controversy to the meddling activities of the national party in the racial affairs of the South, but the major attack on the New Deal was directed at its economic policies and its alleged philosophy of centralism in government. The emergence of the Texas Regular movement reflected a division within the Democratic party along lines of economic philosophy, if one reads correctly the campaign hullabaloo. Latent in the dissension was the makings of a real two-party contest for the Texas electoral votes, although in 1944 the Regulars and the Republicans were unable to get together on a common slate of electors.[4]

Though the leadership of the Regulars in 1944 and the Dixie-

[3] Stanley Schneider, The Texas Regular Party of 1944. (Master's thesis, University of Chicago, 1948), pp. 44-46.
[4] *Ibid.*, pp. 104-5.

crats in 1948 overlapped, the voters who responded were vastly different—suggesting that the spokesmen of the two protests were using such votes as they could find and did not arrive at their positions of leadership solely on a ground swell. The Texas Regular vote was not concentrated in the black belt. The slate polled 11.8 per cent of the state vote. Of 61 counties in which it received more than 12.5 per cent of the votes, 25 were scattered across Texas to the west of the Dixiecratic counties shown in Figure 8. There were 37 counties in which the Regulars received more than 15 per cent of the votes. Their percentages of population that were Negro in 1940 varied as follows:

40-100 per cent	4 counties
30-39.9 per cent	5 counties
20-29.9 per cent	12 counties
10-19.9 per cent	1 county
5-9.9 per cent	5 counties
0-4.9 per cent	10 counties

Looking at the returns another way, many areas where the Regulars were weak were areas with few Negroes, a fact suggesting that usually counties with a relatively large proportion of Negroes did give the Regulars at least a modicum of their votes. The Regulars received less than 5 per cent of the vote in 22 counties. These counties had the following percentages of their population made up of Negroes in 1940:

20-29.9 per cent	1 county
10-19.9 per cent	1 county
5-9.9 per cent	3 counties
0-4.9 per cent	17 counties

In only 59 of Texas's 254 counties was the Regular vote less than 5 per cent or more than 15 per cent of the total vote cast; which fact in itself discloses that the Regulars' appeal, in so far as it went, was a fairly general one geographically.

The Dixiecrats drew only slightly, if at all, from Republicans, because their strength was for the most part concentrated in counties with many Negroes, the areas of traditional Democratic allegiance. If the 1944 revolt was one rooted in economic attitudes, however, it would be reasonable to expect the conservative faction, the Regulars, to draw from the Republicans. Table 23 displays the counties in which the Regulars cast more than 20 per cent of the votes. In almost every instance the Republican percentage dipped sharply in 1944 as compared with 1940 and 1948, suggesting that the Regulars drew at least some of their support from normally Republican voters, in all probability from the fringe Democrats best called "presidential Republicans." [5]

TABLE 23

THE TEXAS REGULARS DREW VOTES FROM THE REPUBLICANS IN 1944

Counties of highest Texas Regular vote, 1944	Texas Regulars, 1944	Republican candidate in: 1940	1944	1948
Washington	52.2	56.3	13.3	50.9
Austin	39.2	49.9	19.4	44.0
Midland	32.0	25.2	10.3	36.9
Colorado	30.2	41.1	20.7	28.5
Matagorda	26.0	23.2	13.4	30.8
Menard	22.3	17.6	8.6	28.6
Lee	21.2	54.7	35.3	21.9
Fayette	20.8	48.4	26.8	32.8
Somervell	20.5	20.6	14.0	15.6
Harris	20.3	22.1	11.4	35.2
Smith	20.2	14.2	9.8	28.1
San Jacinto	20.1	13.5	7.4	13.7
STATE	11.8	19.0	16.8	24.6

[5] See pp. 64-65. Only in Lee County did the Republican vote continue to go down from 1944 to 1948. Though the Republicans were relatively weak all over Texas in 1932 and 1936, it might be pointed out that in the former year Lee County gave Hoover only 5.7 per cent of its votes and in the latter year gave Landon but 19.0 per cent of them.

The ten counties in which the Regulars were weakest, generally more heavily Democratic than those in the table, show no such consistent Republican decline in 1944.[6]

If, as has been suggested in this book, there are portents of a gradually increasing division in sentiment among Democrats in the South based on broad differences in economic philosophy, the bulk of Dixiecratic voters did not express the division in Texas, where just four years before it had assumed its most concrete form in the Texas Regulars. Rather, the Dixiecrats constituted a throwback, a revolt in reverse, among race-conscious whites.

Arkansas. The States' Rights Democrats, as the Dixiecrats prefer to be called, were led in Arkansas by the delta planter-corporation wing of the Democratic party. The initiative was retained from the outset by the officers of the Free Enterprise Association, an organization of plantation operators, Little Rock corporation executives, and their attorneys, with headquarters in Marianna in Lee County (63.3 per cent Negro in 1940).[7] Governor "Business Ben" Laney made vocal his opposition to Federal civil rights legislation but equivocated so confusingly in his stand on bolting the party that no one could predict where he would be found next. Finally, in October 1948 he accepted the post of Dixiecratic state chairman.[8] Moderate, loyal Democrats like Governor-

[6] There was no discernible correlation between urbanism and the strength of the Regulars. Counties with large cities were among their strong and weak supporters alike. Some hint of an economic correlation grows from a comparison of motor vehicle registrations. The median number of persons per motor vehicle in the twelve counties casting their highest vote for the Regulars was 4.11; the median number in the ten weakest Regular counties was 5.56. The suggestion that the counties of Regular strength were a little more prosperous than those in which the Regulars were weak should be taken with considerable caution in view of the factors which might be expected to affect the number of vehicles in a county, such as the degree of urbanism and the kind of rural economy.

[7] The most indefatigable Dixiecrat was the association's executive secretary, John L. Daggett, of Marianna. The association was largely responsible for the adoption of Arkansas' "right-to-work" amendment in 1944.—*Arkansas Gazette* (Little Rock), January 17, August 27, September 16, 1948.

[8] *Ibid.*, October 9, 1948.

nominate McMath, Representative Brooks Hays, and the editor of the *Arkansas Gazette* led in support of the regular ticket.[9]

When the votes were in, Thurmond's counties of greatest strength etched an area corresponding almost exactly to the distribution of the 1940 Negro population along the eastern and southern borders of the state. In fifteen counties he polled more than one-fourth the votes. Negroes comprised more than a quarter of the population in all of them. Of the remaining 60 counties, in all of which Thurmond received less than 25 per cent of the votes, 45 held Negroes numbering less than one fourth of the population. The three counties in which Thurmond received a majority of the votes all contained more Negroes than whites in 1940. Among 41 counties with less than 15 per cent of their population Negro in 1940, Thurmond received less than a fourth the votes in all and less than 15 per cent of the votes in 38.

Between 1944 and 1948 the Republican vote in Arkansas dropped sharply from 29.8 per cent of the total to 21.0 per cent. Despite the fact the Republican vote generally held firm or increased in other southern states where the Dixiecrats were running,[10] the curious might eye the Arkansas Republican decline and attribute it to the 16.5 per cent of the votes which went to the Dixiecrats in 1948. It was true that Republicans lost in all the 15 counties containing 25 per cent or more Dixiecratic voters. The decline in these 15 counties varied widely from one to another, however, and the median decline was 9.9 per cent, as compared with the decline in the state as a whole of 8.8 per cent.

Approaching from the other direction, the median decline from 1944 to 1948 in the 14 counties of the state in which the Republicans polled 40 per cent or more of the 1944 votes was 12.2 per cent. In terms of total Republican strength in the county, the proportionate loss in these relatively strong Republican areas was much less than in the Dixiecratic strongholds where the Republican percentage both years was small. The median Republican

[9] *Ibid.*, May 23, September 30, October 1, 1948.
[10] See p. 279. The table on that page shows that Republican strength increased in Arkansas between 1940 and 1944 more than in other southern states.

vote for the 14 Republican counties in 1948 was 33.8 per cent, and for the 15 Dixiecratic counties, 10.7 per cent. In some Dixiecratic counties the Republican vote was cut as much as two-thirds, even though the decline in the Republican percentage of the total vote may not have been large, indicating that a few black belters may have used a Republican vote in 1944 to protest against the Roosevelt administration.

Tennessee. The southern states with the strongest aggregations of Republicans are Tennessee, Virginia, and North Carolina. Since the Civil War their Blue Ridge counties have harbored tenacious mountain Republicans who have enjoyed local political supremacy but have seldom been able to recruit enough other voters to carry a state election. The competition, nevertheless, has tended to instill in the Democratic party of the three states a sense of unity and corporate responsibility generally nonexistent elsewhere in the South. Just as the mountain redoubts of antislavery sentiment persist in Republicanism, so the heart of Democratic supremacy has been found in the old plantation counties where the descendants of the slaves live most numerously. Some sense of disciplined, party loyalty might be expected in these areas, generated by the constant and sometimes serious threat from an opposition party in state-wide elections. A keen awareness of party responsibility might have offset in part the readiness to desert to Thurmond which in other states sprang from life in close quarters with large numbers of blacks.

We shall see that in North Carolina the locus of Dixiecratic popularity clearly did not lie in the black belt. In Virginia the picture was less clear. In Tennessee, however, which voted Republican in presidential elections twice between 1920 and 1948, the familiar pattern already observed in Texas and Arkansas prevailed. The state's comparatively few Negroes (17.4 per cent in 1940) are concentrated for the most part in the dozen or so counties that fan out from Memphis in the southwestern corner. Table 24 demonstrates that Thurmond was strongest in the black counties and weakest in those with fewest Negroes.

Although Tennessee has consistently polled a higher Republican presidential vote than any other southern state, neither major party possesses the cohesiveness which normally accompanies healthy party competition. Not only are both parties deeply cut by factional fights, not an uncommon condition in two-party states, but a noticeable lack of compulsion exists to close ranks, once the party primaries are over, in order to do battle with the common foe. Formal requirements of party loyalty

TABLE 24

TENNESSEE DIXIECRATS WERE STRONGEST
WHERE NEGROES LIVE

Per cent of total vote Dixiecratic, 1948	Counties: Percentage of population Negro, 1940				
	40-100	20-39.9	10-19.9	5-9.9	0-4.9
40-100	3				
20-39.9	1	7	3	2	
5-19.9		5	9	13	13
0-4.9			1	6	32

governing both candidates and voters have been weaker in Tennessee than elsewhere in the South. Voting across party lines is well known. It is a standard accusation that east Tennessee Republicans are left unbothered by Democrats in their local races, in return for supine activity in the state elections.

In 1948 the candidates of Democratic boss Crump of Memphis were defeated in the primary, rending the party from top to bottom. Mr. Crump announced his support of Thurmond and Wright in the subsequent presidential race.[11] His influence among voters in Democratic primaries beyond Shelby County (Memphis) has been greatest in the western and eastern "grand divisions" of the state. In the 1948 election the weight of his support was therefore added to the presence of Negroes to render the counties surrounding Memphis susceptible to the Dixiecratic siren.

[11] *Commercial Appeal* (Memphis), October 7, 1948.

Democrats in Tennessee predominate not only in the west, but also in the middle grand division, the blue grass "dimple of the universe," where Negroes are not so numerous. Middle Tennessee has traditionally formed the stronghold of opposition to Crump and has somewhat differentiated the Democratic party of Tennessee from that in other southern states by giving it a sizeable area of relative strength among counties of comparatively few blacks. The Dixiecrats did not fare well in those counties of low Negro population and high Democratic loyalty. Neither closeness to matters of race nor Mr. Crump's waning powers of persuasion were present to break down the loyalty of the voters to Truman.[12]

Virginia. As Democratic unity was marred in Tennessee by Boss Crump's defection, the attitude of Byrd organization leaders in Virginia resulted in divided party efforts in that state. The liberal wing of the Democratic party, led by Martin Hutchinson and other Democrats prominent in their opposition to the Byrd machine, early voiced full support of the national nominees of the party. After the national convention, in contrast, Senator Byrd and the organization's Governor Tuck remained silent as to their preferences. Mrs. Byrd, however, was reported openly for the Thurmond-Wright ticket,[13] and the governor was flattering in his introduction of candidate Thurmond at a Dixiecratic campaign rally. Moreover, the Democratic state central committee made a curious picture by announcing it would remain neutral in the presidential contest. The only things that seemed to hold the organization from an all-out endorsement of Thurmond were the races of Senator Robertson and other members of Congress, who had lost no time in seeing a Republican threat and pledging themselves to the national ticket.[14]

In the absence of aggressive Democratic party leadership the

[12] There were 51 counties in 1944 that cast higher than the state average (60.6 per cent) for Roosevelt. Negroes numbered in 1940 less than 5 per cent of the population in 13 of them. None of the 13 gave Thurmond more than 11.6 per cent of its votes and the median percentage was 4.8.

[13] *Times-Picayune* (New Orleans), October 17, 1948.

[14] *Richmond Times-Dispatch*, April 22, September 28, October 9, October 14, October 15, 1948.

presidential race became something of a tug of war. Generally, Thurmond had greatest appeal in counties with the most Negroes, least appeal elsewhere:

Percentage Negro, 1940	Counties: per cent of total vote Dixiecratic, 1948		
	25-100	10-24.9	0-9.9
40-100	6	25	2
0-39.9	0	20	47

Virginia's twenty-four independent cities demonstrated a similar tendency:

Percentage Negro, 1940	Independent cities: per cent of total vote Dixiecratic, 1948 [15]	
	10-100	0-9.9
20-100	9	3
0-9.9	3	9

When examined in detail the correlation is rough, but the trend is the same as in the other states we have examined.

The vote of the cities hinted that maybe the factional division among the Democratic leaders extended down to the voters. Those cities which gave heaviest support to Hutchinson in his race against Senator Byrd in 1946 (the stoutest fight the machine faced for many years up to 1949) returned a markedly lower Dixiecratic vote than those in which Hutchinson had been weakest. Table 25 notes that the median percentage for Thurmond in the ten cities in which Hutchinson polled 45 per cent or more of the 1946 primary votes was 7.95; in the 14 cities in which Hutchinson received less than 45 per cent of the votes, the median Thurmond percentage in 1948 was 14.8. The median percentage of population Negro in 1940 was almost identical for the two groups of cities, the median Republican vote in 1948 was somewhat higher in the cities leaning Dixiecratic. The figures suggest that anti-Byrd

[15] The city of Waynesboro, 6.6 per cent for Thurmond, is not included. It was not independent at the time of the 1940 census.

TABLE 25

In Virginia's Independent Cities, Anti-Byrd Democrats Tended to be Most Loyal to Truman in 1948

Percentage of vote received by Hutchinson in Democratic senatorial primary, 1946	No. of cities	Per cent of total vote Dixiecratic, 1948 High	Low	Median	Median percentage of population Negro, 1940	Median percentage of total vote Republican, 1948
45 or more	10	11.0	4.5	7.95	19.55	30.45
Less than 45	14	29.0	5.1	14.80	20.60	37.55

Democrats in the cities tended to be more loyal to the national party than their neighbors.

There were similar indications in the counties, though the results were less convincing. Virginia has 33 counties which in 1940 were 40 per cent or more Negro. In four of them Hutchinson received more than 40 per cent of the votes in 1946. The median Dixiecratic percentage in those four in 1948 was 12.65. In six of the counties Hutchinson received less than 20 per cent of the 1946 votes. The median Dixiecratic percentage in them two years later was 17.7.[16]

Inclusion of counties of lesser or greater Hutchinson strength produces only inconclusive results. The bailiwick of the Byrd machine has been the counties. Had there been more centers of insurgency among them the contrasts might have been as sharp as among the cities.[17]

[16] Based on the following data:

County	Per cent Negro, 1940	Per cent for Hutchinson in 1946 senatorial primary	Per cent Dixiecratic, 1948
Charles City	77.8	42.6	13.9
Nansemond	67.1	47.6	6.5
New Kent	58.0	43.8	17.9
Prince George	40.2	45.3	11.4
Sussex	67.0	13.3	29.1
Cumberland	58.4	12.1	20.8
Northampton	53.9	12.0	13.0
Caroline	50.2	18.2	13.9
Prince Edward	48.2	17.8	29.7
Buckingham	42.3	18.8	14.6

[17] In the 1946 race Hutchinson received 40 per cent or more of the votes in 13 of the 24 independent cities but in only 21 of the 100 counties. There was but little suggestion in the 1948 returns, however, that the cities were less receptive to the call of the Dixiecrats than counties of similar Negro population. The median Dixiecratic vote of the seven cities containing between 30 and 44.9 per cent population Negro in 1940 was 11.9. The corresponding median for the 23 counties containing similar proportions of blacks was 12.5.

North Carolina. North Carolina shows clearly the effects of a genuine party fight on potential bolters. In that state the Democrats combine into a political force more resembling a real political party than exists anywhere else in the South. The voters are restrained in their enthusiasm for mavericks by genuine appeals to party loyalty and by the hard fact of party discipline. Thurmond drew a smaller proportion of North Carolina's votes than of any other southern state, 8.8 per cent, and in no county received over 27 per cent of the total. He did poorly in the black belt, which in North Carolina has traditionally been a region of liberal protest within the Democratic party as well as that party's region of greatest supremacy over the Republicans. Generally, Thurmond ran strongest in the counties of normal Democratic predominance with relatively few Negroes—in direct contrast to the weak showing he made in the white counties of middle Tennessee.

There was no split in North Carolina's top Democratic leadership as there was in Tennessee and Virginia. Democratic chieftains beat the drums of party regularity. The Dixiecrats were led by David Clark and Philip S. Finn, Jr. Clark had long been viewed by many Democrats as the epitome of reaction.[18] The Dixiecrats' nominal state chairman, Lieutenant Colonel Finn, was relatively unknown. A native of South Carolina, he had lived in Henderson County, North Carolina, since 1946. The moving spirits were described by the archly loyal Democratic *News and Observer* as "the same old crowd" who backed Dewey in 1944 and Willkie in 1940.[19] Opposition to Truman seemed to rest more on longstanding disagreement over economic policy than on concern about civil rights. Prominent Dixiecrats hailed from textile centers in Mecklenburg, Guilford, and Alamance counties.[20] The points of popular support are shown in Figure 9.

[18] Labeled by Jonathan Daniels as "... the reactionary editor of a little textile journal who is not only opposed to civil rights but who was also quite as violently opposed to the abolition of child labor."—*Memphis Press-Scimitar*, March 12, 1948.
[19] July 29, 1948.
[20] *News and Observer* (Raleigh), August 29, 1948.

270

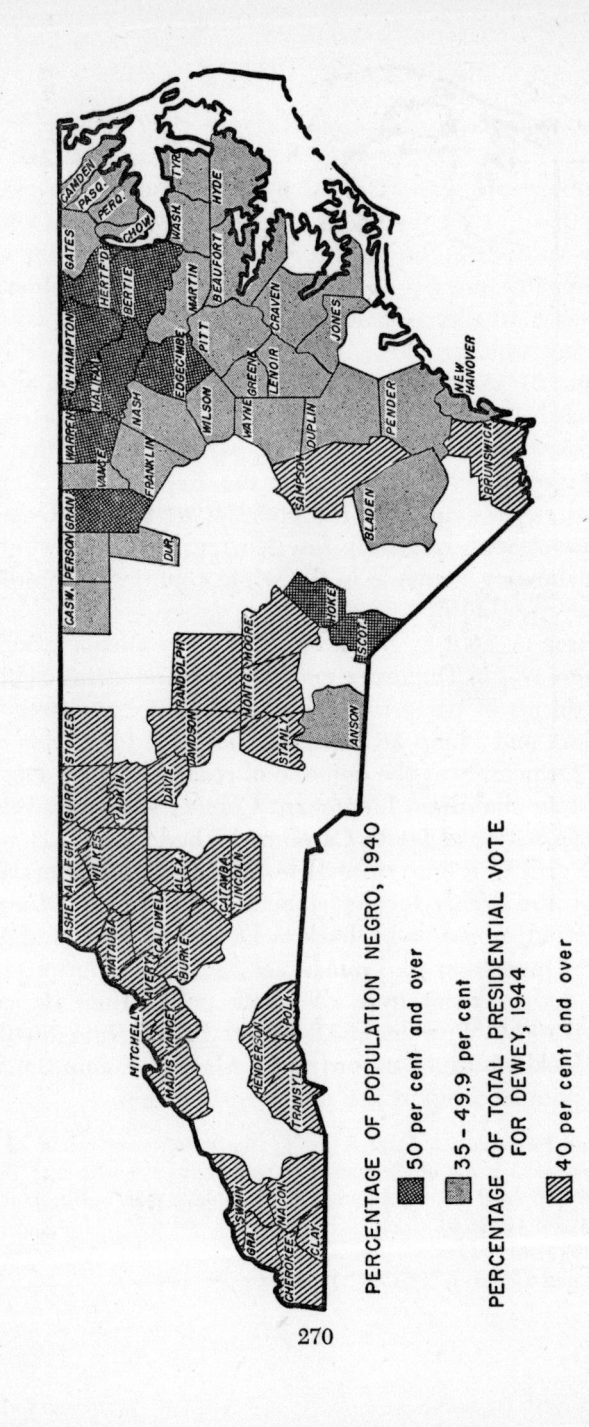

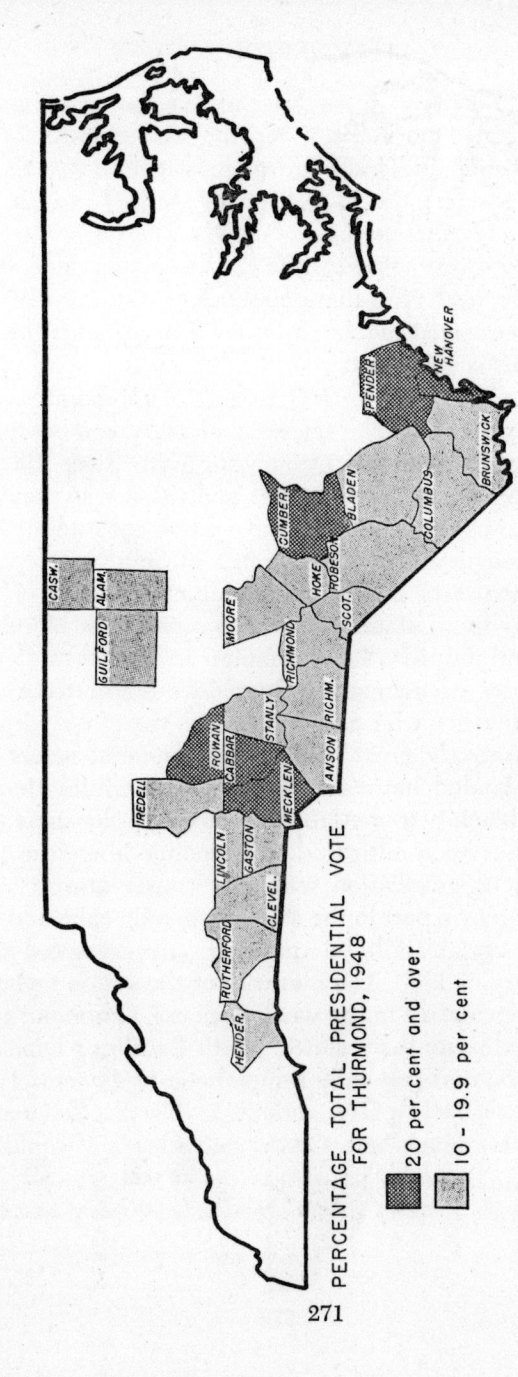

FIGURE 9: NORTH CAROLINA DIXIECRATS WERE STRONGEST IN COUNTIES OF DEMOCRATIC PREDOMINANCE WITH RELATIVELY FEW NEGROES

The figure also contains a map portraying the Negro population as it was distributed in 1940, and the 1944 vote for Dewey. The notable aversion to Thurmond of most counties with large Negro percentages sets the Dixiecrats in North Carolina apart from the movement elsewhere in the South. The Carolinians supporting Thurmond were more akin to the Texas Regulars of 1944. The pull of party loyalty—in these counties of traditionally greatest party loyalty—seemed to take precedence over fears stimulated by the civil rights disturbance.

The atypical behavior of North Carolina's black counties cannot be accounted for alone by the intensity of party competition. In the historic battles within the Democratic party since 1900, between conservative state organizations and those who would depose them, the insurgent candidates have rather consistently found their highest strength among the counties of high Negro population. This fact contrasts with a preponderant tendency of black belts in other southern states to favor conservatives allied with urban finance and industry. Land holdings in the North Carolina plantation counties are comparatively widely distributed and the proportions of tenants who are white, and therefore who may vote, are comparatively great. Among the potential voters there are thus fewer landed barons and more poor whites than, for instance, in the black belt of Alabama. Race consciousness in the black belt has thus been mitigated by economic liberalism rather than bulwarked by association with city conservatism.[21] These factors no doubt play a part in the state's generally calm and tolerant behavior in racial affairs, a tradition only disrupted in the senatorial primary of 1950. The maturity of the state's racial attitudes was itself important in the weak response Thurmond's pleas received. As in other southern states, North Carolina's Dixiecratic strength lay in counties generally sympathetic to the conservative wing of the Democratic party, though in North Carolina they were outside of the black belt. Conservative leaders would have

[21] For a full discussion of the political behavior of North Carolina's black belt, see V. O. Key, Jr., *Southern Politics* (New York: Alfred A. Knopf, Inc., 1949), chap. 10.

opposed Truman even had Thurmond not been running and had there been no civil rights ruckus.

Though many of the relatively strong Dixiecratic counties contained substantial numbers of Republicans, there is little evidence that the bulk of Dixiecratic voters was drawn more from Republicans than from Democrats. Thurmond received more than 15 per cent of the votes in 13 counties. In only seven of the 13 did the 1948 Republican presidential vote differ from that of 1944 by more than 2 per cent of the total vote. The Republican percentage rose in three of the seven and fell in the other four. Only one variation was as great as 8 per cent and that was in Mecklenburg County where the Republican vote rose while the Dixiecrats were receiving 21.6 per cent of the total. The Republican vote in the state as a whole declined 0.6 per cent between 1944 and 1948. It is possible that a major section of the Thurmond vote would have preferred Dewey had Thurmond not been on the ballot, but the lack of consistency from county to county in the effect on the Republican vote of a large Thurmond turnout discourages such an interpretation.

Florida. Dixiecratic strategy called for appropriating wherever possible the regular Democratic label. Efforts to do so failed in the states we have so far examined and in Georgia.[22] In Mississippi, South Carolina, Louisiana, and Alabama, the electors of the Democratic party were pledged to Thurmond and Wright. Only in Florida did the presidential candidates appear on the ballot as individuals, without listing under any party name. No straight ticket could be marked that included a presidential nominee. In a sense the voters had a free choice in Florida, a choice uninfluenced by the appearance of either Truman or Thurmond under the traditional Democratic rallying sign.

Twenty-six of the thirty-three counties that gave Thurmond 20 per cent or more of their votes lie in north Florida, above Ocala, the section of old settlements, the part of the state possessing the Old South features of its neighbors, Georgia and Alabama.

[22] It has not been possible to obtain the 1948 county-by-county Dixiecratic vote for Georgia, hence no detailed analysis is offered for that state.

It is the section that has had the largest proportions of Negroes for the longest period of time. Where there have been migrations the attitudes associated with large Negro concentrations have tended to persist.

All counties in which Thurmond polled 30 per cent or more of the votes contained 35 per cent or more Negroes; among the counties in which he received less than 30 per cent, the chances were five to one the county was less than 35 per cent Negro:

Percentage Negro, 1940	Counties: percentage of vote received by Thurmond, 1948	
	30-100	0-29.9
35-100	8	10
0-34.9	0	49

Mississippi. Thurmond succeeded in winning the electoral votes of all the states where he appeared on the ballot as a Democrat. In these states the character of the Dixiecrats is perhaps best noted by examining the areas which put up the strongest resistance to their lure. Consonant with our general proposition, these areas in Mississippi contained few Negroes as compared with the rest of the state. Such votes as the President received in Mississippi came in large measure from the northeastern corner of the state supplemented by a scattering elsewhere, chiefly in the piney woods of the coastal plain. He did not run well, even relatively, in all counties with few Negroes, but his high points of support were in such counties. Table 26 shows that in only one of the six counties in which he received 30 per cent or more of the votes did Negroes number more than one person in four. The exception is Lafayette, a hill county adjoining counties of both low and high Negro percentages and the home of the University of Mississippi. Of thirty-five counties more than one-half Negro in 1940, all gave Truman less than 20 per cent of their votes and thirty-one gave him less than 10 per cent of them.

It is noteworthy that Truman's greatest popularity was concentrated in and around the district of Representative John Rankin, most vociferous of Mississippi politicians in his concern over matters of race. In four counties in his district the champion of civil rights for Negroes received over 30 per cent of the votes, in another between 20 and 30, and in seven more either in or touching Rankin's bailiwick he polled higher than the state average of 10.1 per cent.

TABLE 26

TRUMAN'S MISSISSIPPI SUPPORTERS IN 1948 WERE STRONGEST IN COUNTIES OF FEW NEGROES

Percentage of population Negro, 1940	Counties: percentage of total vote for Truman, 1948			
	30-100	20-29.9	10-19.9	0-9.9
50-100			4	31
25-49.9	1	1	6	21
0-24.9	5	2	5	6

South Carolina. The distribution of Truman's vote in South Carolina, home of presidential candidate Thurmond, follows that of Mississippi, home of vice presidential candidate Wright. The maps in Figure 10 show that the President ran strongest outside the counties with largest proportions of Negroes. The tendency of the up country of relatively few blacks to divide against the lowlands of many blacks resembled a sectionalism in the politics which has recurred from time to time since the Civil War. It was out of the uplands that Tillman and Cole Blease and Olin Johnston came in their early careers to champion the rights of poor farmers and mill workers. It was among these "red necks" and "lint heads," rather than among the whites of the plantation counties, that the greatest allegiance to the national Democracy was found in 1948.[23]

[23] For maps showing the sectionalism in certain recent South Carolina primaries see Key, *op. cit.*, chap. 7. No figures on the geographical distribution of the vote in a Tillman campaign could be located. Tillman's early campaign appeal to discontented white rural elements, and his bitter attacks against the "cities," especially coastal Charleston, are described in Francis Butler Simkins, *Pitchfork Ben Tillman* (Baton Rouge: Louisiana State University, 1944), chaps. 11, 12, and 14.

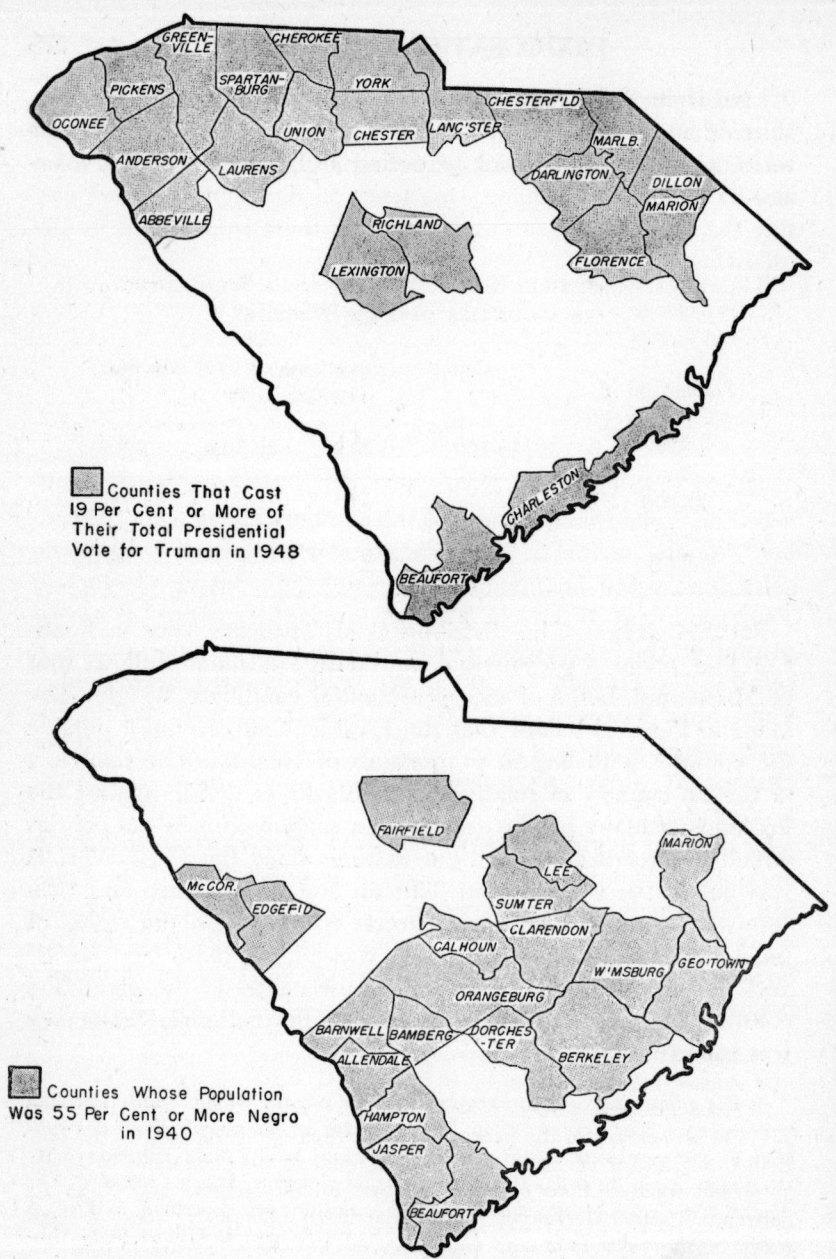

FIGURE 10: THE SOUTH CAROLINA COUNTIES WITH MOST NEGROES FAVORED TRUMAN LEAST

DIXIECRATIC VOTING, 1948

Louisiana. The Louisiana vote contrasts with the neat sectionalism of South Carolina. In Louisiana, the Democratic party split wide open with Thurmond attracting 49.1 per cent of the votes and Truman 32.7. Truman's tendency to find more support outside the heavily black areas than within them is indicated by the following figures:

Percentage Negro, 1940	Counties: percentage of vote received by Truman, 1948	
	0-29.9	30-100
40-100	17	10
0-39.9	14	23

The fight in Louisiana was confused. In April, governor-nominate Earl Long thought some of the southern states were "crowding Truman too much." [24] In September the state Democratic committee voted unanimously to pledge the party's electors to Thurmond and Wright.[25] The governor then called a special session of the legislature which adopted a measure making it possible for Truman to get on the ballot as an independent.[26] There was, however, no clear-cut factional division within the party, at least none which could be discerned by an outsider. Historically, a clear sectionalism has not shown up in Louisiana, even during the campaigns of Huey Long.[27] The importance of religious and linguistic factors not found elsewhere in the South undoubtedly contributes to the peculiar political patterns. Political bossism in such parishes as Plaquemines and St. Bernard upset anticipated correlations. Despite the complexity of factors, however, the effect of the presence of Negroes on Truman's popularity was discernible.

[24] *Memphis Press-Scimitar*, April 12, 1948.
[25] *Atlanta Journal*, September 10, 1948.
[26] *Times-Picayune* (New Orleans), September 23, 1948.
[27] For an analysis of the geographical distribution of the vote in the two 1948 primaries for governor of Louisiana, relating the candidates' strength to several small sections of the state, see Rudolf Heberle and Alvin L. Bertrand, "Factors Motivating Voting Behavior in a One-Party State—A Case Study of the 1948 Louisiana Gubernatorial Primaries," *Social Forces*, 27 (1948), 343-50.

APPENDIX I

Alabama. The nominees of the 1948 Democratic national convention did not appear on the ballot in Alabama. There is no way, therefore, to contrast Truman's pulling power with that of Thurmond in the presidential election.

It seems fairly certain that Thurmond would have had no walk-away. Loyal Democrats, both candidates and voters, were caught in the intricacies of party pledges and, given no alternative, supported Thurmond.[28] Had there been a vote, probably it would have followed the pattern expressed in the popular voting to select delegates to the Democratic National Convention. In the Democratic primaries in the spring of 1948, some candidates for delegate to the convention were pledged to walk out if Truman were nominated, and others urged that Alabama work out its destiny within the party. The delegation elected in the primaries was split 14-12, the majority favoring a walkout and the others either opposed or uncommitted.[29] Districts with heavy Negro population selected delegates favoring a walkout. Districts in the northern and southern extremes of the state, where there are relatively few Negroes, rejected walkout candidates. Again in 1950, in the selection of members of the Democratic state executive committee, the same pattern prevailed. Generally, counties of relatively few Negroes chose committeemen avowedly loyal to the party, whereas the counties with a large proportion of their population Negro chose States' Rights committeemen. The loyalists captured 43 of the 72 seats.

[28] Some Dixiecrats proclaimed that pressure from Alabama voters, rather than the bite of the state Democratic committee's loyalty sanctions, were holding Alabama's normally liberal leaders in line for Thurmond. Note John Temple Graves in *Florida Times-Union* (Jacksonville), July 19, 1948.

[29] *Birmingham News,* June 9, 1948.

APPENDIX II
TABLE 27

REPUBLICAN PERCENTAGE OF THE TOTAL PRESIDENTIAL VOTE, 1916-1948:
THE UNITED STATES AND THE SOUTHERN STATES

	1916	1920	1924	1928	1932	1936	1940	1944	1948
United States	46.1	60.3	54.0	58.1	39.7	36.5	44.7	45.9	45.1
Alabama	21.9	31.9	26.0	48.5	14.3	12.8	14.4	18.2	19.0
Arkansas	28.0	39.1	29.3	38.6	12.5	17.9	21.0	29.8	21.0
Florida	18.1	35.3[a]	28.1	56.8	25.1	23.9	26.0	29.7	33.6
Georgia	7.1[b]	28.8	18.2	44.0[c]	7.8	12.6	14.9[d]	17.2	18.3
Louisiana	7.0[e]	30.5	20.2	23.7	7.0	11.2	14.1	19.4	17.5
Mississippi	4.9	14.1	7.6	17.3	3.5	2.8	4.2	6.4	2.6
North Carolina	41.7	43.2	39.6	54.9	29.3	26.6	26.0	33.3	32.7
South Carolina	2.4[f]	3.4	2.2	8.5[g]	1.9	1.4	1.9	4.5[h]	3.8
Tennessee	42.8	51.2	43.5	55.3	32.5	30.8	32.3	39.2	36.9
Texas	17.4	29.2[i]	19.9	52.0	11.4	12.1	19.0	16.8[j]	24.6
Virginia	32.1	37.9	32.8	53.9	30.1	29.4	31.5	37.4	41.0

[a] Includes 6.5 per cent white Republican.
[b] Does not include 13.0 per cent Progressive.
[c] Includes 15.7 per cent Hoover, anti-Smith.
[d] Includes 7.2 per cent Independent Democratic, favoring Willkie.
[e] Does not include 6.8 per cent Progressive.
[f] Does not include 0.4 per cent Progressive Republican, nor 0.3 per cent Progressive.
[g] Includes 4.6 per cent anti-Smith.
[h] Does not include 7.5 per cent Southern Democratic, opposed to Roosevelt.
[i] Includes 5.6 per cent black-and-tan Republican.
[j] Does not include 11.8 per cent Texas Regular, opposed to Roosevelt.

NOTES

NOTES TO CHAPTER 1

1. See, respectively, Samuel Lubell, *Look*, October 24, 1950, p. 129; Carroll Kilpatrick, *Harper's Magazine*, 186 (1943), 415-21; John Temple Graves, *American Mercury*, 56 (1943), 401-6; Virginius Dabney, *New York Times Magazine*, July 28, 1944.

2. See V. O. Key, Jr., *Southern Politics in State and Nation* (New York: Alfred A. Knopf, Inc., 1949). The relationship between Mr. Key's study and this one is explained in the foreword. The need for studies of party politics has been trumpeted by the Committee on Political Parties of the American Political Science Association in its report, "Toward a More Responsible Two-Party System," *The American Political Science Review*, 44 (1950), supplement, p. 82.

3. Jesse T. Carpenter, *The South as a Conscious Minority, 1789-1861* (New York: New York University Press, 1930), p. 4; see also p. 7.

4. Key, *op. cit.*, chap. 14.

5. Paul W. Wager, *County Government Across the Nation* (Chapel Hill: University of North Carolina Press, 1950), p. 354.

6. Floyd Hunter of the Institute for Research in Social Science, University of North Carolina, has prepared an intriguing study of the power hierarchy in a large southern city.

7. William C. Carleton, "Why Call the South Conservative?", *Harper's Magazine*, 195 (1947), 61-68.

NOTES TO CHAPTER 2

1. *Richmond Times-Dispatch,* September 25, 1948.
2. *Memphis Press-Scimitar,* October 5, 1948; *Birmingham News,* February 8, 1949.
3. *Birmingham News,* April 9, 1949.
4. *Ibid.,* April 14, 1949.
5. Fred Taylor, "Dixiecrats Plan to Give Party Harder Wallop," *Birmingham News,* December 25, 1948; Drew Pearson, "Dixiecrats Plan Comeback," *Birmingham News,* April 16, 1949; also, *Birmingham News,* February 7 and 8, 1949.
6. If any documentation of the relative inflexibility of southern electoral behavior is needed, see Louis Bean, *Ballot Behavior* (Washington: American Council on Public Affairs, 1940), chaps. 5 and 6.
7. *Atlanta Journal,* November 9, 1948.
8. "Capital Comment," issued by the Democratic National Committee, vol. 3., no. 27, August 20, 1949.
9. *Richmond Times-Dispatch,* November 10, 1948.
10. *Birmingham News,* July 14, 1949.
11. For a comprehensive review of this subject, see Clarence A. Berdahl, "Some Notes on Party Membership in Congress," *The American Political Science Review,* 43 (1949), 309-21, 492-508, 721-34.
12. *Atlanta Journal,* November 9, 1948.
13. *Birmingham News,* January 7, 1949.
14. *New York Times,* May 24, 1949.
15. *Birmingham News,* April 29, 1949.
16. "We call upon all Democrats and upon all other loyal Americans who are opposed to totalitarianism at home and abroad . . ."—"Declaration of Principles," text in *Atlanta Journal,* July 18, 1948. "The states' rights movement, by its own nature, must not be a sectional affair." —Dothan declaration, reported in *Birmingham News,* April 9, 1949. At the third annual meeting of the movement in 1950 Governor Fielding Wright declared that "we are not engaged in a sectional fight, but in one that will benefit the nation and the entire world."—*New York Times,* May 11, 1950. "The States Rights feeling in the South fits a home rule sentiment everywhere. What is of greater import, it fits the revolt against 'statism' in general which is swelling through the nation." —John Temple Graves, "Revolution in the South," *Virginia Quarterly Review,* 26 (1950), 196.
17. *Times-Picayune* (New Orleans), October 28, 1948.

18. Computed from official state returns compiled by the Associated Press, appearing in the *Birmingham News*, December 15, 1948.

19. *Memphis Press-Scimitar*, October 7, 1948.

20. *Florida Times-Union* (Jacksonville), August 2, 1948. Italics added.

21. In July, 1949 the Gallup poll asked citizens in seven sections of the country "What do you think is the most important problem facing this section of the country today?" The greatest concern in five sections was unemployment, in another, high cost of living, and in the South, civil rights.—*Birmingham News*, July 24, 1949.

22. Horace C. Wilkinson, States' Rights candidate for presidential elector in Alabama, quoted in *Columbia Record* (S. C.), August 30, 1948.

23. For instance, Fred Taylor in *Birmingham News*, October 24, 1948.

24. V. O. Key speaks about the "safety-valve function" of minor parties. "They operate as a channel for the expression of discontent, which is often dissipated and rendered harmless by the exertions of verbalization and electoral activity."—*Politics, Parties and Pressure Groups* (2nd ed.; New York: Thomas Y. Crowell Company, 1947), p. 244.

25. Arthur N. Holcombe, *The Political Parties of Today* (2nd ed.; New York: Harper & Brothers, 1925), p. 315.

26. For the significance of third parties in "social politics," see Fred E. Haynes, *Third Party Movements Since the Civil War* (Iowa City: The State Historical Society of Iowa, 1916), chap. 30.

27. "Let a whole section begin to feel that its interests are being permanently discriminated against by both old parties, and the time for a plain-spoken third party, organized mainly along sectional lines, is about ripe."—John D. Hicks, "The Third Party Tradition in American Politics," *The Mississippi Valley Historical Review*, 20 (1933), 27-28.

28. "It is almost a law of third party history that the triumph of the third party cause means the death of the third party.... Let a third party once demonstrate that votes are to be made by adopting a certain demand, then one or the other of the older parties can be trusted to absorb the new doctrine."—*Ibid.*, p. 26.

29. For a lucid discussion of the reasons for the two-party system in the United States, see E. E. Schattschneider, *Party Government* (New York: Rinehart and Company, 1942).

30. Cortez A. M. Ewing has computed the state percentages of total

series of three short studies of southern legislatures appearing in *New South* (published by the Southern Regional Council, Atlanta), for 1949; and Emmett Asseff, *Legislative Apportionment in Louisiana* (Louisiana State University: Bureau of Government Research, 1950).

3. *News and Observer* (Raleigh), February 22, 1951.

NOTES TO CHAPTER 6

1. Ben W. Hooper, *Tennessee Elections* (Knoxville: Chandler-Warters Company, 1946), pp. 3-5.

2. Initiated Act No. 3, approved November 2, 1948. See "Arkansas Election Laws" (Simplified), 1950, compiled by the Attorney General, p. 10. For the Republican role in the change, see *Arkansas Gazette* (Little Rock), May 30, 1948.

3. Joseph P. Harris, *Election Administration in the United States* (Washington: The Brookings Institution, 1934), pp. 101-2. State control over primaries has been the subject of controversy in Louisiana in recent years. See Harnett T. Kane, *Louisiana Hayride* (New York: William Morrow & Company, 1941), pp. 106, 160-1.

4. Louisiana's governor appoints two of the three supervisors of elections for each parish in his state.—*Act. No. 224 of 1940* as amended, sec. 11. In Mississippi the law requires the governor, attorney general, and secretary of state to appoint three persons in each county to run the election.—*Code of 1942*, chap. 2, sec. 3204. South Carolina formerly had two sets of officials for the general elections. The governor appointed a board of three members in each county to conduct elections to federal offices and another board of three members to conduct elections to state and local offices.—*Code of 1932*, sec. 2299. By an act approved April 20, 1950, the boards were consolidated. The governor's appointees must be recommended by the county's senator and at least half of its members in the House.—sec. 5-B.

5. *News and Courier* (Charleston), August 9, 1944.

6. North Carolina *General Statutes of 1943*, chap. 163, secs. 8, 11. A handy and excellent compilation of North Carolina election rules is that by Henry W. Lewis, *Guidebook for County and Precinct Election Officials* (Chapel Hill: The Institute of Government, 1950). Tennessee *Code of 1934*, secs. 1967.3, 1967.12, 1970. Virginia *Code of 1950*, title 24, sec. 29. See "Virginia Election Laws," 1950, published by the State Board of Elections, pp. 27-28.

NOTES FOR PAGES 86-94

7. Alabama *Code of 1940*, title 17, sec. 21; *Florida Statutes 1941*, title IX, secs. 98.13, 98.14, 98.15, as amended; Georgia *Code of 1926*, title 2, sec. 52; Louisiana *Act No. 45 of 1940* as amended, sec. 1; Mississippi *Code of 1942*, chap. 2, secs. 3204-5; North Carolina *General Statutes of 1943*, chap. 163, sec. 15; South Carolina Act approved April 20, 1950, sec. 3-C; Tennessee *Code of 1934*, sec. 1999; Virginia *Code of 1950*, title 24, secs. 52-60. Arkansas and Texas had no registration systems, using poll tax roles to identify voters.

8. "BUZZARD NEST METHODS," a pamphlet issued in 1950.

9. Hooper, *Tennessee Elections*, pp. 87-88.

10. *Ibid.*, p. 5.

11. "The Recommendations of the State Board of Elections to the Governor of North Carolina and the General Assembly of 1947," pp. 4-5.

12. *News and Observer* (Raleigh), December 19, 1946.

13. *Ibid.*, January 10, 1947.

14. *Ibid.*, January 18, 1951.

15. *Richmond Times-Dispatch*, February 28, 1948.

16. *Ibid.*, February 12, 1948.

17. *Ibid.*, March 2, 1948.

18. "Arkansas Election Laws" (Simplified), 1950, compiled by the Attorney General, pp. 11-13; *Florida Statutes 1941*, title IX, secs. 99.18, 99.19, 99.20 and chap. 24994 (No. 1) adopted by special session of legislature, September, 1948; Georgia *Act No. 309* adopted by the 1949 legislature; previously Georgia had a permissive secret ballot law that counties could adopt by grand jury action; Louisiana *Act No. 224 of 1940* as amended, secs. 63-81; Mississippi *Code of 1942*, chap. 2, secs. 3258-64; North Carolina *General Statutes of 1943*, chap. 163, art. 20; South Carolina Act approved April 20, 1950, secs. 5-D, 5-E; Tennessee *Code of 1934*, secs. 2060-2062; Virginia Constitution, sec. 28, Virginia *Code of 1950*, title 24, sec. 215.

19. *Code of 1942*, sec. 2304.

20. *News and Courier* (Charleston), August 9, 1944. The party long sought without success to enforce the apparent guarantee of secret voting contained in the state constitution.—*Gardner v. Blackwell*, 167 S.C. 313; 166 S.E. 338 (1932); *Smith v. Blackwell*, 115 F. (2d) 186; *Smith v. Blackwell*, 34 F. Supp. 989.

21. *Columbia Record* (S.C.), May 25, 1948.

22. *Act No. 36 of 1941;* Constitution, art III, sec. III.

23. *Texas Election Laws*, 1946, arts. 2978, 3012.

6. The percentage of the delegates that came from the South was as follows: 1912, 23.3; 1924, 16.5; 1928, 15.3; 1932, 19.5; 1936, 16.5; 1940, 16.9; 1944, 16.4; 1948, 17.3.

7. *Official Report of the Proceedings of the Twenty-fourth Republican National Convention* (1948) (Washington: Republican National Committee), pp. 85-86.

8. See the discussion of Tables 17 and 18 on pp. 125-29. After Hugh D. Scott, Jr., a Dewey man, was removed as chairman of the Republican National Committee, he lambasted Carroll Reece and the national committeemen from Alabama, Louisiana, Mississippi, South Carolina, and Texas for having "sold out" to the Democrats for patronage and power. All six men attacked were Taft supporters and the latter rose to their defense as "among the most conscientious and able Republicans. They command respect of both Democrats and Republicans in their respective states."—*New York Times*, May 30, 1950.

9. *Atlanta Journal*, December 7, 1947.

10. *Ibid.*, June 21, 1948.

11. *Ibid.*, June 22, 1948.

12. See *Manner of Selecting Delegates to National Political Conventions with Information on States Holding Presidential Primaries* (Washington: Government Printing Office, 1948), compiled by the Senate Library. The systems of selecting convention delegates often conduce to ingrown party organizations. For example, in Louisiana, district delegates to the national convention are named by the district committees.—*Times-Picayune* (New Orleans), March 24, 1948. In Florida, until 1948, all delegates were named by party committees—under legislation drawn, it is reliably reported, by a Republican state official to facilitate the smooth working of the party. In 1948 the Republicans were held subject to the mandatory primary legislation and, like the Democrats, selected delegates in primaries.— *Florida Times-Union* (Jacksonville), March 22, 1948.

13. *Toward a New Politics in the South* (Knoxville: The University of Tennessee Press, 1949), p. 66.

14. *Birmingham News*, June 16, 1948.

15. *Richmond Times-Dispatch*, July 8, 1947.

16. *Birmingham News*, March 7, 1947.

17. *Ibid.*, June 22, 1948.

18. The detailed convention balloting is given in the official report of the convention proceedings published after each convention by the national committee.

19. Only occasionally do southern Republican leaders appear deliberately to act in concert. In fact, when questioned, they are likely to protest that they often work more closely with colleagues outside the South. Regional consciousness was shown in the spring of 1947 when high officials of the party from a number of southern states convened for a long week end at "Cobbstead" on Lake Hamilton, home of Arkansas' state chairman, Osro Cobb. "Running through the conference will be the theme of devising ways and means to attract more favorable consideration for the South and its problems," Mr. Cobb said. "This eagerness to contribute to the progress of the South is our best approach to get more Republican votes in the South."—*Arkansas Gazette* (Little Rock), March 10, 1947. The conference proclaimed the intent to obtain important national appointments for southerners and adopted the following resolution: "We endorse the formation of the Southern Republican economic council for the purpose of assisting all agricultural and industrial organizations engaged in promoting interests of the Southern states by advocating to Congress the enactment of legislation fair to the best interests of the South and opposing any and all legislation inimical to the South."—*Ibid.*, March 16, 1947.

NOTES TO CHAPTER 9

1. James Bryce, *The American Commonwealth* (1st ed.; New York: Macmillan and Company, 1888), vol. 1, pp. 540-41. See all of chap. XLVI, "State Politics." The numerous subsequent editions were also published by Macmillan.

2. *Ibid.*, pp. 541-42.

3. For an analysis of this and other features of the American party system, see E. E. Schattschneider, *Party Government* (New York: Rinehart and Company, 1942), especially chap. 6. An eloquent discussion of the party system, especially in relation to Congressional performance, is given by James MacGregor Burns in *Congress on Trial* (New York: Harper and Brothers, 1949). The systems of party bosses that dominate the politics of most states do not flourish in the one-party South. Southern politics is mostly a politics of personalities and fluid factions. Democratic party power, therefore, is less coherently organized in most of the South than in states with a strong bi-party system, and to that extent may be less well prepared initially to meet threats to its position.

3. Jasper Shannon, *Toward a New Politics in the South* (Knoxville: The University of Tennessee Press, 1949), p. 44. Professor Shannon's perceptive and entertaining analysis of the sociology of southern politics conveys the feel as well as the fact of much that is important in the region. See especially chap. 3, "The Governing Class of a Southern County Seat."

4. As one of several examples: An all-white jury in Rome, Georgia, convicted Sheriff Lynch and Deputy Hartline of depriving seven Negroes in Hooker, Georgia, of their civil rights by delivering them into the hands of a robed and masked mob.—*New York Times*, March 19, 1950.

5. The approximate number of Negroes enrolled at certain state universities in the fall of 1950: Texas, 21; Arkansas, 12; Virginia, 3; Oklahoma, 60; Kentucky, 15; Missouri, 9.—*News and Observer* (Raleigh), November 21, 1950. A list of 20 private colleges in southern and border states that formerly accepted only white students but in 1951 admitted Negroes is given by A. A. Morisey in "A New Trend in Private Colleges," *New South*, August-September, 1951, pp. 1-2. On race relations generally in the United States, see the "balance sheet" of group relations put out annually by the American Jewish Congress and the National Association for the Advancement of Colored People.

6. Bureau of the Census, "Population—Special Reports," Series P-45, no. 3, March 29, 1945.

7. The "South" as used in this compilation includes the eleven states of our study plus Oklahoma, Kentucky, West Virginia, Maryland, Delaware, and the District of Columbia.—"Current Population Reports," Series P-20, no. 9, January 19, 1948. Between 1940 and 1950 the southern (same definition) white population increased 16.5 per cent and the southern Negro population 3.1 per cent.—"1950 Census of Population—Preliminary Reports," Series PC-7, no. 3, April 30, 1951.

8. The eleven southern states held 24.6 per cent of the convention seats in 1892, 23.5 per cent in 1944. By adding Kentucky, Maryland, Missouri, and Oklahoma, the respective percentages were 33.2 and 31.6.

9. The thesis that the real tune-callers in southern politics before the Civil War and since have been the whites of the black belts is developed fully by V. O. Key, Jr., in *Southern Politics*.

10. *New York Times*, September 18, 1948.

11. Thomas D. Clark has written four articles called "The Economic

Basis of Southern Politics," appearing in *Forum*, 111 (1949), 261-64 and 332-35; 112 (1949), 5-8 and 83-86.

12. H. C. Nixon emphasized the lack of difference between the South and other regions in "Southern Regionalism Ltd.," *Virginia Quarterly Review*, 26 (1950), 161-70.

13. M. Ostrogorski, *Democracy and the Party System in the United States* (New York: The Macmillan Company, 1910), p. 420.

14. See the notable studies made for the Committee of the South of the National Planning Association: Glenn E. McLaughlin and Stefan Robock, *Why Industry Moves South—A Study of Factors Influencing the Recent Location of Manufacturing Plants in the South* (Washington: National Planning Association, June, 1949); Albert Lepawsky, *State Planning and Economic Development of the South* (Washington: National Planning Association, 1949); Calvin B. Hoover and Benjamin U. Ratchford, *Economy of the South,* Report of the Joint Committee on the Economic Report on the Impact of Federal Policies on the Economy of the South (Washington: Government Printing Office, 1949); and the extended report of Hoover and Ratchford, *Economic Resources and Policies of the South* (New York: The Macmillan Company, 1951).

For another report on industrial development in the South including trends, see Anne E. Hulse and Patrick J. DeTuro, "Economic Problem of the Southeast," *Harvard Business Review*, 27 (1949), 34-52.

15. For the most comprehensive recent report on southern labor in general, see "Labor in the South," *Monthly Labor Review*, 63 (1946), 481-586. For estimates of the extent of unionization in the South, including increases since 1938, see Frank T. de Vyver, "The Present Status of Labor Unions in the South," *The Southern Economic Journal*, 16 (1949), 1-22.

16. Note the comment of one observer: "Instead of a militant labor movement, the first fruits of Southern industrialism have been a rising urban middle class that is almost Republican in its political thinking." —Samuel Lubell, "Has Truman Lost the South?", *Look,* October 24, 1950, p. 134.

17. See Arthur Raper's "The Role of Agricultural Technology in Southern Agricultural Change," *Social Forces,* 25 (1946), 21-30. For a discussion of some of the problems accompanying the new developments, see Lewis W. Jones and Ernest E. Neal, "Changes in the Cotton South," *New South*, October, 1951, pp. 5-8.

18. Using the Census Bureau's 1940 definition of "urban population" (generally persons living within incorporated areas of 2,500 or more population), the following estimated population changes took place between 1940 and 1950:

	Per cent of change in population	
	Urban	Rural
UNITED STATES	18.7	7.4
Alabama	39.3	−5.9
Arkansas	41.9	−15.1
Florida	48.2	40.2
Georgia	28.2	0.3
Louisiana	38.3	−5.2
Mississippi	38.4	−10.1
North Carolina	25.9	8.3
South Carolina	29.8	4.8
Tennessee	22.7	7.1
Texas	58.0	−12.1
Virginia	36.9	14.1

Source: "1950 Census of Population—Preliminary Counts," Series PC-3, no. 10, February 16, 1951.

19. See Marian D. Irish, "The Proletarian South," *Journal of Politics*, 2 (1940), 231-58.

20. Key, *Southern Politics*, examines at length the low levels of southern voting and the causes and consequences thereof. Abolition of the poll tax, incidentally, not only removes a suffrage barrier, but in some areas removes a technique of controlled politics that operates to the disadvantage of the Republican party. On the effect of economic status on electoral participation, see Herbert Tingsten, *Political Behavior* (London: P. S. King & Son, Ltd., 1937), chap. 3 and p. 230.

NOTES TO CHAPTER 11

1. The figure is not based on comprehensive data, but it seems as good an estimate as we have. Charles E. Merriam and Harold F. Gosnell, *The American Party System* (4th ed.; New York: The Macmillan Company, 1949), pp. 141-45. V. O. Key, Jr., concludes: "It is probably not far wrong to estimate that from 75 to 85 per cent of persons voting in two consecutive presidential elections support the same party

both times."—*Politics, Parties, and Pressure Groups* (2nd ed.; New York: Thomas Y. Crowell Company, 1947), p. 601.

2. Daniel Merritt Robison, *Bob Taylor and the Agrarian Revolt in Tennessee* (Chapel Hill: University of North Carolina Press, 1935), p. 53.

3. For a sense of the intensity of emotional reaction required to do this, read William G. Carleton's personal reminiscence of "an exhibition of religious tension, prejudice, and fanaticism there has never been anything in American history" to equal.—"The Popish Revolt of 1928," *Forum*, 112 (1949), 141-47.

4. The development of southern attitudes toward F.D.R. and toward the Democratic nominations for president and vice president is described for the period 1938-48 by Jasper B. Shannon in "Presidential Politics in the South," *The Journal of Politics*, 10 (1948), 464-89. Thomas Sancton has two well-written pieces on the political results of changing economic conditions and New Deal policies in the South. He speaks of the "phony" 1948 revolt and the evidence of unhappiness among economic conservatives that led up to it.—*The Nation*, 167 (1948), 95-98 and 125-28.

5. Stanley Schneider, The Texas Regular Party of 1944 (Master's thesis, University of Chicago, 1948), pp. 44-46, 51-53. Schneider also reports such gestures as those by the "American Democratic National Committee," headed for a while by Harry Woodring, designed to stop Roosevelt's fourth nomination.

6. The Alabama State CIO Political Action Committee felt this rather strongly, calling them "back-door Republicans," people "whose beliefs, sympathies and actions have, for the past several years, paralleled the Republican Party's beliefs, sympathies, and actions on labor, housing, public health and welfare, taxes and prices."—Mimeographed statement, adopted October 17, 1948. The names of Dixiecratic leaders that appeared most often in the press almost without exception fell into the category of well-to-do conservatives, such as "Business Ben" Laney, wealthy former governor of Arkansas; John Daggett, long the driving force of the arch-conservative Arkansas Free Enterprise Association; Sidney W. Smyer, one-time lobbyist for the Associated Industries of Alabama; Frank Dixon, corporation lawyer and former governor of Alabama; Frank D. Upchurch, long-time political foe of Claude Pepper in Florida; and Leander Perez of Louisiana (on the latter, see two articles by Lester Velie called "Kingfish of the Dixiecrats" appearing in *Collier's*, December 17 and 24, 1949). Reports have been repeated in

various places that money interested in state control of tidelands oil helped finance the Dixiecrats. This writer has seen no careful inquiry into Dixiecratic finances. Governor Thurmond is on record as saying early in his campaign that "I know nothing of any attempt by oil interests to make any contribution whatsoever to the States' Rights Democrats."—*Florida Times-Union* (Jacksonville), August 2, 1948. In the forefront of Dixiecratic activity were several shoddy characters whom John Temple Graves explained by saying, "Coming out of the grass roots, the movement could no more have been of one piece in virtue and intent than are the Republican and Democratic parties."— "Revolution in the South," *Virginia Quarterly Review*, 26 (1950), 197.

7. The report made forty-one proposals (not all for Federal action) contained in thirty-five numbered recommendations under six general headings. Mr. Truman's recommendations to Congress incorporated fifteen of the forty-one proposals. The report was published by the Government Printing Office, Washington, D. C., in 1947.

8. Hilary Herbert Vaughan, quoted by John Temple Graves, *Birmingham Post*, September 25, 1948. Some persons reflected that if the consequences of the Truman program would be as disastrous as some felt, the easiest way to kill it would be to put part of it into effect and let public reaction take its course.

9. So reads the text that appeared in the July 26, 1948, issue of *States' Rights,* an official Dixiecratic campaign paper published in Birmingham. The same statement appeared in the manuscript of a talk for delivery in Tuscaloosa, Alabama, on August 9, 1948.

10. See V. O. Key, Jr., *Southern Politics,* part II. Key analyzed the 1928 vote in each state and concluded "that the irreducible core of southern Democracy had its center of gravity in 1928 in the rural, agricultural counties with high proportions of Negro population." Correspondingly, the areas most inclined toward Hoover were those of lowest proportions of Negroes.—*op. cit.*, p. 329.

11. In view of the numbers of voters involved, such a conclusion seems reasonable. It might be modified, however, by more data on the economic status of Dixiecratic voters. No public opinion polls could be located that offered useful data, though the Texas Poll coöperated generously and made available the results of its sample surveys.

12. *Savannah Evening Press,* July 31, 1950.
13. *New York Times,* July 16, 1950.
14. See John N. Popham's report in the *New York Times,* May 11,

1950; also, the editorial in the *Norfolk Virginian-Pilot*, May 12, 1950.

15. See Drew Pearson's column that appeared on August 17, 1950 in the *News and Observer* (Raleigh); and the *New Republic* for March 20, 1950.

16. The view of a leading constitutional scholar, Carl Brent Swisher, in *The Growth of Constitutional Power in the United States* (Chicago: University of Chicago Press, 1946), p. 33.

17. *New York Times*, March 9, 1950.

18. AP dispatch of November 24, 1950.

19. *Savannah Morning News*, July 3, 1950.

20. For example, Ira W. Day, an insurance man, gave $50.00 to the North Carolina Republican campaign fund in 1950. Yet he had been active in the preceding Democratic primaries on behalf of Willis Smith, conservative candidate for the senatorial nomination.—*News and Observer* (Raleigh), October 28, 1950. Samuel Lubell reported from his examination of county and precinct voting in the Florida and North Carolina senatorial primaries of 1950 that the opposition to Pepper and Graham paralleled that to Truman two years earlier. In this he saw something of a Republican-Dixiecratic coalition at the grass roots.—"Has Truman Lost the South?", *Look*, October 24, 1950, pp. 134-36. Precinct election returns and economic and social data suitable for correlational analysis are extremely difficult to obtain. Much work remains to be done in the analysis of southern voting below the county level.

21. See the debate between Senator Mundt and Representative Clifford P. Case, Republican of New Jersey, in *Collier's*, July 28, 1951.

22. *News and Observer* (Raleigh), March 24, 1951.

23. Hodding Carter, "Chip on Our Shoulder Down South," *Saturday Evening Post*, November 2, 1946, p. 19.

24. *News and Observer* (Raleigh), November 3, 1951. See Ralph McGill's article, "What is Jimmy Byrnes Up to Now?", *Saturday Evening Post*, October 14, 1950.

25. For one account of the campaign, written by a labor union official active in it, read David S. Burgess's "Hucksters of Hate," *The Progressive*, February, 1951 (vol. 15, no. 2), 5-8.

26. The suggestions arise from such sentiments as these of the former CIO director for North Carolina as the 1950 senatorial general election in that state approached. Of Willis Smith, the Democratic nominee who had won against the opposition of labor leadership in the primaries, he said: "... no trade unionist, if his union means anything

aged.—"Political Competition will Help the South," *Virginia Quarterly Review,* 26 (1950), 268-76.

20. "Toward a More Responsible Two-Party System," *The American Political Science Review,* 44 (1950), supplement, p. 74. The Committee's report is controversial. See Julius Turner's article, "Responsible Parties: A Dissent from the Floor," *The American Political Science Review,* 45 (1951), 143-52.

21. Dr. Silva probably would disagree with this argument.—"The Lodge-Gossett Resolution," pp. 97-98.

22. See Harold F. Gosnell, *Why Europe Votes* (Chicago: University of Chicago Press, 1930), pp. 183, 187-91.

23. Note the graphs with comments on pp. 533-35 and 608-9 in V. O. Key, Jr., *Southern Politics.*

NOTES TO CHAPTER 13

1. The 1940 and 1947 figures, given below by states, are estimates by the late Luther P. Jackson, "Race and Suffrage In the South Since 1940," *New South,* June-July, 1948, p. 4. They conform to those obtained by this writer in the field. Dr. Jackson's 1947 Texas estimate differs from the 1946 estimate of 184,000 made by the Texas Poll after sampling all the poll tax books in the state.—*Dallas Morning News,* October 27, 1946. The south-wide estimate of 900,000 for 1950 is probably dependable, although it was impossible in some states to confirm the figures on which it was based by conversation or correspondence with reliable informants. The official totals of Negroes registered in Florida and Louisiana, however, are helpful. In Florida in 1948, 85,180 Negroes were registered; in 1950, 116,145. In Louisiana in 1948, 28,177 were registered; in 1950, 51,675. Sound local estimates placed the 1950 Georgia figure at 133,000 and the 1949 Virginia figure at 66,000. Dr. Jackson's estimates of "qualified Negro voters" follow, stated in thousands:

	Ala.	Ark.	Fla.	Ga.	La.	Miss.	N.C.	S.C.	Tenn.	Texas	Va.
1940	2	4	18	20	2	2	35	3	20	30	15
1947	6	47	49	125	10	5	75	50	80	100	48

2. Based on estimates obtained by interview in each state, as follows, stated in thousands:

	Ala.	Ark.	Fla.	Ga.	La.	Miss.	N.C.	S.C.	Tenn.	Texas	Va.
1946	3-5	5	25	90	2.5	2.5	40	—	30	75	15

The North Carolina estimate is for 1944. Negroes in South Carolina voted in Democratic primaries for the first time in recent decades in 1948: to the number of about 35,000. Estimated participation fell in Georgia in that year to 65,000 and rose in Arkansas to 22,000. Some 40,000 Negroes were said to have voted in Little Rock in July, 1950, and between 18,000 and 22,000 in the New Orleans mayoralty race of January, 1950.—*Civil Rights in the United States in 1950* (published by the American Jewish Congress and the National Association for the Advancement of Colored People), p. 16. Samuel Lubell estimated about 60 per cent of Florida's registered Negro Democrats voted in the primary of 1950, *i.e.*, around 64,000—"Has Truman Lost the South?", *Look*, October 24, 1950, p. 137.

3. Robert L. Jack, *History of the National Association for the Advancement of Colored People* (Boston: Meador Publishing Company, 1943), pp. 4-7.

4. Figures provided by NAACP Membership Secretary, letters dated June 15, 1949, April 10, 1951, and April 30, 1951. The figures cover twelve southern states, including Kentucky.

5. Mr. White has written the story of the NAACP in his autobiography, *A Man Called White* (New York: The Viking Press, 1948).

6. *NAACP Bulletin,* October, 1946.

7. Letter to NAACP branches from Harry T. Moore, Executive Secretary, Florida State Conference of NAACP, dated October 11, 1947.

8. The NAACP has not hesitated to oppose individual candidates whom it deemed to have no regard for vital Negro interests. See Walter White's account of its campaign against the United States senators who voted in 1930 to confirm Judge John J. Parker's nomination to the Supreme Court.—*A Man Called White*, pp. 112-13.

NOTES TO CHAPTER 14

1. See Gunnar Myrdal, *An American Dilemma* (New York: Harper and Brothers Publishers, 1944), pp. 771-77.

2. A sketch of Mr. Walden called "Negro Vote-Getter," by Harold C. Fleming, appeared in *The Reporter,* March 28, 1950 (vol. 2, no. 7), 18-20.

3. Donald S. Strong, "The Rise of Negro Voting in Texas," *The American Political Science Review,* 42 (1948), 510-22.

4. Myrdal, *op. cit.*, p. 488.

9. Henry Lee Moon is a Negro journalist who in recent years has had a close view of southern politics as an official of CIO-PAC and as head of public relations for the NAACP. In his book, *Balance of Power: The Negro Vote* (Garden City, New York: Doubleday & Company, Inc., 1949), pp. 194-95, he asserts: "In states where large numbers of Negroes are voting for the first time there has been a strong tendency toward bloc voting. In part this has been due to the new voters' unfamiliarity with the issues, the candidates, and the electoral processes. In need of guidance, they turn to leaders whom they can trust and who have studied the issues and agreed upon candidates to support. Moreover, colored voters are frequently forced into bloc voting by the record and campaigns of such candidates as Talmadge in Georgia and Bilbo in Mississippi. . . . In Tennessee, Virginia, and North Carolina, where Negroes have been voting over a period of years, there is a greater tendency toward the development of factions within the group. Certain leaders, having acquired a personal interest in particular candidates, work for them among Negro voters, much as is done in New York, Philadelphia, or Chicago. In such communities issues are frequently of less importance to the Negro politicians than to the principled leaders in the states farther south, and differences in the communities are much sharper."

10. *Columbus Ledger,* July 17, 1946.

11. A study of Negro voting in Georgia during 1946-47 was published by the Georgia Committee on Interracial Cooperation, "Block Voting." In this state, where Negroes voted more numerously than elsewhere in the South, their performance in six counties or cities was examined. The conclusions were: "1. In state elections the solidifying factor almost invariably is the Negro's right to vote. Negroes will vote in a bloc only when white supremacy is the issue. 2. In county and municipal elections Negroes tend to vote in a bloc against candidates who have demonstrated a disregard for Negro rights and aspirations, and for those who have proved themselves sympathetic. Sometimes, too, local issues may force them into a bloc vote, especially when those issues relate directly to the welfare of the Negro communities. 3. In those few counties where the Negro's right to vote has come to be accepted, and it is the practice for all candidates to bid for the Negro vote as earnestly as they do for the white, there is no Negro bloc."— pp. 2-3.

12. Ralph Bunche, Political Status of the Negro (unpublished

manuscript prepared for the Gunnar Myrdal study, on microfilm in the Library of Congress), chap. XI.

13. Two letters from Negro political groups illustrate the concern of Negroes with state government policy. The first, dated April 6, 1951, from F. A. Dunn, President, and Harry T. Moore, Executive Secretary, Progressive Voters' League of Florida, read as follows:

Members of the Legislature
Governor and State Cabinet
Tallahassee, Florida
Dear Sirs:

At a "legislative clinic" held in Sanford on March 24th, the Progressive Voters' League of Florida voted unanimously to recommend and support the nine proposals listed below. It was decided also to submit a copy of our recommendations to each member of the Legislature, to the Governor, and to members of the Cabinet.

(1) The full appropriation of 120 million dollars to continue the Minimum Foundation Program for public schools.

(2) A constitutional amendment to earmark auto tag money for capital outlay, so that urgently needed school construction can be financed at much lower rates of interest.

(3) A state law to require *every* county to pay teachers equal salaries, solely on the basis of training and experience. This law should eliminate rating systems that permit some counties to practice unfair discrimination against Negro teachers.

(4) A state law against lynching and mob violence, similar to the one enacted in Texas two years ago. Florida needs such a law for greater security against disturbances like we had around Groveland in 1949, and to make it easier to mete out justice in lynchings like we have had in Suwannee, Madison and Jackson Counties during recent years.

(5) Measures to outlaw the Ku Klux Klan, which has established a long record of violence and intimidation.

(6) A law to make cities liable for any police brutality practiced by their officers. Florida citizens—particularly Negroes—are often victims of such brutality. Recently a Riviera Beach Negro, charged only with a misdemeanor, was shot *in the back* and killed by a policeman. This officer is still on the force. If it is made possible for victims or their relatives to sue cities for damage in such cases, the cities would automatically tighten up on the behavior of their officers.

(7) No change in voting laws to require a literacy test for prospective voters. Such a change might permit wholesale discrimination against Negroes, as did the "Grandfather Clause".

(8) Tightening of welfare laws to make fathers of illegitimate children responsible for their support, thus leaving more money available for deserving old age pensioners.

(9) Plans for the immediate opening of the new home for delinquent Negro girls at Ocala. Negro citizens will look with much disfavor on any efforts to deny or further delay the use of this home by Negro girls.

We solicit your favorable consideration and support of these recommendations.

Respectfully yours,

The other letter, from R. L. Battle, President, and Leon R. Williams, Acting Secretary, Alabama Political Primary Council, read in part as follows:

To Whom It May Concern:

The Negro Representatives and Registered Voters from communities in all sections of the State of Alabama, assembled in the City of Montgomery, March 30, 1946 hereby make the following statement of their beliefs and principles on matters affecting Social, Economic, Political and Educational development of the Negro in the State of Alabama. . . .

In view of the foregoing beliefs, we feel that the government of the State of Alabama should take definite steps to see that the Negro gets his just share of these things which are essential to his development, on the same basis as they are extended to all other people.

1. We feel that in the allocation of funds for education a definite sum should be earmarked for the Negro, based on his needs and population ratio;
2. We urge that Negro Supervisors for Veteran affairs be appointed to look after Negro Veterans' welfare, and that in large metropolitan centers there be appointed local advisors to guide and direct men who have recently and are still being discharged from the armed services;
3. We strongly urged that Negro parole officers be connected with the Parole Board to look after Negro parolees, and to

see to it that these men be properly guided in getting adjusted to civilian life;
4. We are convinced and strongly urge that Negro Social Workers should be employed in the Department of Welfare to look after the needy who are serviced by this department. It is our feeling that a Negro is in better position to understand needs of the Negro and will do more to get for him the security provided in the law. We are convinced that Negroes as a whole would be more intelligent on matters pertaining to the work of this department if there were colored Social Workers employed;
5. We urge the appointment of Negroes to the Employment Service which is now under the United States Government; and should the Employment Service be turned over to the several states, we urge that Negroes be continued as functional members of the Employment Service;
6. We feel that a Negro labor conciliator should be appointed to help in the settlement of labor difficulties and to give guidance to Negro labor groups in industrial employment;
7. We favor an extension of security to provide laborers not covered under the present law;
8. We favor a state minimum wage law sufficiently high to provide all laborers with a decent standard of living;
9. We favor the repeal of the poll tax and strongly oppose the Boswell amendment. It is our belief that the registration laws should be administered indiscriminately. Many boards as now constituted discourage a large segment of the citizens of Alabama from voting. Such descouragement is contrary to the principles of democracy to which we are sincerely devoted;
10. We urge equalization salaries for school teachers and adequate transportation for Negro school children. The Negro is suffering in the state of Alabama from unequal educational opportunities; we strongly urge that such inequality be corrected immediately;
11. We look upon the Bradford Act as being unfair to organized labor and we urge its repeal.

In conclusion, we wish to state our beliefs that the Negro has been blocked too long in making his full contribution to the development of the natural and human resources of the great State of Alabama. We feel that it is incumbent upon the State legislature, the governor, and local county and city officials to see that the Negro is allowed a larger share than he now has in the development of our State. Such is possible we believe, only if opportunities increasingly are granted Negroes which are enjoyed by other citizens of the State.

14. Litchfield found in Detroit that prior to 1936 race consciousness rather than class consciousness seemed to characterize Negro voting. In 1936, however, economic lines began to crystallize within the racial group.—Edward H. Litchfield, *Voting Behavior in a Metropolitan Area* (Ann Arbor: University of Michigan Press, 1941), pp. 40-41. In a further analysis he focused his attention specifically on Negro ballot behavior. His findings should be weighed heavily by those seeking to envision the southern politics of the future. "In summarizing the major party affiliation of the Negro groups it may be said: (1) that whereas in 1930 the group as a whole was the least Democratic of the city's many elements, in 1940 it is one of the most Democratic; (2) that the poor Negro voter is coming to vote more and more like the poor man in other race and ethnic groups and less like his middle class neighbor.... In short, the story of Negro voting behavior seems to show above all else, that the Negro is at last becoming politically average. His participation, while once very small, has gradually approached the average; his party affiliation, once a paragon of rigidity, has shown an ability to adapt to changing ideas within the community in a normal manner; his third party voting, which was once atypical has now moved well into the average pattern."—"A Case Study of Negro Political Behavior in Detroit," *Public Opinion Quarterly*, 5 (1941), 273-74. It is important that studies of this type be made of Negro voting under the one-party conditions in the South. Negro voting behavior in the general elections of northern states may rest on conditions different from those obtaining in southern primaries.

15. There are inevitable exceptions. In 1947 a Negro named Armstrong qualified as a candidate in the Democratic primary for the Jacksonville, Florida, city council from the fifth ward. He was immediately disavowed in a resolution "drafted by officers of the Roosevelt Democratic Club, the Duval County Voters League, and the Negro Chamber of Commerce, and by Rev. A. V. Weaver, pastor of the Day Springs Baptist Church, Rev. A. B. Coleman of the Shiloh Baptist Church, Rev. G. W. Washington of the Central Colored Methodist

Episcopal Church, and Ertha M. M. White, representing the Negro women voters of the Fifth Ward. ... The Fifth Ward is predominantly Negro, having 2,214 qualified colored voters as against 1,178 white.... The group does not feel, the statement said, after a conference with Armstrong, that he is 'representative of the race for the position he is aspiring.' The signers of the resolution 'further believe that Armstrong's action was prompted by some radical group or groups; and that his entry into the race at such an inopportune time will do much harm not only to the Negro in Jacksonville, but in the State at large ... The announcement of the endorsement of the negro people's choice ... will be made known in the very near future.... We ... wish it generally known ... that we do not and will not endorse a candidate because of his race or creed but solely on his qualifications plus his willingness to serve to the best of his ability the best interests of all the people whom it will be his duty to serve." The three other candidates were white.—*Florida Times-Union* (Jacksonville), March 20, 1947. A Negro explained that Armstrong insisted on running "when the time was not ripe," i.e., when a white primary bill was expected to come up in the legislature. Armstrong's filing fee was paid by the National Negro Congress, allegedly a Communist connected organization.—J. Erroll Miller, "The Negro in Present Day Politics With Special Reference to Philadelphia," *The Journal of Negro History*, 33 (1948), 339.

16. James M. Hinton, in a letter to Senator Olin D. Johnston, quoted in *Columbia Record* (S. C.), April 26, 1948.

17. *Columbia Record* (S. C.), June 9, 1948; *Richmond Times-Dispatch*, August 7, 1947.

18. *Journal and Guide* (Norfolk), November 15, 1947.

19. *Ibid.*, May 10, 1947.

20. *New South*, August-September, 1951, p. 7.

21. *Nashville Tennessean*, April 22, 1951.

22. *News and Observer* (Raleigh), November 8, 1946.

23. *Journal and Guide* (Norfolk), May 10, 1947; *News and Observer* (Raleigh), April 10, 1951; *New South*, January-February, 1950, p. 7.

24. *Richmond Times-Dispatch*, August 7, 1947.

25. *The Texas Spectator* (Austin), April 19, 1948.

26. "Negro Candidates for Congress," *New Republic*, June 12, 1950, pp. 7-8.

NOTES TO CHAPTER 17

1. Henry Lee Moon, *Balance of Power: The Negro Vote* (Garden City, New York: Doubleday & Company, Inc., 1949), p. 68.

2. This point is commented on in various places. See for example, Andrew C. McLaughlin, *A Constitutional History of the United States* (New York: Appleton-Century-Crofts, Inc., 1935), pp. 651, 655. Until the time of Bryan, of course, the strength of the two major parties was extremely close.

3. Hampton's Negro support has been noted by scholars, but it is sometimes forgotten that he created quite a stir in South Carolina by dining with Negroes and urging that the University of South Carolina be combined with a Negro college. Note the interesting period piece, *Red Shirts Remembered*, by William Arthur Sheppard (published by the author, Spartanburg, S. C., printed by the Ruralist Press, Inc., Atlanta, 1940), pp. 264-65 and *passim*. Negro support for Woodrow Wilson in his first campaign is discussed by Arthur S. Link in "The Negro as a Factor in the Campaign of 1912," *The Journal of Negro History*, 32 (1947), 81-99.

4. Paul Lewinson, *Race, Class, and Party* (New York: Oxford University Press, 1932), p. 170; Moon, *op. cit.*, pp. 79-80.

5. Willie D. Halsell (ed.), "Republican Factionalism in Mississippi 1882-1884," *The Journal of Southern History*, 7 (1941), 84-101.

6. Judson C. Ward, Jr., "The Republican Party in Bourbon Georgia, 1872-1890," *The Journal of Southern History*, 9 (1943), 196-209.

7. Lewinson, *op. cit.*, p. 171.

8. E. Merton Coulter, "The Attempt of William Howard Taft to Break the Solid South," *The Georgia Historical Quarterly*, 19 (1935), 134-44.

9. Victor Rosewater, *Back Stage in 1912* (Philadelphia: Dorrance and Company, Inc., 1932), pp. 64-65. One reporter of the convention proceedings was William Jennings Bryan: "The X, or unknown quantity, in the Republican situation is the colored vote from the South. It is the weakness of the Taft cause. It is a weakness not only because it does not represent a voting strength proportionate to its influence in the convention but a weakness also because it cannot be depended upon to stand tied.... One of the Mississippi delegates has returned some money which was given to him for travelling expenses for the delegates, but there are Taft supporters who are uncharitable enough to charge that this money would not have been returned had not a

larger sum been received from 'sources unknown.' "—*A Tale of Two Conventions* (New York: Funk and Wagnalls Company, 1912), pp. 7-8.

10. Letter to Julian Harris dated August 1, 1912.—Arthur S. Link (ed.), "Correspondence Relating to the Progressive Party's 'Lily White' Policy in 1912," *The Journal of Southern History*, 10 (1944), 487. George E. Mowry has written on "The South and the Progressive Lily White Party of 1912," *The Journal of Southern History*, 6 (1940), 237-47. The Progressive Party convention of 1916 nominated Roosevelt for president and John M. Parker of Louisiana for vice president, a gesture to the white south. Roosevelt declined the nomination but Parker did not, receiving 41,894 votes, of which 20,653 were cast in Georgia, 10,172 in New York, and 6,349 in Louisiana.—Edward Stanwood, *A History of the Presidency from 1897 to 1916* (rev. ed.; New York: Houghton Mifflin Company, 1928), pp. 346, 374.

11. "The Republicans and the Black Voter," *The Nation*, 110 (1920), 757-58.

12. The election returns for governor of Florida in 1920 show 103,407 votes received by the Democrat, 23,788 by the Republican, and 2,654 by the "Republican, white." The Arkansas gubernatorial returns for the same year show 123,604 votes for the Democrat, 46,339 for the Republican, 15,627 for the "Negro Independent" candidate, and 4,543 for a Socialist.

13. Ralph Bunche, Political Status of the Negro (unpublished manuscript prepared for the Gunnar Myrdal study, on microfilm in the Library of Congress), p. 1181. According to the official returns the Negro Republican, John Mitchell, Jr., received 5,036 votes and Anderson 65,933, results somewhat at variance with those reported in the Bunche manuscript. The Democratic candidate received 139,416 votes. See Lewinson, *op. cit.*, p. 159.

14. Lewinson, *op. cit.*, pp. 171-76. For detailed descriptions of the black-and-tan vs. lily-white conflicts in several states, counties, and towns, see Bunche, *op. cit.*, pp. 1175-1226.

15. Bunche, *op. cit.*, pp. 1176-77. Useful in making the shift was the well-known investigation led by Senator Brookhart of Iowa. The Brookhart report contains abundant testimony on corruption and patronage practices among Republicans in the South.—United States Congress, Senate Subcommittee of the Committee on Post Offices and Post Roads, 70th Congress, 2nd Session, *Influencing Appointments to Postmasterships, Hearings*, parts 1-6 (Washington: Government Printing Office).

16. In the six presidential contests from 1928 to 1948, the Inde-

pendent Republicans led the recognized faction four times. The vote in 1948: regular Republican, 2,595; Independent Republican, 2,448.

17. The percentages that the number of Negro delegates from the South was of the number of southern seats in Republican national conventions from 1912 to 1940 were as follows: 1912, 25.0; 1916, 9.5; 1920, 12.0; 1924, 17.5; 1928, 21.0; 1932, 6.2; 1936, 17.0; 1940, 9.5. The sharp drop in 1932 resulted not only from the Hoover lily-white policy but also from the increase in southern delegates that followed the cracking of the solid South in 1928. Whites took the new seats that were awarded. There were Negro alternates in some years, their number usually running behind the number of Negro delegates. Sources of number of Negro delegates by states, for 1912-36, *Negro Yearbook* (published by Tuskegee Institute, Alabama); for 1940, *Negro Handbook* (New York: W. Malliet and Company).

18. More was involved in the trade, of course, as set out by Vann Woodward in *Reunion and Reaction* (Boston: Little, Brown and Company, 1951).

19. Moon, *op. cit.*, pp. 95-97.

NOTES TO CHAPTER 18

1. In another state, a Negro saw in the CIO the only bridge over the divide of color that separates whites and Negroes of common occupational and economic interests.

2. See, for example, Harold F. Gosnell, "The Negro Vote in Northern Cities," *National Municipal Review*, 30 (1941), 264-66.

3. Harry T. Moore, Executive Secretary of the Progressive Voters' League of Florida, Inc., in a release to Negroes of Florida dated March 1, 1948.

4. Negroes of all ages find it distasteful to vote the Democratic primary ballot of Alabama which carries the legend "white supremacy."

5. Arkansas Democratic Party Rules, 1948, sec. 2 (b), (c): "Party Membership . . . shall consist of only legally qualified white electors . . . No person who is not a member of the Party may . . . be nominated as a candidate of the Party. . . . Nor . . . act as a party official or serve on the membership of any committee of the Party, or participate in any Party convention."

6. *New South*, January-February, 1950, p. 7.

7. Donald S. Strong, "The Rise of Negro Voting in Texas," *The American Political Science Review*, 42 (1948), 512.

8. *Constitution and By-Laws* (October 10, 1928), Article II.

9. Strong, *op. cit.*, p. 515.

10. Resolution #11 adopted by the 1946 state convention read that: "This organization continue, making firm efforts to increase its membership among white citizens and in elections devote its strength to candidates appearing to be the least prejudiced and most able to render impartial services to all citizens; that where advisable, this party shall sponsor its own candidates they being chosen without distinction as to race, creed, or color."

11. A letter from Mrs. Andrew W. Simkins to B. L. Brooks, dated April 3, 1947.

12. These benefits, as expressed in the 1944 platform of the Progressive Democratic party, included (1) prosecution of the war, (2) elimination of freight rate differentials, (3) federal aid for education, (4) elimination of poll tax for voting, (5) enactment of a Federal anti-lynching law, (6) fair employment practices on Federally financed jobs, (7) "more equitable distribution of Federal funds to be used for developmental purposes in the various states, with special reference to the Southeastern area," (8) re-election of F.D.R. The resolutions adopted by the 1946 state convention included a plea for "firmer and more positive action of this government in settling an unhealthy number of strikes and strifes between industry and labor"; a plea on behalf of freedom for nations under the control of more powerful nations; and the request that the United States government "reallocate the number of congressmen in states which circumvent or disbar free voting of all citizens."

13. *Richmond Times-Dispatch,* September 16, 1948.

14. This last seems a fair conclusion, though the writer has seen no statistical support for it.

15. See Wilson Record, *The Negro and the Communist Party* (Chapel Hill: University of North Carolina Press, 1951), especially chap. 8, "Red and Black: Unblending Colors." The present writer's skepticism of the success of any third party movement is expressed in chapter 2, above.

16. The Myrdal study speculated on a "reorganization" of the American party system which would include two parties, one liberal, carrying on the tradition of the New Deal, and the other conservative. "If we assume that such a new system will materialize, it seems fairly certain that the great majority of Negroes are going to adhere to the liberal party, provided it be consistently liberal with respect to the

Negro problem and manifests its liberalism not only in words but also in deeds." The comment was added that if such a realignment occurred many Negro politicians would be released from the dilemma of double loyalty to a party and to the Negro group. "This would remove to a certain extent one of the fundamental causes of political cynicism and corruption among Negro politicians."—Gunnar Myrdal, *An American Dilemma* (New York: Harper and Brothers Publishers, 1944), p. 511.

17. Along with the tendency of Negro voters to follow national election trends.—J. Erroll Miller, "The Negro in Present Day Politics With Special Reference to Philadelphia," *The Journal of Negro History*, 33 (1948), 342.

18. "Texas Republicans Monday joined southern Democrats in denouncing President Truman's proposed civil rights legislation. A resolution condemning the President's action was approved unanimously by the Republican state executive committee..."—*Dallas Morning News*, February 17, 1948. "The Republican state convention [of Tennessee] went on record today against a federal civil rights program."—*Memphis Press-Scimitar*, April 30, 1948. "Arkansas Republicans joined Southern Democrats yesterday in denouncing President Truman's proposed Fair Employment Practices Act as a platform including opposition to the measure was unanimously adopted by delegates to the state Republican convention...."—*Arkansas Gazette* (Little Rock), May 12, 1948. "John A. Wilkinson of Washington, N. C., Republican candidate for the United States Senate, ... promised to oppose the civil rights proposals if elected to the Senate."—*News and Observer* (Raleigh), June 11, 1948.

NOTES TO CHAPTER 19

1. W. G. Carleton questioned the need for a two-party system in "Why Call the South Conservative?", *Harper's Magazine*, 195 (1947), 61-68.

2. A convenient inventory of voting behavior studies appears in chap. 19 of V. O. Key, Jr., *Politics, Parties, and Pressure Groups* (2nd. ed.; New York: Thomas Y. Crowell Company, 1947). See the critical discussion by Samuel J. Eldersveld, "Theory and Method in Voting Behavior Research," *The Journal of Politics*, 13 (1951), 70-87.

3. See, for example, Charles E. Merriam and Harold F. Gosnell, *The American Party System* (4th ed.; New York: The Macmillan Company, 1949), pp. 119-21, on the persistence of "neighborhood"

attitudes; also, Paul F. Lazarsfeld, *The People's Choice* (New York: Duell, Sloan and Pearce, 1944), chap. 9.

4. Dayton David McKean, *Party and Pressure Politics* (New York: Houghton Mifflin Company, 1949), p. 101.

5. Jackson, of course, ran strongly in low country as well as up country. The difference in outlook appeared rather clearly in the subsequent Whig-Democratic elections. Invaluable in understanding the struggles of the post-Jackson period is A. C. Cole's classic study of *The Whig Party in the South* (Washington: American Historical Association, 1913). The appendix contains a series of instructive maps, of which the author says: "In general, they show that from the election of 1836 to the election of 1852 there was a continuance of Whig and Democratic strength or weakness in certain definite regions. The regions of Whig strength are to be identified with those districts which were drawn by economic interests to the support of the 'American system,' or with those in which the negro-slave-plantation system predominated. ... [A] comparison of the maps plotting the presidential votes with the one indicating white or negro-slave preponderance shows that wherever there was a negro majority or significant minority there could be found, with no important exceptions, a Whig majority or uncertain Democratic control."—p. 367. As the author himself acknowledges, there are apparent exceptions to his generalizations that require special explanation, especially in the distribution of Whig strength in North Carolina.

6. "Our parties seek to be as inclusive as possible without actually crumbling because of the very incongruity of the constituent elements." —Pendleton Herring, *The Politics of Democracy* (New York: W. W. Norton & Company, Inc., 1940), p. 248. A dissent from the conventional view expressed in the text has been rendered by Samuel P. Huntington in "A Revised Theory of American Party Politics," *The American Political Science Review*, 44 (1950), 669-77. Mr. Huntington argues that Democrats from two-party areas more consistently voted "liberal" and Republicans from two-party areas more consistently voted "conservative" than their fellow party members from other areas. Therefore, stiff party competition tends to accentuate the differences between the parties rather than to make them more nearly alike. It seems to this writer that the phenomenon Mr. Huntington observes is a heightening of party loyalty in two-party areas, and as such does not necessarily reflect "qualitative" differences between the parties, i.e., the extent of differences in party policies. In the House of Com-

mons, for example, where party discipline is great, Laborites unanimously, and Conservatives unanimously, may oppose each other in a long string of divisions, yet what the two parties stand for in public policy may not be widely different.

7. Louis H. Bean, *How to Predict an Election* (New York: Alfred A. Knopf, Inc., 1948), chap. 8, "Political Patterns."

8. Quoted by Charles Seignobos, *Die geographische verteilung der parteien in Frankreich* (Sonderabdruck aus der Frankfurter Zeitung), p. 18. See André Siegfried, *Tableau Politique de La France de L'Ouest sous la Troisième République* (Librairie Armand Colin, 103 Boulevard Saint-Michel, Paris, 1913).

9. Pierre Maillaud, quoted in David Thomson, *Democracy in France: The Third Republic* (New York: Oxford University Press, 1946), p. 52.

10. This book is written, deliberately, without much exposition of the analytical methods employed. Essentially, the book assumes the validity of a cross-pressure analysis of individual behavior. David B. Truman has expounded systematically the concept of group membership and of overlapping, multiple memberships as sources of multiple interests, and therefore of diverse pressures, on individuals. See *The Governmental Process* (New York: Alfred A. Knopf, Inc., 1951), especially chap. 6.

11. See especially two of Holcombe's early books, *The Political Parties of To-day* (2nd ed.; New York: Harper & Brothers, 1925) and *The New Party Politics* (New York: W. W. Norton & Company, Inc., 1933).

12. "The Influence of Metropolitan Party Pluralities in Presidential Elections Since 1920," *The American Political Science Review*, 43 (1949), 1189-1206.

INDEX

Absence voting, 89-92
Acuff, Roy, 104
AF of L, 155; *see also* Labor
Afro-American, 232
Agrarianism, *see* Populism
Agriculture, *see* Social and economic conditions
Alabama: Democratic factionalism in, 15; Democratic loyalty requirements, 140; Dixiecratic vote, 1948, analyzed, 278; Dixiecrats, 22-23, 161-63, 164; financing of primaries, 107n; Heflin, Tom, 138; NAACP in, 186; Negro politics, 190-91, 210, 225, 308-10; Negro registration in, 86; Negro voters, number, 302; Populism, 48; registration officials, 86; Republican campaign quota, 116; Republican candidates, 288; Republican leadership, 111; Republican primaries, 106; and secret voting, 94; "white supremacy" on ballot, 314; *see also* Democratic party; Dixiecrats; Negro politics; One-party system in South; Republican party; Republicans, southern
Alabama Political Primary Council, 308-10
Alamance County, N.C., 218, 269

Albany State College, Ga., 305
Alexander County, N.C., 78
American Jewish Congress, 294
American Political Science Association, Committee on Political Parties, 176, 281
Anderson, Henry, 224, 313
Anniston, Ala., 190-91, 205
Anti-lynching, *see* Civil rights proposals
Arkansas: Democratic loyalty requirements, 138-40; Dixiecratic vote, 1948, analyzed, 261-63; Dixiecrats, 164; election officials, 84-85; lily whiteism, 224; Negro politics, 194-95, 202-03, 224, 225, 229, 230; Negro voters, number of, 302-03; poll tax, 86-87; presidential Republicans, 141-42; Republican candidates, 1948, 103n; Republican politics, 100, 111, 111n; Republican primaries, 106; Republicans, distribution, 56; Republicans, presidential race and state politics, 135, 137; secret voting, 93; vote for governor, 1920, 313; *see also* Democratic party; Dixiecrats; Negro politics; One-party system in South; Republican party; Republicans, southern

319

INDEX

Arkansas Free Enterprise Association, 261, 297
Arkansas Gazette, 262
Arkansas Negro Democratic Association, 194-95, 202-3, 230
Armstrong, candidate, 310-11
Arnall, Ellis, 210
Asheville, N.C., 218
Ashmore, Harry S., x
Asseff, Emmett, 286
Associated Industries of Alabama, 297
Athens, Tenn., 87n-88n
Atlanta, Ga., 147, 184, 192, 205
Atlanta Urban League, 192
Attorney General, U.S., 207
Augusta, Ga., 218

Bailey, Joseph, Jr., 258
Baker, Howard H., Sr., 109
Ballot, secrecy, *see* Voting, non-secret; Absentee voting
Baltimore, Md., 232
Baton Rouge, La., 186, 229
Battle, R. L., 308
Bean, Louis H., 243, 282
Bellinger, Valmo, 195
Berdahl, Clarence A., 282
Bertrand, Alvin L., 277n
Biggs machine, in Tennessee, 88n
Bilbo, Theodore, 166, 210, 304, 306
Birmingham, Ala., 147, 190, 201
Birmingham Dixiecratic "conference," 21
Black-and-tan Republicans, *see* Negro politics; Republicans, southern
Black belts: 8-9; and Dixiecrats, 27, 160, 163-64, state by state, 251-78; *see also* Intimidation of Negroes; One-party system in South, origins; Race relations; Population shifts
Blackwell, Gordon W., x
Blease, Cole, 275
Bloc voting, and minority groups, 210
Bloc voting, Negro: 201, 209-19, 306, 310-11; "balance of power," 215-16; criticism of, 209-10; continuing bases for, 216; disrupted easily, 213; on economic and social issues, 214-15; in future, 232-33; for government services, 210-15, 305, 307-10; group interests at stake, 210-15; for Negro candidates, 216-19; studies of, needed, 210, 216-17, 310; when whites compete for votes, 214
Blue Ridge Mountains, Republican heartland, 40-41, 242
Booze, Mary, 225
Boston, Mass., 210
Boswell Amendment, in Alabama, 86, 210
Brevard County, Fla., 186
Brewer, Basil, 301
Brewer, J. Mason, 304
Brookhart, Smith W., 288, 313
Brooks, B. L., 315
Browning, Gordon, 104, 109
Bryan, William Jennings, 312
Bryce, James, 134
Bunche, Ralph, 195, 215, 313
Buncombe County, N.C., 50n
Bureau of Public Administration, University of Alabama, vii, ix
Burgess, David S., 299
Burlington, N.C., 218
Burns, James MacGregor, 291
Burruss, Mary Helen, x
Butler, Marion, 45
Byrd, Harry F., 69, 99, 158, 165, 265, 266
Byrd, Mrs. Harry F., 265
Byrd machine, 99, 142, 196, 265-68; *see also* Virginia
Byrnes, James F., 164, 165-67

Čadek, Sara H., x
Calvert, Robert W., 257
Campaign finance: Dixiecratic sources, 298; and Lodge-Gossett Amendment, 173; Negro, *see* Negro politics; and southern Republicans, 103, 116-17, 129, 137, 143
Campaign organization, *see* Negro voters' leagues; Republicans, southern
Candidates, *see* Primaries; Negro politics; individual parties
Cantrell machine, in Tennessee, 87n-88n

INDEX

Carleton, William G., 16, 297, 300, 316
Carmichael, James V., 205-7, 210, 304
Carpenter, Jesse T., 281
Carter, Hodding, x, 144, 166, 171
Carter, J. W., 218
Case, Clifford P., 299
Chapel Hill, N.C., 211
Charleston, S.C., 219, 275n
Charlotte, N.C., 77, 196, 305
Chattanooga, Tenn., 198
Chicago, Negro politics in, 306
Childs, Marquis, 122
Chilton County, Ala., 48
CIO, 155, 197, 198, 228, 297, 299-300, 314; *see also* Labor
Citizens' Democratic Club, in Savannah, Ga., 203-5
Citizens' Progressive League, in Savannah, Ga., 204-5, 213-14
Civil rights proposals: and Dixiecrats, 21, 26-27, 29-30, 160-64; future of, 233; reaction in South to, 18, 151-53; southern Republicans oppose, 233, 316
Civil War, *see* One-party system in South, origins; Republicans, southern origins
Clark, David, 269
Clark, Thomas D., 294
Clay County, N.C., 90
Clearwater, Fla., 201
Cobb, Osro, 291
Cole, A. C., 317
Coleman, A. B., 310
Collins, Charles Wallace, 32n
Colmer, W. M., 24
Columbia, S.C., 230, 231
Columbia Record, The, on Negro bloc voting, 209
Columbus, Ga., 215
Communist party, 232, 311
Confederate states, 6
Congressional elections, Republican competition in South, 70-73
Conscription, Confederate, 41, 44, 50
Constitutional Democrats of Texas, 158, 257-58
Convention, Democratic National, 150; *see also* Democratic party

Convention, Republican National: apportionment of seats, 119; caution on interpreting votes, 125; competition for delegates, 119-23; contests, 120-22; fraud, 122-23; independence of southern delegates, 121; selecting delegates, 121-22, 290; significance of South in, 122; South in, 96-97, 99; southern Negro delegates in, 314; 1940, southern voting in, 123-25, 127-28; 1948, southern voting in, 125-27; *see also* Republican party; Republicans, southern
Conventions, Republican, state and local, 100-2
Conway, S.C., 215
Corruption, political: reason for among Negroes, 315-16; among southern Republicans, 223-24, 312-13; *see also* Absentee voting; Election officials; Gerrymandering; Negro politics; Registration officials; Republicans, southern
Coudert, F. R., Jr., 300
Coulter, E. Merton, 312
County government, in South, 13
Crawford, William R., 218
Creager, R. B., 107, 111, 112-13, 126
Crisis, on Negro politics, 223
Crossing party lines, *see* Parties, political, cooperation between
Crump, E. H., 108-9, 196, 264-65
Cullinan, Gerald, 113
Cuney, Norris Wright, 222
Curtis, Charles, 96
Curtis, Francis, 285

Dabney, Virginius, 281
Daggett, John, 261n, 297
Dallas, Texas, 195, 201, 257
Daniels, Jonathan, 269n
Daniels, Josephus, 285
Davis, B. J., 123, 182, 225
Day, Ira W., 299
Daytona Beach, Fla., 201
Democratic National Committee, acts against Dixiecratic members, 23
Democratic National Convention, 150; *see also* Democratic party

Democratic party: changed position in South, 163-64; decreasing importance of South to, 17-19; divided by social and economic policies, 152-54; Dixiecratic factionalism, 21-24; and Dixiecratic future, 28-32; Dixiecrats, disciplining of, 23-25; factionalism in South, varieties of, 14-15; future of, and South, 168; hereditary allegiances, 243; historic liberal role, 18; effects of Lodge-Gossett Amendment on, 172-78; loyalty requirements, 137-38, 140; Negro officers in, 230; and Negro welfare, 150-52; Negroes, shift of to, 226, 228; old-time Negro support, 221-22; political success, bases of, 153-54; southern influence in, 150-51; supreme in the South, 7; two-thirds rule, 150; and whites of black belt, 8-9; *see also* Corruption, political; Dixiecrats; Factionalism; Future, the; Negro politics; One-party system in South; individual states
Detroit, Mich., 158, 310
DeTuro, Patrick J., 295
Devane, W. P., 218
de Vyver, Frank T., 295
Dewey, Thomas E., *see* Republicans, southern, factionalism among; Convention, Republican National
Dies, Martin, 104
Disfranchisement, *see* Suffrage
Dixiecrats: accomplishments in 1948, 27-29; alliance with Republicans, 165-66; 1948 vote analysis, state-by-state, 251-78; campaign finance, 298; 1950 convention, 165; decline after 1948, 164-65; Democratic label used by, 1948, 22-23, 273; desertions to, 152; differ from usual minor parties, 31; disciplinary measures against, 23-25; economic status, 298; as emotional outlet, 29; future of, 28-32, 246-47; goals of, 1948, 19; leadership, nature of, 159-60, 246-47, 297; and Lodge-Gossett Amendment, 178; national appeal of, 25, 165; nature of movement, 20-25; not channel to party politics, 32; as obstacle to Republican growth, 31; racist appeals, 26-28, 160-64; Republican vote, effect on, 65; and Republicans, 21-2, 28, 165, 299; significance summarized, 246-47; and states' rights, 27, 165; as stepping-stone to Republicanism, 29; Truman, reasons opposed to, 29; variations within South, 25-26; voters, nature of, 27, 160, 163-64, 251-78; *see also* Future, the; individual states
Dixon, Frank, 26-27, 163, 297
Dothan, Ala., Dixiecratic meeting, 21
Dougherty, Harry, 123
Douglass, Frederick, 221
Du Bois, W. E. Burghardt, 223-24
Dunn, F. A., 307
Duplin County, N.C., 48-49
Durham, N.C., 196-97, 218, 305
Durham Committee on Negro Affairs, 196-97, 201
Duval County Voters League, Fla., 310

Eastland, James O., 24
Economic changes, influence on South, 247-48; *see also* Social and economic conditions
Edmonds, Helen G., 304
Effingham County, Ga., 52
Eisenhower, Dwight D., 167
Eldersveld, Samuel J., 244-45, 316
Election laws, and southern Republicans, 74-95
Election officials: and fraud, 83-84, 87-89; and Lodge-Gossett Amendment, 177-78; partisan control of, 84-89
Election reform, 94-95
Elections: contested by Republicans, 57-58; primary, *see* Primaries; *see also* Democratic party; Dixiecrats; Negro politics; Republican party; southern Republicans; individual offices
Electoral behavior, *see* Political behavior; voter-interest
Electoral college: abolition, votes on, 169, 171, 173; criticisms of, 169-70; Georgia electors, 301; and party programs, 174-75; proposed changes in, 170-72; significance of, 169-78, 246; and southern dissatisfactions,

170; *see also* Electors, presidential; Lodge-Gosset Amendment
Electoral votes, of South, 1880-1948, 117
Electors, presidential, independence of, 22, 31, 159, 170, 284; *see also* Dixiecrats; Electoral college; Texas Regulars
Ewing, Cortez A. M., 283

Factionalism: effect of party competition on, 15-16
Factionalism, Democratic: and Dixiecrats, 21-24, 28-29, 251-78; in Louisiana, 293; since 1936, 158-68, 257-58; over civil rights, 150-52; over social and economic policies, 152-54; in state politics, as source of two-party politics, 133-35; in Texas, 293; varieties in South, 14-15; in South before 1861, 8
Factionalism, Republican: history, 222-26; among Negroes, 229; and national convention, 120-22; personal, 102; and revitalization efforts, 111-14; in Tennessee, 104, 108-9
Fair Deal, *see* Democratic party
Fannin County, Ga., 106
Farmer, Hallie, 285
Farm Security Administration, 153
Fayetteville, N.C., 218
FEPC, *see* Civil rights proposals
Ferguson, Homer, 301
Ferguson, Miriam A., 68n, 69, 136
Fesler, James W., x
Finn, Philip S., Jr., 269
Flanders, R. E., 300
Fleming, Harold C., 303
Florida: Democratic factionalism in, 15; Democratic loyalty requirements, 140; Dixiecratic vote, 1948, analyzed, 273-74; Dixiecrats avoided in, 164; elections, timing of, 135; lily whiteism in, 224; NAACP in, 186; Negro politics in, 188-90, 203, 211, 212, 215, 219, 225, 228, 229, 230, 307-8, 310-11; Negro registration, 86, 229; Negro voters, number of, 302-3; presidential Republicans important, 141-42; Republican campaign quota, 116; Republican candidates, 1948, 103n; Republican gains, 114; Republican leadership, 112; Republican organization in, 100; Republican primaries in, 106; Republicans in, distribution of, 56; Republicans, and recent settlement, 53, 63; vote for governor, 1920, 313; *see also* Democratic party; Dixiecrats; Negro politics; One-party system in South; Republican party; Republicans, southern
Flowers, Harold, 195
Foreign policy, U.S., requirement of, 232
Fort Worth, Texas, 195, 257
Foster, Roy, 120-21
France, hereditary politics in, 243-44
Fraud: local differences in, 87; *see also* Corruption, political
Fulbright, J. W., 300
Fusion politics, *see* Populism
Future, the: of Dixiecrats, 28-32; and Lodge-Gossett Amendment, 172-78; and Republican-Dixiecratic coalition, 165; for southern Democrats, 158, 167-68; of southern Negro politics, 181, 226, 232-35; of southern politics, 239-49; for southern Republicans, 158

Gabrielson, Guy, 165
Gallup, George, 301
Gallup Poll, 171, 283
Galveston, Texas, 195
Garcia, Gus, 219
Gardner v. Blackwell, 287
Garner, John N., 258
George, J. Z., 222
Georgia: county-unit system, 155; Democratic loyalty requirements, 138; Dixiecratic vote, 1948, not analyzed, 273n; and Dixiecrats, 164, 165; lily white-ism, 225; Negro politics in, 191-92, 202, 203-7, 210, 213-14, 215, 218, 222, 225, 229, 230, 300; Negro voters, number of, 302-3; presidential electors, 301; Progressive ticket in 1916, 62, 313; Republican campaign quota, 116; Republican factionalism in, 120-21; in Republican National Conven-

Georgia (*Cont.*)
  tion, 120-21; Republican primaries in, 105-6; Republicans on coast, 52; suffrage requirements, increased, 146-47; W. H. Taft in, 223; *see also* Democratic party; Dixiecrats; Negro politics; One-party system in South; Republican party; Republicans, southern
Georgia Association of Citizens' Democratic Clubs, 191-92, 202, 205-7, 215, 230
Georgia Committee on Interracial Cooperation, 306
Gerald, J. Bates, 126
"German" counties, Texas, 49-52 (map), 256
Germans, in Virginia, 285
Gerrymandering, 76-82
Glass, Carter, 69
Good Government Ticket, 58n, 67n
Gosnell, Harold F., 296, 302, 314, 316
Gossett, Ed, 171
Government, and social-economic setting, 145-46
Governor, elections of: Republican vote in South, 55, 66-69; effects on of presidential campaign, 68n, 135-37; *see also* Presidential Republicans
Graham, Frank P., x, 148, 210, 304
Graham, N.C., 218
Graves, John Temple, 21, 278, 281, 282
Great Britain, politics in, 243-44, 248
Greensboro, N.C., 218, 305
Groveland, Fla., 307
Guilford County, N.C., 269
Guill, Ben, 113

Halsell, Willie D., 312
Hamblen, W. B., 258
Hampton, W. M., 218
Hampton, Wade, 221, 312
Hardin County, Texas, 256
Harris, Joseph P., 286
Harris, Julian, 313
Hartline, Deputy, 294
Haynes, Fred E., 283
Hays, Brooks, 262
Heberle, Rudolf, 277n

Heer, David M., 252n
Heflin, Tom, 138
Henderson County, N.C., 269
Hereditary politics, 157-58, 163-64, 229, 241-44, 263, 316-17; *see also* One-party system in South, origins; Party loyalty; Political behavior; Republicans, southern, origins
Herring, Pendleton, x, 317
Hesseltine, William B., 284
Hicks, John D., 283
Hill, Lister, 29, 164
Hill, Oliver W., 218
Hill County, Texas, 257
Hinton, James M., 311
Hoey, Clyde R., 300
Holcombe, Arthur N., 29-30, 244, 245, 248
Holland, Lynwood Mathin, 288
Holland, Rush, 123
Holley, Joseph Winthrop, 305
Hooker, Ga., 294
Hooper, Ben W., 83-84, 88-89
Hoover, Calvin B., 295
Hoover, Herbert C., 224-25
Hopkins, George, 289
House of Representatives, U.S., voting for, 135
Houston, Texas, 195, 257
Howard, Perry W., 111, 123, 126, 225
Hub, the, in Savannah, Ga., 204
Hubbell, William K., ix
Huff, Dr., 215
Hulce, Mr., 186
Hulse, Anne E., 295
Hunter, Floyd, 281
Huntington, Samuel P., 317
Hutchinson, Martin, 265-68

Illinois: 81; presidential Democrats in 1944, 292-93
Independent Democrats, Georgia, 222
Independent Republicans, Mississippi, 55n
Industry, *see* Social and economic conditions
Institute for Research in Social Science, University of North Carolina, viii, ix, 281

INDEX 325

Intimidation of Negroes, 184, 205-7, 217, 251, 307; *see also* Black belts; One-party system in South, bases of; Race relations; Social and economic conditions
Irish, Marian D., 296
Ivins, T. Burkett, 88n

Jack, Robert L., 303
Jackson, Andrew, 8, 242
Jackson, John E., 123
Jackson, Luther P., 195, 302, 304
Jackson, Miss., 165, 191
Jackson County, Fla., 307
Jacksonville, Fla., 219, 310-11
Jennings, John, Jr., 109
Jester, Beauford, 50, 257
Jocher, Katherine, x
Johnsen, Julia E., 300
Johnson City, Tenn., 108
Johnston, Olin D., 164, 171, 275, 311
Jones, Jesse, 144, 153, 160
Jones, Lewis W., 295
Jones, Sam, 25
Jones County, Miss., 44
Journal and Guide, 232

Kane, Harnett T., 286
Kefauver, Estes, 84, 109, 300, 301
Kentucky, Dixiecrats in, 25
Key, V. O., Jr.: mentioned, vii, ix; cited, 272n, 275, 281, 284, 292, 294, 296, 298, 302, 316; on consequences of one-party system, 10-13; on "safety-valve" function of third parties, 283
Kilgo, John W., 105, 109
Kilpatrick, Carroll, 281
Kirby, John Henry, 258
Kiss-of-death, Negro endorsement as, 202, 206
Knight, Newt, 44
Knoxville, Tenn., 109
Krock, Arthur, 300, 301
Kytle, Calvin, x

Labor: and Negro politics, 206, 218-19, 247-49; and southern politics, 155-56, 167-68; *see also* AF of L; CIO

Labor party, British, 248
Lafayette County, Miss., 274
Lake Wales, Fla., 188
Lamar, L. Q. C., 222
Lambeth, Robert Bolling, x
Laney, Ben, 164, 261, 297
Langer, William, 171
Laski, Harold, 293, 300
Lawrence, William, 218
Lazarsfeld, Paul F., x, 317
Leadership, *see* individual parties and groups
Lee County, Ark., 261
Legislatures, state, apportionment in, 79-82, 155
Lepawsky, Albert, 295
Lerner, Max, 300
Lewis, Henry W., 286
Lewison, Paul, 312, 313
"Lily-black" candidate, 224
Lily white-ism, 221-26; *see also* Negro politics
Link, Arthur S., 312, 313
Litchfield, Edward H., 310
Little Rock, Ark., 111n, 194, 229, 303
Lodge, Henry Cabot, 171, 173, 300, 301
Lodge-Gossett Amendment: changes proposed by, 171-72; and Committee on Political Parties, 176; effect on party policies, 175-76; effects on South, 173-78, summarized, 176-78; and election administration, 177; and Federal intervention, 177-78; Gallup poll on, 171; newspaper support of, 171; opposition to, 172-73; and party discipline, 175-76; and proportional representation, 178; results summarized, 176-7; southern support for, 171; and suffrage, 177; Truman attitude toward, 172; and voter-interest, 177; votes on in Congress, 169, 171, 173; *see also* Electoral college
Long, Earl, 277
Long, Huey, 48, 277
Long, M. M., 92
Long, Russell, 164, 293
Louisiana: Democratic factionalism, 133, 293; Dixiecratic vote, 1948, analyzed, 277; Dixiecrats, 22-23, 164;

INDEX

Louisiana (*Cont.*)
NAACP in, 186; Negro politics in, 225, 229; Negro voters, number of, 302-3; Populism in, 48; Progressive ticket in 1916, 62, 313; Republican candidates in, 102; Republicans in, 53; *see also* Democratic party; Dixiecrats; Negro politics; One-party system in South; Republican party; Republicans, southern
Lubell, Samuel, 281, 295, 299, 303
Lucey, J. F., 113
Lutz, Earle, 92
Lynch, Sheriff, 294

McCarran, P. A., 300
McCray, John H., 209
McDonald, "Goose Neck Bill," 182, 224-25
McGill, Ralph, 299
McGrath, J. Howard, 23
Mackay, James, x
McKean, Dayton D., 242
McKellar, Kenneth, 108
McLaughlin, Andrew C., 312
McLaughlin, Glenn E., 295
MacLean, Marrs, 289
Macmahon, Arthur W., x
McMath, Sid, 164, 262
McMinn County, Tenn., 87n-88n
Madison County, Fla., 307
Madison County, N.C., 89n
Mail Ballots, *see* Absentee voting
Maillaud, Pierre, 318
Marianna, Ark., 261
Martin, Roscoe C., vii, ix, 285
Mecklenburg County, N.C., 77, 269, 273
Memphis, Tenn., 196, 198, 215, 263, 264
Mencken, H. L., 96
Merriam, Charles E., 296, 316
Mexican-Americans and Negro politics, 219
Miami, Fla., 219, 229
Middle class, in South, 167, 295
Migrants, Republican, 53, 75, 112
Miller, J. Erroll, 311, 316
Milton, George Fort, 198
Mims, Fla., 189

Mississippi: anti-Roosevelt Democrats, 1944, 159; Democrats endorse Lodge-Gossett Amendment, 171; Dixiecratic vote, 1948, analyzed, 274-75; Dixiecrats, 22, 23-24, 31; financing of primaries, 170n; lily white-ism in, 222, 225; Negro politics in, 191, 203, 210, 225, 229, 306; Negro voters, number of, 302; oil in, 155; Republican campaign quota, 116; Republican factional vote in, 313-14; Republican leadership, 111; Republican organization, 100; Republicans in, 1928, 53; Republicans in national convention, 121n; seats in Republican National Convention, 119; *see also* Democratic party; Dixiecrats; Negro politics; One-party system in South; Republican party; Republicans, southern
Mitchell, John, Jr., 313
Mobile, Ala., 186, 190, 201
Model City Improvement League, in Anniston, Ala., 190-191
Montgomery, Ala., 190, 308
Moon, Henry Lee, 306, 312, 314
Moore, Harry T., 189, 189n, 303, 307, 314
Morisey, A. A., 294
Morse, Wayne, 300
Mound Bayou, Miss., 225
Mountain Republicans, *see* Republicans, southern
Mowry, George E., 313
Mundt, Karl, 165, 299
Muscogee County, Ga., 215
Myrdal, Gunnar, 303, 304, 315-16

NAACP: 217, 232, 294; founded, 183; advocate of "full citizenship," 184; funds, 184; getting-out-vote, 186; goal in southern politics, 200; influence varies, 183; and legal rights, 183; membership, 183-84, 189, 191, 195; and Negro political consciousness, 183, 191; and Negro politics, 182-87; and Negro voters' leagues, 187, 188-99; non-Negro membership, 184; nonpartisan, 183, 186-87; political program, 184-85; political role varies,

INDEX

197-98; registration drives, 185-86; white attitude toward, 191
Nansemond County, Va., 218
Nashville, Tenn., 196, 198, 202, 218, 229-30
National convention, see Convention, Democratic National; Convention, Republican National
National Negro Congress, 311
National Planning Association, Committee of the South, 295
Navarro County, Texas, 257
Neal, Ernest E., 295
Neely, M. M., 300
"Negro Independent" candidate, 224, 313
Negro politics, southern: three phases for study, 182; increasing activity, 181-82; balance of power, 235; benefits sought, from state and local government, 210-12, 228, 315; "cleaning up the vote," 201-7; corruption in, 196-99, 200-1; in Democratic party organization, 230; old-time support of Democrats, 221-22; future of, 232-35; group consciousness, 182, 227-28; independence of, 220, 227, 230-32; inexperience, 202; and labor, 218-19; leadership, nature of, 190, 202, 204, 205, 306; and liberal party recruits, 232, 234-35, 315-16; and Mexican-Americans, 219; nature varies, 207; Negro candidates, 216-19; in 19th century, 208; in 1940's, basic facts of, 208; and party preferences, 227-35; personal orientation of, 196, 201, 215, 306; political potential, changes in, 182; pro-Talmadge Negroes, 305; and registration, 86; Republican appeal, decline of, 226, Republican factionalism in, 229; Republican history of, 220-26; in Republican National Convention, 229, 314; Republican party organization, 229-30; Republican preferences, sources of, 229; Republican strength, and disfranchisement, 63; variations in South, 194, 207; voter-interest in, 202, 207, 217-18, 251-52;
voters in South, number of, 181, 302-3; Negro welfare and the parties, 150-52; and white primary, 146-47, 148-49, 156; see also Bloc voting, Negro; Intimidation of Negroes; NAACP, Negroes, southern; Negro voters' leagues; Suffrage
Negro population, and Dixiecrats, 251-78
Negro voters' leagues: activities, chiefly local, 205; campaign organization, 203-7; "cleaning up the vote," 209; in Democratic primaries chiefly, 230-31; endorsements, 201-2; goals of, 200, 201; independent channel of political expression, 187, 207, 208-9, 227, 230-32; leadership of, 190; membership in, 189, 191, 192, 194, 196-97, 202-3; and NAACP, 187, 188-99; nature of organizations and origins, 188-99, 220; in rural areas, 205, 218; significance of, 207; in urban areas, 205; variations, 194
Negroes, southern: and Dixiecrat origins, 26-28; educational status, 148; Federal concern with, 30, 151; group consciousness, 210; and origins of one-party system, 6-9, 145-46; population shifts, 149-50; progress, 148; and Republican party history, 8, 40-41; residential segregation, 211, 218; in southern universities, 294; white attitudes toward, 19, 147-50; see also Civil rights proposals; Intimidation of Negroes; NAACP; Negro political leagues; Negro politics; Suffrage
New Deal, see Democratic party
New Hampshire, hereditary Democrats in, 242
New Orleans, La., 186, 303
New York: 81; Negro politics in, 306; Progressive vote in 1916, 313
News and Observer (Raleigh): on absentee voting, 90; on Dixiecrats, 269
Nixon, H. C., 155, 295
Nominations, see Conventions; Primaries; Republican national leadership

INDEX

Norfolk, Va., 79, 218, 232
North Carolina: absentee voting, 89-91; atypical black belt, 269-73; Buncombe County, 50n; Democratic factionalism in, 15; Dixiecratic vote, 1948, analyzed, 269-73 (maps); Dixiecrats avoided, 164; election officials, 85; elections, timing of, 135; fusion forces, 45, 48; gerrymandering, 76-78; Negro politics in, 195-98, 203, 210, 211, 214, 218, 225, 230, 231, 306; Negro registration, 86; Negro voters, number of, 302-3; party spirit, 269; Populism, 45, 48-49; presidential Republicans, 141-43; racist appeals, 1950, 167; Republican headquarters in east, 104; Republican legislators, 57, 80-81; Republican primaries, 106; Republican state convention (1948), 101-2; Republican state headquarters, 285; Republicans above fall line, 40; Republicans and Democratic state government, 99; Republicans, financial aid to, 117; Republicans in coastal areas, 52; Republicans in Sampson County, 45, 48-49; seats in Republican National Convention, 119; slaveholders and secession, 41, 42-43 (map); State Board of Elections, 89; and Truman nomination, 1948, 151; *see also* Democratic party; Dixiecrats; Negro politics; One-party system in South; Republican party; Republicans, southern
North Dakota, Dixiecrats in, 25
North Little Rock Democratic City Central Committee, 206

O'Daniel, W. Lee, 50, 104, 289
"Office mass meetings," 101
Ogden, Frederic D., x
Ohio, voter-interest in, 292
Olden, Samuel B., Jr., x
One-party system in South: bases of, changing, 146-56, 247-49; bases of, historic, 145-46; bosses, lack of, 291; change, obstacles to, 239-40; summarized, 245-46; complaints against, sources of, 17; consequences for national politics, 16-17; consequences for state politics, 10-13; difficulties of comparing with two-party systems, 9-10, 13; Dixiecrats and black belts, 251-78; and electoral college reform, 169-78; evolution of, 245-49; Democratic factionalism and two-party growth, 133-35; since 1936, 158-68; future of, 239-49; future of Democrats, 167-68; future of Negro party preferences, 232-35; future of Negroes, 226, 227-38; lily-white-ism, origins, 221; origins, 6-9, 145; party loyalty requirements, 137-38, 140; and political issues, 133-35; satisfaction with, 239-40; social and economic conditions, changes in, 133, underlying, 145-46; effects on factionalism, 156, 167; object of study, 3-4; need to study, 5-6; varieties of, 14-15; *see also* Party system
Orlando, Fla., 229
Ostrogarski, M., 154-55
Ozark Mountains, Arkansas, and Republicans, 40

Parker, John J., 303
Parker, John M., 313
Parties, political: cooperation between, 99, 104-4, 107-9, 113-14, 138, 222, 224, 233; minor, fate of in U.S., 30-31; race and religious basis, 29-30; state regulation of procedures, 100n; *see also* Party system; individual parties
Party loyalty: Democratic requirements, 137-38, 140; Tennessee requirements, 264; *see also* Hereditary politics
Party organization, *see* conventions; Republicans, southern; individual parties
Party spirit, in Upper South, 263
Party system: and administrative efficiency, 13; in ante-bellum South, 317; Lord Bryce on, 134; effects of competition on factionalism, 15-16; effects of compeition on South, 18-19; and democratic government, 239; federal character, 135; national-

INDEX

state relations, 133-35; Negroes as source of minor party strength, 232; non-rational alignments, 241-44; realignment, 32, 144-45, 156, 168, 233, 235, 247-49, 315-16; reform proposed, 176; relation to social structure, 13-14, 145-46, 247-49, and changes in, 244-45; U.S. success with, 239
Patronage: denied Dixiecrats, 24-25; and southern Republicans, 96, 99
Pearson, Drew, 122-123, 282, 299
Penniman, Howard R., 288
Pepper, Claude, 29, 297
Percy, Leroy, x
Perez, Leander, 164, 297
Petersburg, Va., 218, 230
Philadelphia, Negro politics in, 306
Phillips, Dayton, 109
Pine Bluff, Ark., 195
Pinellas County, Fla., 215
Plaquemines Parish, La., 164, 277
Political attitudes, *see* Political behavior
Political behavior: determinants of, 158, 227-28, 240-44, 318; *see also* Hereditary politics
Political parties, *see* Parties, political
Polk County, Tenn., 49n, 87n-88n
Poll tax: effect of abolition, 156; and Republicans, 86-87; *see also* Civil rights proposals
Popham, John N., 298
Population shifts, Negro, 149-50
Populism: 221, 242, 248; and Republicans, 48-49; southern weakness, 31; as threat to white supremacy, 9
Populist party, *see* Populism
Port Arthur, Texas, 195
Porter, Jack, 113, 293
Power structure, *see* Party system, relation to social structure; Social and economic conditions
Presidential elections: 1880-1948, southern electoral vote, 117; 1904, location of Republican strength in South, 46-47 (map); 1916-48, Republican vote in South, 59-66, 61 (chart), 279; 1940-48 shifts in southern Republican voting, 64-66; 1944, location of Republican strength in South, 38-39 (map); 1944, Republican vote in South, 55; 1944, strongest preferences in South, 5 (map); 1948, Dixiecrats in, 25; 1948, results in South, 25-26; Republican attitude toward in South, 115-118; and Republican state voting, 135-37; southern and national fluctuations, 60-62; and voter-interest, 68; *see also* Electoral college
Presidential electors, *see* Electors, presidential
Presidential politics, South not isolated from, 60
Presidential Republicans: 56, 137-43; 1920-48, 140-42; 1948, 139-40; difficulties of analysis, 293; increase in, necessary for two-party growth, 140; and Presidential Democrats in Vermont and Illinois, 292-3; and Texas Regulars, 260-61; types of, 143
Primaries: loyalty requirements, 137-38, 140; mandatory, 106-7; presidential, 105, 121; privately financed, 106-7; use of by southern Republicans, 105-7
Progressive Democratic Council, Birmingham, Ala., 190
Progressive Democratic Party, South Carolina, 192-94, 209, 219, 231-32, 315
Progressive Movement, of T.R., 223
Progressive party, 1916, 313
Progressive Voters' League: (Florida), 188-90, 211, 212, 231, 307-8; (Mississippi), 191, 203; (Texas), 195, 230
Proportional representation and Lodge-Gossett Amendment, 178
Pulaski County, Ark., 111n

Quebec, compared with South, 32n, 210

Race issue, in American politics, 31, 232
Race relations: and lily white-ism, 221-22; Negroes in southern colleges, 294; in South, changing, 147-50; *see also* Racist appeals

Racist appeals: to divide opposition, 167; by Dixiecrats, 160-64; and Lodge-Gossett Amendment, 178; and Populist-Republican fusion, 221; used by "Southern Democrats," 158-59
Raleigh, N.C., 196, 218, 305
Rankin, John, 274-75
Raper, Arthur, 295
Ratchford, Benjamin U., 295
Rayburn, Sam, 24
Record, Wilson, 315
Reece, Carroll, 105, 108-9, 121, 122, 290
Regional sentiment, southern: 145-56, 166; and Lodge-Gossett Amendment, 174-75; *see also* One-party system in South, origins
Registration: officials, partisan control of, 86-87; *see also* NAACP
"Regular Democrats," Mississippi, 159
Religion, and politics, 52, 62, 297
Remmel, H. L., 111n
"Republican, white," ticket, Florida, 67, 224, 313
Republican Club of Texas, 113
Republican national leadership: and South, 115-29; financial aid to South, 116-17; and southern oligarchies, 119-20, 122, 127-29; and southern presidential campaigns, 115-17, 129
Republican National Committee: 116, 225; Executive Director of, 293
Republican National Convention, *see* Convention, Republican National
Republican party: lily white-ism, 221-26; effects of Lodge-Gossett Amendment on, 172-78; Negro politics and history of, 220-26; Negro politics in South, future of, 232-35; Negro preference for, 229-30; and Negro suffrage, 8; Negro support, loss of, 226; Negro vote, loss of, 228; and Negro welfare, 152; Negroes at National Convention, 314; South Carolina Negroes, and national leadership of, 231; Negroes in organization, 229-30; 1948 gains, 114; 1952 drive in South, 115; origin, 8, 40-41, 243; southern Democrats, coalition with, 21-22, 28, 165-66; *see also* Convention, Republican National; Conventions, Republican, state and local; Republicans, southern; individual states

Republicans, southern: and absentee voting, 89-92; campaign finance, 103, 116-17, 129, 137; campaigns, state, 104-5; candidates, failure to run, 102-4; candidates offered, 57-58; civil rights program, opposed to, 233, 316; in coastal areas, 52; continuity of strength, 44-45; in convention, national, 96-97, 118-19, 123-28, 223, 312-13; conventions, state and local, 100-2; Democratic control of local legislation, 82; Democratic state government, satisfied with, 99; Democrats, cooperation with, 104-5, 107-9, 113-14; distribution within states, 56-59; and Dixiecrats, 262-64, 273; and election laws, 74-95; and election officials, 84-89; and electoral reform, 94-95; factionalism among, 102, 104, 108-9, 120-22, 222-26; in "German" counties, Texas, 49-52; and gerrymandering, 76-82; hereditary, 37-53, 157-58; in highlands, 40-45; leadership, nature of, 94-95, 96-114, 225; location in 1904, 46-47 (map); location in 1944, 38-39 (map); effects of Lodge-Gossett Amendment on, 172-78; in Louisiana, 53; migrants, 53, 75, 112; in Mississippi, 53; and national party leadership, 96-98, 115-29; and party organization, 99-100, 102; Negro disfranchisement, effect on, 63; and Negro politics, 220-26; and Negro support, 181, 227-35; and nonsecret voting, 92-94; origins, 37-53; and poll tax, 86-87; former Populists, 45, 48-49; prejudices and sanctions against, 74-75; presidential elections, interest in, 135-37; and primaries, mandatory, 106; and presidential primaries, 105; primaries, use of, 105-6; reform of party in South, 223-26; regional consciousness among, 291; and registration officials, 86-87; in Rio Grande Valley, 53; in state

INDEX

legislatures, 57-58, 79-82; Taft, support of, 120-29; in Texas, 53; and Texas Regulars, 259-61; types of, 37, 40; unimportant to national victory, 98-99; variations among, 127, 142; voting for governor, 1920-50, 66-69; voting for president, 1916-48, 59-66, 61 (chart), 279; voting for president, 1940-48, 64-66; voting for president and governor, 1944, 55; voting in primaries, low, 106; voting for U.S. Representatives, 70-73; voting for U.S. Senator, 1920-50, 69-71; voting trends, 59-73, 142, 293; *see also* Negro politics; Republican party
Richland County Republican Committee, S.C., 231
Richmond, Va., 186, 218
Richmond Times-Dispatch, on absentee voting, 92
Ries, Siegfried H., x
Rio Grande Valley, Republicans in, 53
Rivers, Ed, 210, 304
Riviera Beach, Fla., 307
Robertson, Willis, 265
Robinson, E. E., 284
Robinson, J. M., 194
Robinson, Joseph T., 194, 221, 230
Robison, Daniel Merritt, 284, 297
Robock, Stefan, 295
Robson, C. B., ix
Rockefeller Foundation, vii, ix
Rome, Ga., 294
Roosevelt, Eleanor, 233
Roosevelt, Franklin D.: services to Negro, 214-15; *see also* Democratic party
Roosevelt, Theodore, 157, 223, 226, 313
Roosevelt Democratic Club, Florida, 310
Rosewater, Victor, 312
Russell, Richard B., 28, 165

St. Bernard Parish, La., 277
St. Petersburg, Fla., 186, 215
Sampson County, N.C., 45, 48-49
San Antonio, Texas, 195
San Antonio Junior College, 219
Sancton, Thomas, 297

Sanford, Fla., 307
Savannah, Ga., 203-5, 211, 213-14
Schattschneider, E. E., 283, 291
Schneider, Stanley, 258n, 297
Scott, Hugh D., Jr., 290
Secession: in Jones County, Mississippi, 44; in North Carolina, 41, 42-43 (map); southern opposition to, 41, 44; *see also* One-party system in South, origins
Secret ballot, 92-94, 159
Sectionalism: in politics, 243-249; within southern states, 253-78; *see also* One-party system in South; Social and economic conditions
Segregation, *see* Civil rights proposals
Seignobos, Charles, 318
Senator, U.S., elections of, Republican vote in South, 69-71
Shannon, Jasper B., 122, 145, 168, 297
Shelby County, Tenn., 264
Sheppard, Muriel Earley, 284
Sheppard, William A., 312
Shugg, Roger W., x, 304
Siegfried, André, 243-44
Silva, Ruth C., 172-73, 292, 302
Simkins, Mrs. Andrew W., 315
Simkins, Francis Butler, 275n
Simms, Henry H., 285
Slaveholders: influence in Democratic party, 8; and secession, 41-45
Smith, Edward B., 289
Smith, H. A., 300
Smith, Samuel D., 304
Smith, Willis, 299-300
Smith v. Blackwell, 287
Smyer, Sidney W., 297
Social and economic conditions: changing in South, 154-56, 167; changing, effects summarized, 247-49; and future of one-party system, 74, 129, 133, 240, 245-49; underlying one-party system, 145-46; urbanism in South, 296
Solid Block Club, Nashville, 198, 202
South, the: defined, 6; decreasing importance of, to Democratic party, 17-19; social and economic changes in, 154-56; *see also* Future, the

INDEX

South Carolina: Democratic loyalty requirements, 138-40; Dixiecratic vote, 1948, analyzed, 252n, 275-76 (maps); Dixiecrats, 22, 23, 24; election officials, 85; general ballot in 1944, lack of, 159; Johnston-Thurmond primary, 164; lily white-ism, 225; Negro politics in, 192-94, 209, 215, 219, 225, 229, 230, 231; Negro voters, number of, 193, 302; registration officials, 86; Republican campaign quota, 116; seats in Republican National Convention, 119; Republicans in national convention, 121n; and secret voting, 93; "Southern Democratic" electors, 1944, 158; suffrage requirements increased, 146-47; *see also* Democratic party; Dixiecrats; Negro politics; One-party system in South; Republican party; Republicans, southern
South Carolina, University of, 312
Southern Conference for Human Welfare, 198, 206
"Southern Democratic" electors, South Carolina, 158
Southern Regional Council, 305
Southern Weekly, The, on Democratic-Republican coalition, 152-53
Spades, C. C., 112
Sparkman, John, 164, 300
Stanwood, Edward, 289, 313
State legislatures in South, Republicans in, 57-58
States' Rights Democrats, *see* Dixiecrats
States' rights sentiment: 27, 29, 160, 165; *see also* Dixiecrats
Steele, George S., x
Stennis, John C., 300
Strong, Donald S., viii, x, 303, 314
Suffrage: 146-47, 156, 167-68; and Lodge-Gossett Amendment, 177; Negro, in 19th century, 221; *see also* Civil rights proposals; NAACP; One-party system in South; White primary; Voter-interest
Supreme Court, U.S., 146-47, 188
Sutton, G. J., 219
Suwannee County, Fla., 307

Swain County, N.C., 90
Swisher, Carl Brent, 299

Taft, Robert A., 120-29, 172; *see also* Republicans, southern, factionalism among
Taft, William Howard, 223, 226
Talmadge, Eugene, 15, 192, 205, 210, 304, 306
Talmadge, Herman, 164
Tampa, Fla., 186
Taylor, A. A., 304
Taylor, Alf, 158
Taylor, Bob, 158
Taylor, Fred, 282, 283
Taylor, Joseph H., x
Tennessee: corrupt elections in, 83-84, 88-89; Democratic factionalism in, 14, 15; Dixiecratic vote, 1948, analyzed, 263-65; election officials, 85; fraud in elections, 87-89; Negro politics in, 195-96, 198, 202, 218, 225, 229, 306; Negro voters, number of, 302; party spirit in, 263-64; Polk County, 49n; presidential elector, votes for Thurmond, 25; presidential Republicans, 141-42; Republican candidate in, financial aid to, 117; Republican Congressional districts in, 70, 81; Republican-Democratic deals, 99, 107-9; Republican factionalism, 104; Republican legislators in, 57, 79-81; Republican primaries, 106; Republican state campaigns in, 104-5; Republicans, presidential race and state politics, 135, 137; Taylor brothers in, 158; *see also* Democratic party; Dixiecrats; Negro politics; One-party system in South; Republican party; Republicans, southern
Texas: Constitutional Democrats of, 158; Democratic bolters, 68n, 69, 293; Dixiecratic vote, 1948, analyzed, 253-61 (maps); factionalism among Democrats, 1936-40, 257-58; lily white-ism, 222; money to oppose F.D.R. from, 116; Negro politics in, 195, 219, 225, 230-31; Negro voters, number of, 302; 1951 election law, 94n; party leaders

INDEX

endorse Lodge-Gossett Amendment, 171; and poll tax, 86-87; presidential Republicans important, 135-37 (chart), 141-42; Republican candidates in, 104-5; Republican-Democratic cooperation, 104-5, 113-14; Republican factionalism, 112-14; Republican leadership, 111-13; Republican primaries, 107; Republican vote, and recent settlement, 63; Republicans in "German" counties, 49-52; Republicans in Rio Grande Valley, 53; secret voting, 93-94; *see also* Democratic party; Dixiecrats; Negro politics; One-party system in South; Republican party; Republicans, southern

Texas Club of Democratic Voters, 195, 230

Texas Poll, 298, 302

Texas Regulars, 55n, 65, 114, 159, 253, 258-61

Thompson, Katherine Wade, x

Thomson, David, 318

Thurmond, J. Strom, 20-21, 27, 160-61, 164, 298; *see also* Dixiecrats

Tillman, Ben, 275

Tingsten, Herbert, 296

Titusville, Fla., municipal election in, 212-13

To Secure These Rights, 162

Tolbert, "Tieless Joe," 121n, 182

Townsend, Wallace, 111n

Trade union, *see* Labor

Trends, voting, *see* Republicans, southern

Truman, David B., 318

Truman, Harry S., *see* Civil rights proposals; Democratic party; Dixiecrats

Tuck, William, 265

Tucker, Roscoe, 120-21

Turner, Julius, 302

Tuscaloosa, Ala., 211

Tuskegee Institute, 148

Two-party system: value of, 4; need for studies of, 9, 13

Two-thirds rule, 150

Tyler County, Texas, 256

Unions, *see* Labor

Upchurch, Frank D., 297

Urbanism, *see* Social and economic conditions

Vance, Rupert B., x

Vaughan, Hilary Herbert, 298

Velie, Lester, 297

Vermont, presidential Democrats in 1944, 292

Virgin Islands, 229

Virginia: absentee voting, 91-92; Democratic factionalism in, 14, 15, 133; Dixiecratic vote, 1948, analyzed, 265-68; election officials, 85-86; financing of primaries, 107n; gerrymandering, 79; lily white-ism, 224; NAACP in, 186; Negro politics in, 195-96, 198-99, 218, 225, 230, 231, 306; Negro voters, number of, 302; presidential Republicans, 141-42; Republican candidates, 103; Republican conventions, 101; Republican gains, 114; Republican leadership, 111-12; Republican legislators, 57, 80-81; Republican primaries in, 106-7; seats in Republican National Convention, 119; U.S. senators, 69; vote for governor, 1921, 313; Wise County, 49n; *see also* Byrd, Harry F.; Byrd machine; Democratic party; Dixiecrats; Negro politics; One-party system in South; Republican party; Republicans, southern

Virginia Voters' League, 199

Voter-interest: and economic status, 16; and labor unions, 16; and Lodge-Gossett Amendment, 177; among Negroes, 202, 207, 217-18; and presidential elections, 68, 135, 292; and party competition, 16; *see also* NAACP; Suffrage; White primary

Voter registration, *see* Registration officials

Vote-trading, *see* Parties, political, cooperation between

Votes cast, *see* Individual offices and states

Voting, non-secret, in South, 92-94, 159

INDEX

W. Lee O'Daniel News, 289
Wager, Paul W., 13
Walden, A. T., 192
Wallace, Schuyler C., x
Ward, Judson C., Jr., 312
Washington, Booker T., 184, 223
Washington, G. W., 310
Washington, George, 239
Washington, N.C., 218
Washington County, Texas, 65
Watauga County, N.C., 77
Waynesboro, Va., 266n
Weaver, A. V., 310
Weaver, John B., 284
Wechsler, Herbert, 301
West v. Bliley, 304
Whig party, 8, 317
White, Ertha M. M., 311
White, Melvin Johnson, 285
White, Theodore H., 87n-88n
White, Walter, 184, 232, 303
White primary: future of, 233; invalidated, 146-47, 156, 188; Negroes, and entrance to, 206-7, 230; Negroes in before 1944, 195-96, 198-99; *see also* NAACP; Suffrage
White Republican Clubs, Texas 222
White supremacy, *see* Dixiecrats; One-party system in South, origins; Negroes, southern; Race relations; Racist appeals; White primary
Wilkins, Josephine, x
Wilkinson, Horace C., 283
Wilkinson, John A., 316
Willbern, York, viii, x, 284
Williams, Kenneth R., 218
Williams, Leon R., 308
Williams, Robert E., 288
Williams, Wilson, 105, 111
Willkie, Wendell, *see* Convention, Republican National
Wilmerding, Lucius, Jr., 300
Wilson, Woodrow, 226, 312
Winn Parish, La., 48
Winston County, Ala., 111
Winston-Salem, N.C., 218
Wise County, Va., 49n, 92
Wood County, Texas, 256
Woodhouse, Edward James, x
Woodring, Harry, 297
Woodward, Vann, 314
Wright, Fielding, 21, 171, 282
Wurzbach, Harry M., 50
Wythe County, Va., 79